Feeding the Dead

Feeding the Dead

Ancestor Worship in Ancient India

MATTHEW R. SAYERS

OXFORD
UNIVERSITY PRESS

OXFORD
UNIVERSITY PRESS

Oxford University Press is a department of the University of Oxford.
It furthers the University's objective of excellence in research, scholarship,
and education by publishing worldwide.

Oxford New York
Auckland Cape Town Dar es Salaam Hong Kong Karachi
Kuala Lumpur Madrid Melbourne Mexico City Nairobi
New Delhi Shanghai Taipei Toronto

With offices in
Argentina Austria Brazil Chile Czech Republic France Greece
Guatemala Hungary Italy Japan Poland Portugal Singapore
South Korea Switzerland Thailand Turkey Ukraine Vietnam

Published in the United States of America by
Oxford University Press
198 Madison Avenue, New York, NY 10016

Library of Congress Cataloging-in-Publication Data
Sayers, Matthew R.
Feeding the dead : ancestor worship in ancient India / Matthew R. Sayers.
pages cm
Includes bibliographical references and index.
ISBN 978-0-19-989643-1—ISBN 978-0-19-991747-1 1. Ancestor worship—India—
History. 2. Sraddha (Hindu rite)—History. I. Title.
BL2015.A6S28 2013
294.5'388—dc23
2013012872

1 3 5 7 9 8 6 4 2
Printed in the United States of America
on acid-free paper

डेनिस् रे सेयर्स् एतत्ते ।
रे व्हिल्बर् सेयर्स् एतत्ते ।
राबर्ट् सेयर्स् एतत्ते ।

Contents

List of Tables

Acknowledgments

ṛṇáṃ ha vái jāyate yó 'sti | sá jā́yamāna evá devébhya
ṛ́ṣibhyaḥ pitṛ́bhyo manuṣyébhyaḥ
—*Śatapatha Brāhmaṇa* 1.7.2.1

Dicebat Bernardus Carnotensis nos esse quasi nanos, gigantium humeris insidentes, ut possimus plura eis et remotiora videre, non utique proprii visus acumine, aut eminentia corporis, sed quia in altum subvenimur et extollimur magnitudine gigantean.
—John of Salisbury, *Metalogician*

THE *ŚATAPATHA BRĀHMAṆA* tells us that man is born a debt, and I suggest that a scholar too is born a debt. As the Brahmin is born a debt to his Ancestors, so the scholar is a born a debt to his gurus. The citations throughout this book evidence my debt to those upon whose work I have relied; as Bernard of Chartres said, "we are like dwarfs on the shoulders of giants, so that we can see more than they, and things at a greater distance, not by virtue of any sharpness of sight on our part, or any physical distinction, but because we are carried high and raised up by their giant size." But just as the son's debt to his more distant ancestors is less immediate than the debt to his father, so my debt to the classical works of Religious Studies and Indology are less immediate than those to the teachers who taught me directly.

Patrick Olivelle and Joel Brereton have had a profound impact on my education, and if I succeed in being half the teacher, mentor, and example that each of them has been for me, I will feel my debt to them acquitted. For the moment I offer them heartfelt gratitude for the seemingly limitless generosity of time, advice, and support they extended me from the moment I set foot on the University of Texas at Austin campus and continue to give me today.

Many other mentors, colleagues, and friends have helped me become the scholar I am today; to each of them I offer my thanks: Stephen J. Vicchio, Steven Fine, Willie Bediako Lamousé-Smith, Carlos Lopez, Kathleen Erndl, Bryan J. Cuevas, Aline Kalbian, John Kelsay, Kevin Vacarella, Arthur Remillard, Oliver Frieberger, Cynthia Talbot, Janice Leoshko, Martha Selby, Traude Harzer, Rupert Snell, Tracy Buck, Cary and Ashley Curtiss, Mark McClish, Jarrod Whittaker, Dave Brick, Elliott McCarter, Neil Dalal, Urmila Patil, Jennifer Tipton, Michael Roemer, Burt Estes, Amy Hyne, and Peter Knapczyk. My colleagues at Lebanon Valley College, particularly Jeffrey Robbins, have been invaluable in the transition from student to teacher-scholar, and I am reminded daily of how lucky I am to work here.

James Egge generously gave me extremely valuable feedback on an early draft of this work. The constructive criticism offered by the reviewers improved my work significantly. Jeffery Long and Jeffrey Robbins both read the final manuscript, and this work is much better because of their sage advice. Any shortcomings that remain in this book are due not to the learned scholars who endeavored to help me but to my inability to integrate their constructive criticisms and suggestions.

To my family and friends, who—though ignorant of the detail, process, time frame, or even the point of my work—gave me encouragement, love, and support, I offer my love and gratitude. My son Ze'ev accepted that I had work to do more graciously than I would have at his age; for this I thank him with all my heart. To Margery, without whom I would not have survived graduate school, who put my needs above her own far too often, and who endured more relocations, ambiguity, and general stress than anyone deserves, I offer far too little: eternal gratitude, undying love, and an ardent desire for her happiness.

Abbreviations

Primary Texts

A	*Aṅguttara Nikāya*
AB	*Aitareya Brāhmaṇa*
ĀpDhS	*Āpastamba Dharmasūtra*
ĀpGS	*Āpastamba Gṛhyasūtra*
ĀpŚS	*Āpastamba Śrautasūtra*
ĀśGS	*Āśvalāyana Gṛhyasūtra*
ĀśŚS	*Āśvalāyana Śrautasūtra*
AVP	*Atharva Veda Paippalāda*
AVŚ	*Atharva Veda Śaunaka*
BDhS	*Baudhāyana Dharmasūtra*
BGS	*Baudhāyana Gṛhyasūtra*
BhGS	*Bharadvāja Gṛhyasūtra*
BhŚS	*Bharadvāja Śrautasūtra*
BrP	*Brahmāṇḍa Purāṇa*
BŚS	*Baudhāyana Śrautasūtra*
CU	*Chāndogya Upaniṣad*
D	*Dīgha Nikāya*
GDhS	*Gautama Dharmasūtra*
GGS	*Gobhila Gṛhayasūtra*
GM	*Gayā Mahātmyā*
GP	*Garuḍa Purāṇa*
HGS	*Hiraṇyakeśin Gṛhyasūtra*
JGS	*Jaimini Gṛhyasutra*
JB	*Jaiminīya Brāhmaṇa*
KaU	*Kaṭha Upaniṣad*
KhGS	*Khādira Gṛhyasūtra*

KŚS	*Kātyāyana Śrautasūtra*
LŚS	*Lāṭyāyana Śrautasūtra*
M	*Majjhima Nikāya*
MBh	*Mahābhārata*
MDhŚ	*Mānava Dharmaśāstra*
MkP	*Mārkaṇḍeya Purāṇa*
MS	*Maitrāyaṇī Saṃhitā*
MŚS	*Mānava Śrautasūtra*
PB	*Pañcaviṃśa Brāhmaṇa*
PGS	*Pāraskara Gṛhyasūtra*
PU	*Praśna Upaniṣad*
Pv	*Petavatthu*
PvA	*Paramatthadīpanī nāma Petavatthu-aṭṭhakathā*
RV	*Ṛg Veda*
S	*Saṃyutta Nikāya*
ŚBK	*Śatapatha Brāhmaṇa Kaṇva*
ŚBM	*Śatapatha Brāhmaṇa Mādhyaṃdina*
ŚGS	*Śāṅkhāyana Gṛhyasūtra*
ŚŚS	*Śāṅkhāyana Śrautasūtra*
Sn	*Suttanipāta*
TĀ	*Taittirīya Āraṇyaka*
TB	*Taittirīya Brāhmaṇa*
Thag	*Theragāthā*
TS	*Taittirīya Saṃhitā*
VaitS	*Vaitānasūtra*
VS	*Vājasaneyi Saṃhitā*
VDhS	*Vasiṣṭha Dharmasūtra*
ViSmṛ	*Viṣṇu Smṛti*
YS	*Yājñavalkya Smṛti*

Publications

IIJ	*Indo-Iranian Journal*
JAOS	*Journal of the American Oriental Society*
HoD	*History of Dharmaśāstra*
KEWA	*Kurzgefaßtes etymologisches Wörterbuch des Altindischen*
PAPS	*Proceedings of the American Philosophical Society*
PED	*Pāli-English Dictionary*
RoSA	*Religions of South Asia*

Feeding the Dead

Introduction

THE CENTRALITY OF reincarnation to the contemporary conception of Hinduism in particular and South Asian religions more generally belies a long and rich history of ancestor worship in South Asia. The funerary offerings made to one's deceased parents in contemporary India are the survivals of a tradition that stretches back to the Vedas, a tradition that revolves around the ritual translation of the deceased to the next world. David Knipe calls this "one of the great spiritual dramas of man," yet laments that "it is one of the least studied aspects of Hinduism" (Knipe 1977, 112). The veneration of the Ancestors (*pitṛ*, literally "father") is one half of the soteriological dichotomy at the heart of classical Hinduism. What is the ultimate goal of the individual in Hinduism? Liberation from rebirth? An eternal place in heaven? The tension between the ascetically oriented soteriology of liberation and that of the ritualist tradition that aims at heaven is at the core of Hindu practices relevant to the ultimate end of the religious life. This tension arises from the contestation between the Brahmins,[1] who advocate the tradition of sacrifice that goes back to the *Ṛg Veda,* and the Brahmanical advocates of renunciation of ritual and worldly life for the attainment of salvation. The ritualists endorse ritual activity as the way to the ultimate goal, an eternal stay in heaven. The renunciates promote the abandonment of worldly attachments with the aim of liberation from rebirth. This book aims to shed some light on the less-examined side of this soteriological debate: the long tradition of ancestor worship.

Despite the ubiquitous nature of the doctrine of transmigration in contemporary Hinduism there still exists the widespread practice of rituals that purport to transport the deceased to the world of the Ancestors (*pitṛloka*), that is, a heavenly realm where the Ancestors live on the food offered to them in ritual. Not only has the ritual performed to sustain the Ancestors' stay in heaven persisted for more than two thousand years after the development of the concept of transmigration, it has also thrived and grown considerably from its description in the domestic ritual manuals as one of the sacred ceremonies (*saṃskāras*), rituals that themselves have older Vedic precedents. The fully elaborated, complex ritual process described by Knipe (1977) and Kane (*HoD* 4:334ff.) is the product of centuries of religious discourse about the practice of ancestor worship, discourse that thrives alongside, perhaps in spite of, the assumption that one's Self (*ātman*) transmigrates according to the law of *karma*, the immutable process of retributive justice that determines one's rebirth.

The tradition is not ignorant of the tension between the two soteriological ends envisioned for the religious actor, that is, the world of the Ancestors and liberation from rebirth (*mokṣa*). In the Upaniṣads, early philosophical texts, we find evidence of a prolonged debate about the ultimate end of man, which Bodewitz (1996a) has described in detail. Ultimately, this led to the fully developed notion of reincarnation with liberation from rebirth as the desired end to the cycle of repeated birth. For the most part the ritual literature ignores or rejects the idea of rebirth for at least a few centuries (Bronkhorst 2007, 137–159), but the tension does appear in the literature concerned with *dharma*.[2] The *Baudhāyana Dharmasūtra*, for example, combines the notion of rebirth with the understanding that one's Ancestors are sustained in heaven by ritual performance of the *śrāddha*-rite, the classical form of ancestor worship in Hinduism. The author says that a man who misuses sesame will be reborn as a worm and "plunge into a pile of dog shit together with his ancestors" (*BDhS* 2.2.26, Olivelle 2000, 249).[3] More explicitly, the *Brahmāṇḍa Purāṇa* asks how Ancestors can bestow the benefits of performing the ancestral rites if they have been reincarnated, specifically in hell (*BrP* 2.9.10).

How then does this rich tradition of ancestor worship develop and thrive alongside a contradictory ideology? There is not a switch-over moment when the tradition makes an either-or choice, nor is there a gradual shift from one soteriology to the other. Advocates of each ideology assert the superiority of their understanding, producing texts that describe the way to the specific soteriological end they champion. The *Mahābhārata*, the great Indian Epic poem, and the *Purāṇas*, encyclopedic compendia of religious lore, draw equally upon both of these ideologies to construct classical Hinduism, and after many centuries there arose efforts to synthesize the two soteriologies,[4] the heaven-oriented soteriology of those Brahmins that advocated ritual as the primary expression of the proper religious life and the liberation-oriented soteriology of the renouncer tradition. This book describes the historical development of the rituals of ancestor worship, which rests on the heaven-oriented soteriology.

Vedic Ritual and Religion

A brief review of the Vedic religion will help contextualize the following discussion of ancestor worship in ancient India. The Vedic religious tradition developed in the culture of the Indo-European speaking peoples that migrated into the subcontinent around the middle of the second millennium before the Common Era. Their world is available to us only through the extant texts, described in the section entitled "The Sources," and those texts come from a culture primarily concerned with the practice of sacrifice (*yajña*). The rituals described in these texts are called the solemn rites (*śrauta*). The term *śrauta* (related to *śruti*, that is, related to revelation) refers primarily to the practice of large-scale, public ritual sacrifice.

The ritual inherited from the older tradition that composed the *Ṛg Veda* is "the ideally portable religion" (Jamison 1991, 17) in that the liturgy is memorized by those who enact it and the materials used in the ritual are implements used in everyday life or created for that particular instance, such as the ritual space and the fire. Specific places are not recognized as sacred; rather the ritual space in which the ritual will occur is created through a meticulous demarcation of sacred space.

At the center of Vedic ritual are the ritual fire and the offerings made into the fire. From the simplest ritual—the Fire Offering (*agnihotra*), offerings of milk and similar products into a single fire and involving only a single priest—to the most complex, involving many offerings and numerous priests, the central action of the ritual is offering food or drinks into the fire. In these rituals all other actions are subordinate to, leading up to or from, the offerings made into the fire.

The conceptual basis of these offerings is the Vedic emphasis on hospitality. The gods (*deva*) are invited into the ritual space and invited to sit on the seat of honor. Priests praise the gods with hymns (*ṛc*) and songs (*sāman*) and offer them food. The sacrificial fire (*agni*)—both the physical fire itself and the deified god of fire Agni—transfers the offering to the particular god of this ritual and the priests invite him or her to partake of it. More praise is heaped upon the divine guests and they are ceremoniously asked to withdraw. The hospitality of the sacrifice engenders the qualities of generosity and benevolence in the gods, and they in turn provide the benefits of sacrifice: long life, worldly wealth, prosperity, sons, protection, success, and so forth.

The human focus of the sacrifice is the patron of the ritual, the Sacrificer (*yajamāna*), who derives all the benefits won through the ritual. The title *yajamāna*—literally meaning sacrificing on his own behalf—as well as the translation Sacrificer are somewhat misleading, because he is responsible for very little work of the actual ritual. While he is the patron of the sacrifice and all the benefit of its performance goes to him, the priests perform the ritual, that is, chant, sing, make offerings, and so forth. In return for their work in the ritual, the priests receive compensation, the sacrificial gift (*dakṣiṇā*). Usually this gift takes the form of livestock or gold, but the appropriate gift is designated by the ritual.

The primary requirement for being a Sacrificer, in addition to being married and a member of the top three classes (*varṇa*), is that he must be someone who has established the fires (*āhitāgni*), that is, he must have performed a ritual that establishes the three ritual fires, allowing him to maintain them in his household. This qualifies him to perform the solemn rites, which require three sacred fires. The three fires are the householder's fire (*gārhapatya*), the offertorial fire (*āhavanīya*, literally "to be offered into"), and the southern fire (*dakṣiṇāgni*). It is unlikely that any but a small percentage of those eligible to maintain all three sacrificial fires did so, because maintaining the fires and performing the larger solemn rites involved considerable expense. Most households probably maintained only the householder's fire, which is required for domestic rituals.

The three fires are central to the ritual space created for ritual. The ritual is oriented toward the east, where the gods dwell, so the offertorial fire—which is square—is in the east of the ritual space. On the east-west axis behind the offertorial fire is the altar (*vedi*), a shallow, hourglass shape space dug out of the ground. Further west is the householder's fire, which is round. The southern fire, in the shape of a half-moon, lies to the south of the central axis created by the two fires, closer to the householder's fire.[5] In the ritual, the altar is strewn with *barhis* grass as a seat for the gods who are to be invited. The altar also serves as the resting place of implements and offerings. This ritual space is created by the priests commissioned by the Sacrificer to perform the sacrifice.

The four classes of priests employed correspond to the four Vedas. The Hotṛ and his followers recite the verses from the *Ṛg Veda*. The Adhvaryu and his assistants recite the ritual formulas from the *Yajur Veda* and are responsible for most of the ritual actions undertaken during the sacrifice. The Brahman, the priest of the *Atharva Veda*, was added to the older, original Vedic sacrifice later in the Vedic period (Oldenberg 1894, 395; Jamison 1991, 21). His role is to oversee the ritual and silently recite *mantras* (a sacred verse or formula) to correct any mistakes. In the Soma rituals, the Udgatṛ sings the songs of praise (*stotra*) set to melodies from the *Sāma Veda*.

There are several classifications of ritual, and rituals in different categories share characteristics with those in others, but the rituals are often divided into two classes, the Soma Sacrifices (*somayajña*) and those rites called the *haviryajña* (literally "a sacrifice with an oblation") (Keith 1925, 316). The former differ from the latter in the offering of Soma and the inclusion of the Udgatṛ and his songs. The Haviryajña most often employs oblations of dairy products (for example, clarified butter, milk, different varieties of curds) and vegetables (gruels and cakes made from different grains), but animal sacrifices (most often a goat, but including cows) are classed in this group as well. The Soma Sacrifices center on the offering of the divine substance, *soma*, which, according to tradition, imbues the drinker with incredible strength and poetic inspiration (Jamison 1991, 22).[6]

These classifications, however, belie commonalities in the basic structure and patterns of Vedic ritual. Certain rituals serve as models for other rituals and rituals can be "nested or embedded in other rituals, building larger and increasingly intricate ritual structures" (Jamison 1991, 23). Looking at the basic types within the two-fold classification just described, there are seven fundamental forms, from which other rituals derive. The first is the Establishment of the Fires (*agnyādheya*), in which the Sacrificer qualifies himself to perform sacrifice.

The next five are periodic rituals that follow the rhythm of the calendar. The Agnihotra consists of twice-daily offerings made into the fire. The New and Full Moon Sacrifices (*darśapūrṇamāsa*) occur, as is clear from the name, on the new and full moons. They also serve as the model for the class of rituals called the *iṣṭi*, which are undertaken to achieve a particular end. The Four-Monthly Sacrifices (*cāturmāsya*), also called the Seasonal Sacrifices, occur at the beginning of the three main seasons: the Vaiśvadevas are offered in the spring, the Varuṇapraghāsas are offered in the rainy season, and the Sākamedhas are offered in the autumn. The First-Fruits Sacrifices (*āgrayaṇa iṣṭi*) are those offerings made before partaking of the crops. The normal offerings include rice in the spring and barley in the fall. A man who has established the sacrificial fires should offer the Animal Sacrifice (*paśubandhu*) before he eats meat. Thereafter he performs the rite annually or every six months, depending on the authority. The rite is modeled on the New Moon Sacrifice and involves tying the sacrificial victim to a ritually prepared post and killing it in such a way as to avoid bringing into the ritual the negative connotations of the necessary violence (Keith 1925, 325).[7] The fact that there is an Animal Sacrifice in the Soma rite is but one example of the imperfect nature of the classification of ritual.

The final type is the Soma Sacrifice, the central ritual cycle of the *Ṛg Veda*. The Agniṣṭoma, the one-day Soma sacrifice, serves as the model for this sacrifice. In this ritual Soma is offered in the morning, at midday, and in the evening. All the multiday sacrifices involving Soma are variants of this model. Keith outlines several other types of sacrifice, some subtypes of those here outlined, others defying the two classification systems used here (Keith 1925, 332–357). Significant for their place in the later tradition are the Consecration of the King (*rajasūya*), the Horse Sacrifice (*aśvamedha*), and the Piling of the Fire Altar (*agnicayana*). The first two incorporate Soma Sacrifices and draw upon that ritual as a model; additionally, they are held up as standards of Vedic sacrifice by the later tradition.[8] The Piling of the Fire Altar, Keith tells us, "is regarded as being always available for performance along with the Soma sacrifice" (1925, 354) but was infrequently performed because of the elaborate procedures involved.[9]

This general picture of Vedic sacrifice is drawn from the liturgy of the Vedic Saṃhitās, the ritual exegesis of the Brāhmaṇas, and the detailed instructions of the Sūtra literature, texts complied roughly in that chronological order over almost a millennium. This tradition, however, does not remain fixed over this period. While much of the technical terminology appears in the oldest layers of texts (Jamison 1991, 25) some change over the period of composition of these disparate texts is evident (Keith 1925, 252). The exact nature of the changes is difficult to determine given the sparse evidence available to us.

One feature central to the Vedic religious imagination, at least by the time of the Brāhmaṇas, is the tendency to understand the human realm as linked to the cosmic realm through homologies established in the ritual realm. Ritual exegetes of the Vedic tradition emphasize the establishment and recognition of certain equivalences (*bandhu*), which establish an identity between the ritual elements and their corollaries in the human and cosmic spheres (Smith 1989, 31–34). "Participants and objects in the ritual stand for, embody, and indeed actually *become* participants and objects in the larger sphere of human life and in the cosmos..." (Jamison 1991, 25). Through the manipulation of participants and objects in the ritual realm, the ritual manipulates their equivalents in the human and cosmic realm.

Control of the microcosm, the ritual space, enables control of the macrocosm, the human and divine realms. Sacrifice confers upon the performer the ability to transform and transcend the human world.

It should be clear from this brief review that two features of later Indian religious practice are conspicuously absent, namely, temples—or other permanent ritual places—and images that represent the divine. The primary mode of religious behavior was sacrifice; these other features commonly associated with Hinduism arise much later. Much of the liturgy of the *R̥g Veda* and the commentary of the Brāhmaṇas relate mythic accounts of the divine, the former through allusion and reference, the latter in somewhat more fulsome fashion. Although none of these texts outlines the cosmos in great detail, the central gods and their major exploits are well-known.

Indra—the hard-drinking, relentless warrior god—occupies the minds of the poets more than any other deity in the hymns of the *R̥g Veda*. This is fitting for the nomadic, cattle-herding culture of the Aryans. He is the deification of the ideal Aryan warrior and his main activity is smashing foes with his mighty weapon, the *vajra*.[10] Often hymns speak of him as exhilarated by Soma and call upon him to inspire similar heroic deeds in his followers. His most famous exploit is the destruction of the Vr̥tra (literally "obstacle"), the great snake that trapped the primordial waters. He often engages in cattle raids, the most well-known of which against Vala, who hid his stolen cattle in a cave.

Second only to Indra, is Agni, fire personified. While he is praised less frequently in the *R̥g Veda* than Indra, he is far more central to the practice of sacrifice. He is fire in all its manifestations, the most important of which is the sacrificial fire. Agni is the priest of the gods, the eater of the oblations, and the mediator between this world and the world of the gods; in the ritual he is the divine counterpart to the human priests. He conveys the oblations to the gods worshiped in the ritual and brings the gods to the ritual space to sit and enjoy the hospitality of the Sacrificer. It is through Agni that the householder is able to make offerings to both the gods and his Ancestors.

Like the deified fire, the primary offering of the Soma Sacrifice is divinized. Soma is the personification of the Soma drunk in the ritual and the plant from which the sacrificial drink is pressed. Soma most often appears in pairs with Indra, Agni, and other gods. He is sometimes described as swift and compared to a fast steed. The central Soma myth revolves around its theft from heaven.

These three gods, Indra, Agni, and Soma, are the most important gods in the *Ṛg Veda* and are central to both myth and ritual activity. Indra is invoked most often and a substantial mythic cycle is available to us. Agni is the primary divine ritual actor and is involved in every ritual in at least his role as mediator. Soma is central to both the myth and ritual of the *Ṛg Veda*, because the majority of the liturgy of that text is concerned with the Soma Sacrifice. Many other gods populate the Vedic pantheon, and occupy a rich storehouse of myth.[11]

Particularly relevant for this work are the Vedic conceptions of life-after-death and the Ancestors. References to life-after-death in the *Ṛg Veda* are scarce, as are references to the Ancestors. Bodewitz (1994) has shown that the earliest layers of the *Ṛg Veda*, the Family Books, make little mention of man's destiny after death at all. The highest goal attainable by ritual performance throughout most of the older hymns is a longer life here on earth, not the immortality that the gods in heaven possess (1994, 27). The most common reference to the afterlife mentions a dark underworld. The latest layers of the text, books nine and ten, increasingly consider life in heaven the ideal for the Sacrificers, and that is promised them by the poets. Bodewitz suspects that the promise of an eternal life in heaven came to replace the older goal of continuing life here on earth, though he points out that this development was probably not linear (1994, 36). However it developed, the notion of a heavenly realm promised by the poets in the Vedic period influences the conception of the world of the Ancestors mentioned in the funerary rites and sought in ancestral rites.

This summary describes the key aspects of the Vedic religion described by Brahmins; it is the culmination of the Vedic culture of the Brahmins that moved into northwest India during the second millennium B.C.E. (Witzel 1997). This culture thrived and composed religious texts for the next millennium. Toward the end of the Vedic period—from the middle of the first millennium up to the last few centuries before the Common Era—Brahmins called their sphere of influence the land of the Āryas (*āryāvarta*), and it is in this area that the texts of Classical Hinduism were composed (Bronkhorst 2007, 1–3; *HoD* 2[1]:11–18). Beyond their self-defined boundaries—to the east of confluence of the Gaṅgā and Yamunā rivers—was an area outside the influence of the Brahmanical culture. Bronkhorst (2007) calls this area Greater Magadha and argues that the acceptance of rebirth and karmic retribution, the use of round funerary mounts, and certain forms of ascetic practice were manifestations of the religious culture of that area. It is in this context that Buddhism developed.

Early Buddhism

During the middle centuries of the last millennium before the Common Era, the Brahmanical culture's self-described hegemony was challenged. The challenge to the dominant Brahmanical worldviews came from within the Brahmanical culture and from without.[12] This rich period of challenge, rebuttal, and general contestation—indicative of competing worldviews and practices—developed out of the widespread *śramaṇa* movement, which emphasized the renunciation of the worldly life with the aim of finding some higher goal.[13] The hallmarks of this largely ascetically oriented movement—the internalization of religion, the ethicization of ritual concepts, and the rejection of the Veda as an authority and sacrificial models of religiosity—occur in both Brahmanical and non-Brahmanical discourses. Out of this movement grew the traditions of Buddhism, Ājīvikism, Jainism, and asceticism-oriented movements within the Brahmanical culture.

In this work I speak only to the Buddhist contestations of Brahmanical hegemony and, within that, restrict myself to the Buddhist reflections on ancestral rites, but a general introduction to early Buddhism will contextualize this discussion. The popular conception of Buddhism as a reformation of Brahmanical religion is a dangerous simplification of the complex religious milieu of religious contestation in the last few centuries before the Common Era. Buddhism reflects one reaction to the variety of alternatives being explored during the *śramaṇa* period.

The Buddhist tradition ascribes its core ideas to the founder, Siddartha Gautama. We are told he mastered various forms of religious practice and found them lacking, then, taking rest beneath a tree in Uruvelā, entered a deep state of mediation and eventually achieved *nirvāṇa* (the end of the cycles a rebirth, literally "extinguishing"). Through the keen insight into the nature of existence attained in meditation he was awakened (*buddha*) to the true nature of reality. The Buddha is the source of all insights, thus the early corpus of Buddhist literature revolves around the teachings of the Buddha; often these are embedded in narrative tales of his encounters with various religious practitioners, monks, and others.

In broad terms the Buddha taught that which is "conducive to the holy life and to peace and enlightenment" (Bronkhorst 2009, 9); he was primarily concerned with the end of human suffering. In terms used by the tradition, the teachings of the Buddha are often summed up as the Middle Path, and this implies not merely the rejection of the extremes of hedonism and the harshest of ascetic practices, but also an understanding of reality as real, but devoid of permanence. The Buddha diagnosed the human condition—in the four noble truths: life is suffering; suffering has a cause: craving; to end suffering end craving; to end craving follow the Eightfold Path—and outlined the method to end the innately painful cycle of worldly existence. The goal, to achieve *nirvāṇa*, became the ultimate goal of the teachings of the Buddha and the path of personal development and meditation outlined in the Eightfold Path.

The Buddhists accepted the notions of *karma* and reincarnation, but they reinterpreted both significantly. Whereas other *śramaṇa* groups emphasized the attainment of liberation through knowledge of the self, the Buddha distinguished himself by denying this (Bronkhorst 2009, 25). While the question of whether the Buddha himself formally denied the existence of the self (the doctrine called *anatta*), as the later tradition did, or not is uncertain (see Bronkhorst 2009, 23 for sources on this debate), but the early tradition denies a permanent self. Restraining from identifying ourselves with any one aspect of our existence, for example, our body, is central to the Buddha's teachings. The doctrine of conditioned origination—the assertion that no event is without a cause or an effect, which implies a perpetual cycle of becoming and dissolution—describes a world in which nothing is permanent, including the self. This doctrine is often said to be the key to attaining liberation. If one were to understand the impermanence of reality and, because of that, stop craving that which is transitory, then one can end suffering—and by no longer craving existence, cease to be reborn in this world.

While this is the traditional account of the main points of Buddhism, the early Buddhist texts paint a much more complicated picture of both the practices and ideas advocated by those who preserved the texts ascribed to the Buddha. One practice that shapes the early Buddhist community is the extension of the common ascetic rain retreats—ascetics could not easily move about and seek alms during the rainy season—into permanent establishments, which gradually grew into monasteries. The Buddhist Saṅgha (monastic community) consists of monks, and later nuns, who serve as a repository for knowledge and source of merit-making for the laity of all persuasion. Throughout the Pāli Canon, the earliest collection of Buddhist texts available to us, wealthy householders and kings make gifts to the Buddha and the Saṅgha. This indicates one key religious practice for the laity, giving material support to the monastic community, the religious experts, in exchange for some benefit; this benefit is expressed explicitly in some places and implicitly in others (Samuels 1997, 232–233). However, the patronizing of religious experts is not uniquely Buddhist. Evidence in the Pāli Canon—as well as the Brahmanical literature—suggests that religious experts of various groups were the object of religious gifting.[14]

The Buddha frequently speaks to the practice of ritual among householders, often condemning the violence inherent in sacrifice, but condoning, if not advocating, ritual that does not involve violence (e.g., *S* i.75–76 and *A* ii.4–43).[15] The Buddhist authors did not reject the ubiquitous ritual practices of the householder (hospitality, divine rites, and ancestral rites); they merely reinterpreted them in various ways, for example, reconceptualizing their underpinning assumptions or offering a moral interpretation (Egge 2002; White 1986, 203). The Buddhist texts incorporate a wide variety of religious practice, including those gradually incorporated into the Brahmanical texts during this period. The preoccupation of the early Buddhist literature with conversion stories indicates the efforts to include various religious practitioners in the Buddhist fold. The nature of the specific narratives of conversion and other interactions between Buddhists and non-Buddhists demonstrate an intense rivalry and competition as well as efforts to portray the Buddha in as recognizable a form as possible and express a nonthreatening inclusivistic community (Bailey 1998). The Buddhists reacted to the religious environment in which they operated and sought to compete with others offering religious services.

However, the Buddhist authors were not only reactionary in their competition for the role of religious expert; they were also proactive in reconceptualizing the religious life. Some of their efforts produced reactions within Brahmanical theological circles. Olivelle has convincingly argued that Buddhists used the term *dharma* as part of their appropriation of royal symbols and language and subsequently incorporated it as a central part of "a new imperial ideology." Further, Brahmanical efforts to define *dharma* found in the Dharmasūtras, the Law Codes, and the *Mahābhārata* were a "direct consequence of the Buddhist and Aśokan reforms" and represent the creation of "an authoritative means to know *dharma*" (2004a, 505–506). Similarly, I have argued that the establishment of the Hindu pilgrimage place of Gayā may have been inspired by the older Buddhist associations there (2010). The author of the *Bhagavad Gītā* incorporated several ideas from Buddhism into that most highly respected text of the Hindu tradition (Upadhyaya 1971). John Clifford Holt has described the political dimension of such religious transformations going in both directions (Holt 2004).

Throughout their history Buddhist and Brahmanical theologians have reflected upon their competitors' works and inconsistently appropriated, incorporated, rejected, and ridiculed the ideas, languages, and practices of the other groups (see Ben-Herut 2009). The appropriation by all parties intensified the competition between rival religious ideologies. The competition between these rival groups had the highest stakes: the livelihood of those who market themselves as the religious expert best able not only to serve the daily religious needs of the average religious actor but also to guide the religious practitioner to the ultimate goal of human life.

This multiplicity of religious expert seeking patronage naturally set up a competitive religious marketplace. The religious literature produced in each of these religious communities is rife with evidence that they were consciously marketing themselves to the primary religious consumer, the householder, for the householders performed ritual to propitiate the divine and their ancestors. I use the term *marketing* in the sense that Bailey and Mabbett do: "By marketing we understand the deliberate application of a panoply of techniques to parade, in an intentionally persuasive manner, the ideology each group claimed to embody and its corresponding lifestyle" (2003, 109). The descriptions of the proper religious experts in both traditions—as well as disparaging comments about others who claim the role of religious expert—should be understood as one of the techniques aimed at convincing the householder that the author's worldview and ethos are best suited for the householder.

We must take into account here not only the audiences of the texts, but the authors as well. The Brahmins are not a monolithic group that share the same concerns; nor are the Buddhists. Certainly the Brahmins did not write for a general audience, nor did the Buddhists authors. But I assert that we can understand the concerns that underlie their literature as reflective of a certain appropriative stance toward the householder and indicative of a mindset that includes marketing as Bailey and Mabbett use the term.

The religions just described are largely available to us through the texts composed by the educated among both groups.[16] The following summary contextualizes the sources from which most of the evidence throughout this work is drawn.

The Sources

The Vedic religion as just described is known to us through the textual production of an educated class of Brahmins living in the north of modern-day India from the end of the second millennium B.C.E. through the beginning of the first millennium of the Common Era. These texts were all composed and preserved orally until the very end of the period under discussion. The oldest evidence available to us comes from the *Ṛg Veda Saṃhitā*, a compilation of sacred hymns said to embody the revelatory knowledge "heard" by the ancient Vedic seers (*ṛṣi*)—the later term for the Vedic ritual tradition, *śruti*, derives from the verb *śru*, to hear. The *Ṛg Veda Saṃhitā* (literally "collection of sacred knowledge in verse") is one of four texts, each associated with one of the four classes of priests employed in the sacrifice: The *Ṛg Veda*, the *Yajur Veda*, the *Sāma Veda*, and the *Atharva Veda* collectively describe the roles of these four classes of priests. The *Ṛg Veda* is a collation of 1028 hymns to various deities collected into ten books. The youngest hymns belong to a period just before the compilation of the *Ṛg Veda* sometime around 1000 B.C.E.; the oldest are centuries older (Witzel 1989; 1997). The text serves as the primary liturgical collection for the Vedic ritual cycle, especially the extensive Soma rites. The *Sāma Veda* records songs of praise (*sāman*) largely derived from the hymns of the *Ṛg Veda*. The *Yajur Veda* is a collection of sacred ritual formulas (*yajus*) used in the ritual. The *Atharva Veda* includes much beyond that which is directly relevant to the solemn ritual performance, including magical and healing rites. Within the priestly traditions that correspond to each Veda there arose theological schools (*śākhā*, literally "branch") that composed the subsequent literature that describes, interprets, and comments upon the Vedic ritual cycle. Table I.1 outlines the theological schools that developed around the four Vedas.

Each theological school composed several genres of literature reflecting on the ritual. The earliest works in these traditions were called Brāhmaṇas and include extensive commentary related to the Veda of that theological school. The Brāhmaṇa commentaries on Vedic ritual follow the ritual cycles and include direct glosses, etymological analysis, extensive mythic references, and prose reflections on the purpose and function of the ritual. The dating of these texts is notoriously difficult, but scholarly consensus is that the earliest Brāhmaṇas were composed in the first several centuries of the first millennium B.C.E. (Witzel 1989).

The further development of this reflective tradition appears in the subsequent genres of texts, the Āraṇyakas and the Upaniṣads. While there

Table I.1 Theological schools of the *Ṛg, Yajur, Sāma*, and ***Atharva*** Vedas

Veda	*Saṃhitā*	Brāhmaṇa	Śrautasūtra	Gṛhyasūtra	Dharmasūtra	Smṛti
Ṛg	Ṛg	Aitareya	Āśvalāyana	Āśvalāyana	Vasiṣṭha	
		Kauṣītaki	Śāṅkhāyana	Śāṅkhāyana	Gautama	
Yajur	Taittirīya	Taittirīya	Baudhāyana	Baudhāyana	Baudhāyana	Vādhūla
	Maitrāyaṇī		Mānava	Mānava	Mānava	Mānava
	Kāṭhaka	Kaṭha	Kāṭhaka	Kāṭhaka		Viṣṇu
	Vājasaneyi	Śatapatha	Āpastamba	Āpastamba	Āpastamba	Yājñavalkya
			Bharadvāja	Bharadvāja		
			Kātyāyana	Pāraskara		
			Hiraṇyakeśin	Hiraṇyakeśin		
Sāma	Kauthuma	Pañcaviṃśa	Maśaka	Gobhila		
	Rāṇāyanīya	Ṣaḍviṃśa	Kalpasūtra	Khādira		
				Lāṭyāyana		
	Jaiminīya	Jaiminīya	Jaiminīya	Jaimini		
Atharva	Śaunaka	Gopatha	Vaitān	Kauśika	Sumantu	
	Paippalāda		aĀgastya	Paithīnasi		

is no clear distinction between these genres in the tradition—in fact, they usually form part of the Brāhmaṇas—they are distinguished by an increasingly speculative philosophy and a developing interest in the truth of reality that lies beyond the ritual itself. The Upaniṣads develop the alternative theologies related to reincarnation and the nature of the self—specifically the conception of the *ātman* as the eternal Self and its identity to the underlying substrate of reality called *brahman*. Olivelle dates the oldest Upaniṣads, which were composed in prose and are likely pre-Buddhist, to the seventh or sixth centuries B.C.E. (1996, xxxvi). Subsequent Upaniṣads were composed in verse; the oldest of these likely date to the last few centuries before the Common Era (Olivelle 1999, xxxvii). Finally, two late Upaniṣads, composed in prose, appear in the early centuries of the Common Era.

Following these Vedic materials, there arose within the Vedic theological schools expert discourse aimed at preserving all the knowledge supplementary to the performance of the sacrifice. The *Vedāṅgas* (literally "limbs of the Veda") are generally classified into six categories: collections of ritualistic rules, grammar, astronomy, etymology, phonetics, and metrics (e.g., *ĀpDhS* 2.8.11). Educated Brahmins concerned about preserving their culture recorded their traditions in compendia of ritual expositions called the Kalpasūtras. These collections included the *Śrautasūtras*, the *Gṛhyasūtras*, and the *Dharmasūtras* addressing the solemn rites, the domestic rites (*gṛhya*), and *dharma*, respectively.

The *sūtra* texts consist of a series of brief aphorisms—the word *sūtra* means "thread" and evokes the image of beads strung on a thread, each aphorism a bead. [17] The *sūtras* are organized in a terse style; the paradigmatic ritual is described in detail, but the description of each subsequent ritual mentions only the variations from the paradigmatic rite.

The Śrautasūtras describe the major solemn ritual cycles and they largely agree with the Brāhmaṇas with respect to their understanding of the ritual (See Bhide 1979, Einoo 1988, and Gonda 1977b). There are some significant differences between the rituals described here and in the older material—and differences in performance between theological schools are evident—but in general the rituals are understood to be variants within the same broad Vedic tradition. The Śrautasūtras date to the middle of the first millennium B.C.E. (Gonda 1977b, 476–477).

The Gṛhyasūtras similarly describe ritual behavior in *sūtras*, but their object is significantly different. The domestic rituals largely concern themselves with the private, domestic ritual life of the twice-born man, primarily that of the Brahmin. The series of twelve sacred ceremonies to be performed during one's life address life-cycle events and rites of passage, for example, birth, naming, initiation, marriage, death rites. One significant difference between solemn and domestic rituals is the dramatically reduced role played by the Vedic priests of the older ritual cycle. The householder takes on the primary responsibility for the ritual actions.

For the first time in the Gṛhyasūtras there appears a new role for a religious expert. The educated Brahmin is invited to the ritual to act as a professional guest; the householder asks his permission to make the oblations, he is fed, and he pronounces the success of the ritual endeavor. In addition, as I will argue later, this new role employs the Brahmin as a mediator, ensuring the efficacious exchange enacted through ritual between the householder and the entities he seeks to propitiate through ritual, that is, the gods or the Ancestors.

The domestic rituals described in the Gṛhyasūtras form the core of the religious practice for the subsequent development of Hinduism. The Gṛhyasūtras presuppose the solemn model for several key rites and model a significant portion of the rituals on the solemn ritual cycle (Oldenberg 1967, xxx), but the authors also introduce rites and modes of religious practice previously unexpressed in the textual tradition. The Gṛhyasūtras in general follow the Śrautasūtras chronologically, but few of the domestic ritual manuals in the different theological schools are contemporaneous with each other, that is, the genre develops unevenly within the theological traditions. While some Kalpasūtras are attributed to single authors, for example, Āpastamba and Baudhāyana, these texts are generally composite works drawing on older traditions and often including newer material (Olivelle 2000, 4; Oldenberg 1967, xxxiii). Internal evidence found in the Gṛhyasūtras suggests that they include similar additions and interpolations (Oldenberg 1967). The Gṛhyasūtras were probably composed from sometime between the middle and the last few centuries of the first millennium B.C.E.; the earliest texts of this genre probably overlap with the Śrautasūtras and the latest with the Dharmasūtras.[18]

The later Gṛhyasūtras were coming into their current form during the composition of the Dharmasūtras, which can be dated with a little more precision that the earlier literature. The earliest Dharmasūtra, Āpastamba, was probably composed at the beginning of the third century B.C.E. and the latest, Vasiṣṭha, around the turn of the millennium (Olivelle 2000, 10). The Dharmasūtras record a tradition of scholarly reflection on the nature of *dharma*. They evidence an educated class of Brahmin reflecting, and often debating, views on topics including ritual procedures, life-cycle ceremonies, dietary restrictions, regulations for social behavior and organization, and the duties of the king. They are squarely situated in the tradition of Brahmins who understand ritual as central to the proper life.

Out of this early discursive tradition on *dharma* arose the more fully developed Law Codes (*dharmaśāstra*). These works also address *dharma*, but include much more detail on the king's duties and the judicial procedure. More significantly, whereas the Dharmasūtras *describe* what constitutes the proper life, the later authors *prescribe* the proper *dharma*. Additionally, the tradition ascribes far greater authority to the Law Codes than to the *Dharmasūtras*. For example, the *Mānava Dharmaśāstra*, the *Law Code of Manu*, is ascribed to Manu, the mythological progenitor of mankind. This Law Code, the earliest of the legal treatises, was composed sometime in the first or second century of the Common Era (Olivelle 2004, xxiii).

Olivelle has ably argued that the construction of elaborate treatises on *dharma*—like the *Mahābhārata*, which is similarly concerned with religious duty—appears to indicate a strident and urgent defense of Brahmanical privilege. Likely this came as a reaction to the historical memory, at least for these Brahmins, of the broad displacement of Brahmins from their privileged position in society by so-called Śūdra kings such as Aśoka (Olivelle 2004a; 2004b, xli–xlv; see also Bronkhorst 2007, 97). This is one factor in the efforts made in this period by the Brahmins to define their worldview as hegemonic. They are reacting to competition for the role of religious expert between, among others, the Brahmins and Buddhists. It is in this context that the most ardent discursive works on the proper religious life are composed. Most of the early Law Codes that follow Manu rely heavily, occasionally slavishly, on him.

The last few centuries before the Common Era and the first few centuries thereof saw tremendous textual production.[19] The *Law Code of Manu* draws upon the ancient Indian treatise on statecraft the *Arthaśāstra*, therefore some version of this work must have come into being at least shortly before Manu's work (Olivelle 2004b, xx; see also Kangle 1988, 3:59ff.). In addition, it is in this period that the *Mahābhārata* began to come into its present form (van Buitenen 1973, xxv; Bronkhorst 2007, 95).

The Buddhist material is far less extensive, both in time span and in volume, but the Pāli Canon—the earliest collection of Buddhist texts, composed in the literary language of Buddhists—was under formation during the last few centuries before the Common Era. The version of that compendium of early Buddhist literature we have available today is a reflection of the canon first written down in the first century B.C.E. (Norman 1983, 5). There was certainly a long period of development before its commitment to writing (Hinüber 1996, 5), but debate over the manner and degree of success in preservation has courted controversy. Norman argues that Pāli grammarians of the twelfth century had some influence on the commentators, whose opinion sometimes had a bearing of the readings scribes preserved (1983, 6). Schopen suggests we can know little for certain of the Pāli Canon before the redaction known to Buddhaghosa in the fifth or sixth century C.E. (1997a, 24), but it is difficult to accept this level of skepticism, since other material datable to a period before the fifth century C.E. demonstrates an awareness of the Pāli Canon. This does not eliminate the real possibility of changes to the content of those texts, but Norman's assertion that there is evidence the texts were already being written down before the first century—and that the linguistic changes in the language at that time suggest a slowing of the changes in the language (1983, 5)—suggest a conservative tradition.

From the Pāli Canon I draw primarily upon the texts most relevant to my argument, which demonstrate that the *śrāddha*-rite did have a significant place in the Buddhist discourse on the proper religious life of the householder. I rely primarily on the older sections of the *Sutta Piṭaka*—a collection of *suttas,* texts that are generally narrative in form—and the *Petavatthu*—a collection of ghost stories from the *Khuddaka Nikāya* aimed at warning the readers about the dangers of immoral behavior—for the early Buddhist perspective on ancestral rites as a part of the ritual life of Buddhists and about the *śrāddha*-rite specifically. These didactic tales aim to reinforce the religious practice of giving, particularly to the Saṅgha, but they can be read with an eye to revealing cultural assumptions about and practices related to the deceased. The *Petavatthu* exists today embedded in its commentary, the *Paramatthadīpanī* of Dhammapāla. The *Petavatthu* dates between the second century B.C.E. (Obeyesekere 2002, 139) and the first century C.E. (White 1986, 190n7), but the commentary of Dhammapāla dates to somewhere between the fifth (White 1986, 190n7) and the seventh century C.E. (Cousins 1972, 159).[20]

The texts from the Pāli Canon grant us a perspective on the earliest expressions of Buddhism. Though their exact chronological provenance is unclear, they are roughly coeval with the Brahmanical sources in which the construction of ancestral rites and the role for a new religious expert occur. In the end, though caution is advised, the dating of all the texts from this period is a fluid enterprise, and my arguments do not rest on firm, clear-cut relative dating, let alone absolute chronology. Romila Thapar suggests that to separate Brahmanical and Buddhist traditions "in viewing the ideological concerns of the mid-first millennium B.C. is to pull a historiographical situation out of alignment" (1982, 273). Further the "Brahmanical and Buddhist world-views presented both a dialectical and inter-face relationship" (273). Similarly, Jamison and Witzel note "conceptual overlaps" with the late Vedic materials and recommend comparison between the later Vedic and "slightly later evidence of the Pāli Canon" (Jamison and Witzel 2003, 105). I aim to do just this—uncover the shared ideological concerns by comparing and relating the discursive efforts made by the two traditions—by understanding the relationship between texts in relative terms and avoid the trap of relying on or insisted upon exact dating, which is impossible.

Ancestor Worship

The earliest reference to ancestor veneration occurs in the tenth book of the *Ṛg Veda*, among the youngest material of this liturgical text (Witzel 1997). The poet's use of the term *pitṛyajñá* (Sacrifice to the Ancestors), may indicate a broader tradition of ancestor worship, but its context in the funeral hymn (*ṚV* 10.16) reveals little about the cult of the dead. The funerary hymns, including offerings to one's deceased father as an Ancestor, are a later inclusion in the collection of hymns used primarily in the Soma cult of the ancient Aryans and suggest the late incorporation of ancestral rites into the Vedic sacrificial cycle. The fuller treatment of such offerings to the dead in the *Atharva Veda* indicates that text's greater investment in things beyond the central Vedic sacrificial cycle, though that text still does not offer a complete picture of the practice of ancestor worship.

It is only in the Brāhmaṇas that the tradition addresses the ancestral rites in a comprehensive fashion. Understood through their exposition in the Brāhmaṇas, the *pitṛyajña*—which is certainly different from the rite hinted at in the *Ṛg Veda*—and the *piṇḍapitṛyajña* (Rice-ball Sacrifice to the Ancestors) represent a full ritual cycle of offerings to one's Ancestors. In brief, both rituals aim at feeding the Ancestors and follow the basic paradigm of the New and Full Moon Sacrifice, though they differ in important ways.

The *piṇḍapitṛyajña* occurs on the afternoon of the new moon. After the preliminaries, which are shared with the other rites, the rite deviates from the usual paradigm, by offering not to Agni and Soma, the deities of the new and full moon rites, but to the Ancestors. Instead of cakes, they offer rice-balls (*piṇḍa*)[21] cooked on the southern fire, collyrium, ointment, and wool (which symbolizes clothing). After these rice-balls are symbolically consumed by the Ancestors, they are consumed by the priests, as is the offering in the model ritual.

The *pitṛyajña* occurs during the Four-Monthly Sacrifices performed in the fall. It follows the same preliminaries, but involves a conscious synthesis of divine and ancestral offerings, accompanied by the shifting of one's sacred thread, which marks the mode of worship. This rite does include the offering of rice-balls, but it does not include gifts of collyrium, ointment, or wool.

The differences briefly mentioned here point to the synthesis of the model of sacrifice paradigmatic for the Vedic religion and a fuller, originally domestic, tradition of ancestor worship. The *śrauta* tradition of sacrificial ritual is attested throughout the texts available to us and Gonda and Oldenberg demonstrate there was a strong culture of domestic ritual in the Brāhmaṇas (Gonda 1977b, 547; Oldenberg 1967, xv–xxii), but little is known about the practice outside the ritual texts. The integration of the domestic rites involves an infusion of concerns previously not central to Vedic sacrifice into the texts of the theological tradition and the śrautification of the domestic ritual behavior. Drawing upon the wealth of domestic practice to enrich their ritual repertoire, they synthesize the Vedic ritual tradition with this lively cult of ancestor worship that developed alongside the centuries-old tradition described in the texts. Knipe, in the context of the *sapiṇḍīkaraṇa śrāddha*-rite—the ritual promotion of the deceased to the ranks of the Ancestors—refers to such synthesis as the "conflation of vedic-Hindu liturgical practice and probable indigenous folk religion" (Knipe 1977, 121). I agree with him provided we resist the temptation to understand the latter as belonging to a different cultural system. Bronkhorst's (2007) characterization of the Greater Magadha culture would preclude them as candidates for the infusion of this ritual tradition. The introduction of ancestral rites into the textual tradition is a synthesis of different streams within the Vedic religious milieu, not of Aryan and non-Aryan practices.

Within the context of the solemn ritual, I argue, the *piṇḍapitṛyajña* incorporates a tradition of feeding the dead into the Vedic ritual cycle and introduces several ritual elements uncommon in Vedic sacrifice. The *pitṛyajña*, on the other hand, shows signs of being a more fully integrated rite, that is, the Brahmanical authors adapted the Vedic sacrifice and oriented it toward the Ancestors. The veneration of the Ancestors was structured in ways more akin to the divine rite than the *piṇḍapitṛyajña* and its presumed extra-textual model. The *piṇḍapitṛyajña* and the *pitṛyajña* represent two phases of the incorporation of the practice of ancestor worship into the Vedic sacrificial model. Whereas the *piṇḍapitṛyajña* is more clearly a hybrid ritual, the *pitṛyajña*, suggests a more fully integrated Vedic ancestral rite.

The Brahmanical tradition that infused the rituals of ancestor worship into the solemn ritual, the large-scale, public rites, also drew upon this vast cultural reservoir in the textualization of the domestic rituals, the small-scale, domestic rites. A tradition of domestic ritual certainly predated the composition of the Gṛhyasūtras, the domestic ritual manuals, but the incorporation of these rites into the textual tradition of the Brahmins demonstrates more strongly the synthesis of the textualized and untextualized ritual traditions. The discourse on domestic ritual reflects on both the inherited textualized version of ancestor worship and the broader untextualized tradition, gradually integrating them into a single ritual cycle of ancestral rites known as the *śrāddha*-rite. This new tradition of ancestral rites differs in scale, its principal human actors, and the manner of ritual interaction. It becomes the paradigm for ancestral veneration for the subsequent tradition.

This new form of ancestor worship, the *śrāddha*-rite, is very influential on the development of the theological discourse on *dharma* that develops in the period subsequent to the Gṛhyasūtras. The authors of the Dharmasūtras and the Dharmaśāstras accept the *śrāddha*-rite as the paradigmatic rite of ancestor veneration, and gradually it becomes a central part of their prescription for the proper religious life. The broader arguments between Brahmins that advocate a ritual-oriented life and Brahmins that champion liberation (*mokṣa*) won through renunciation as the goal of a religious life permeate the *dharma* literature, and the soteriology upon which the *śrāddha*-rite rests is central to the tension between ritualists and renouncers. The former accept a heaven won through ritual as the ultimate goal for a human life, whereas the latter advocate the renunciation of worldly life in order to transcend the cycle of rebirth, that is, to achieve liberation. Brahmanical theologians who composed the *dharma* literature mount a staunch defense of the ritualist soteriology.

In retrospect we can mark the Gṛhyasūtras as the locus of a radical shift from the religious practice advocated in Vedic corpus of the *Ṛg Veda*, the Brāhmaṇas, and the Śrautasūtras to that which defines Classical Hinduism as expressed in the Dharmaśāstras, the Epics, and the Purāṇas, a period coincident with the origins and early development of Buddhism.

Both Brahmanical and Buddhist thinkers participate in the transformational construction of a new form of religiosity, often in direct competition with each other (e.g., Bailey and Mabbett 2003). One of the most salient features that distinguishes the earlier and the classical forms of Indian religiosity is the tremendous increase in forms of religious activities described in the theological literature, for example, pilgrimage.

I do not suggest that the traditions that Brahmanical authors describe are new or that they are practiced by more people; we have no way to determine how widespread these rituals were, before or after their textualization. Nor do I suggest that the Vedic rituals or ancestor worship are *replaced* by the domestic rites—Vedic peoples practiced both solemn and domestic rites before the domestic rites were textualized, so we have no reason to believe the Vedic rites were simply eliminated. However, the domestic model of ancestor worship, specifically the *śrāddha*-rite becomes more central to the tradition's understanding of the householder's ritual obligations. Classical Hinduism grows out of the gradual synthesis of Vedic discourse found in the texts and religious practices introduced into the theological discourse of educated Brahmins during this period. This synthesis is apparent in the repeated appropriation and, by means of discursive construction of proper religious behavior, authorization of disparate religious practices, for example, ancestor worship, funerary rituals, pilgrimage, and so forth. Buddhism too develops by means of a perpetual synthesis of disparate views, sometimes narrowly defined as Brahmanical and "popular" (e.g., DeCaroli 2004) or, in the case of Vedic domestic ritual, "Popular and Hieratic" (Keith 1925, 55–57). However, the social milieu in which these two traditions existed and defined themselves was far too complicated to be captured by a simple dichotomy.[22]

The development of the practice of ancestral rites in both traditions derives from the periodic incorporation—which both appropriates and authenticates—of previously untextualized ancestral rites into the elite, educated religious discourse of Brahmins and Buddhists, but this should not be understood to imply a distinction between the practice of the authors as "elite" and that of others as "popular." Neither Brahmins nor Buddhist authors are separated from the world in which they live. Neither the "world" generated by the texts nor "world on the ground" are uniform or homogenous; both are diverse and dynamic.[23] In this complex cultural environment, authors argued for particular practices against many other perspectives, those in the texts and those encountered in the real world. Read in this way, the discourses on ancestor worship in both Brahmanical and Buddhist literature can be understood as expressing meaningful and intentional authorial decisions to synthesize disparate religious practices in the on-going construction of their ideology as the proper perspective on efficacious religious practice and their religious experts as the key to the success of that practice. Their religious literature, among other aims, works to market the religious expert described therein as the only proper expert. At stake is the livelihood of the Brahmin acting as ritual expert and the Saṅgha as recipient of religious gifts.

While this is instrumental in understanding the development of the classical rites of ancestor worship, left in this general form this approach would not alter our broader understanding of religious development in ancient India. However, I argue that the rituals of ancestor worship are central to this development. The transformation of religious expression just described revolves around the debate over the ultimate soteriological goal of religious men and relies upon the redefinition of the role of the religious expert, specifically the mode of mediation that the religious expert was said to effect between the ritualist and the supernatural entities he sought to propitiation through ritual.

The soteriological debates in the *dharma* tradition indicate a growing concern with the efficacy of the rites and these concerns center on the religious expert said to mediate the exchange effected in the ritual or the materials exchanged. The authors of the Gṛhyasūtras do not exhibit any doubts about the rites, they simply prescribe the proper behavior—this is likely a feature of the genre—but the authors of the Dharmaśāstras react to challenges leveled against the presumption that ritual is the pinnacle of proper religious behavior. Read in this light the point of the lengthy discussions of the proper method and materials for performing the ancestral rites becomes clear; the authors respond to the challenge by championing the efficacy of the rituals said to win one an eternal stay in heaven. Brahmanical authors respond to the challenge of the renouncer tradition that the rites do not win an eternal world and to Buddhist challenges that the Saṅgha more effectively guarantees success in ritual activity by vehemently asserting that the rites do indeed win an eternal heaven when performed by Brahmins.

One key feature of the development of the ritual tradition in this period is the effort made by both the Brahmanical and Buddhist traditions to recreate the role of religious expert as mediator. In the solemn ritual tradition the Vedic priests mediated between the Sacrificer and the gods in the sacrifice. They made offerings to Agni, who carried them to the gods and the

Ancestors. The Brahmin authors involved in the redefinition of the ritual tradition worked to create a new religious expert, but they did not draw upon the model of the Vedic priest, instead they drew upon the model of and used metaphors related to Agni—the god of Fire, who is himself called priest[24]—as the paradigmatic intermediary. In this way, they constructed a new role for themselves in the ritual life of the householder, an alternative to the Vedic priest. The creation of this new role generated the need to identify who was qualified to act as mediator. Theologians denied birth rite as a qualification, so they needed to describe the person who was qualified to act as mediator. This sparked considerable debate about who was qualified to act as mediator. Authors in both traditions advocated learning and morality, but described those qualifications differently, narrowly circumscribing the conception of the proper ritual expert to exclude competitors.

These discussions grew to epic proportions in the descriptions of the ritual expert employed in ancestor worship. The Brahmanical authors of the *dharma* tradition were preoccupied with the role of mediator in their discussions of the *śrāddha*-rite, while in the Buddhist traditions the cultural memory of *śrāddha*-rite informed the tradition of religious gifting (*dāna*). Selections from the Sutta literature shows that at least some Buddhist householders still engaged in the *śrāddha*-rite, though the authors works to change the moral implications of its practice. The tales of the *Petavatthu* reveal the influence of the practice of *śrāddha*-rite on the conception of religious giving advocated early in the Buddhist tradition.

Both of these threads, soteriology and mediation, occupy central places in the discussion of ancestor worship in both traditions and drive the transformation from Vedic forms of religion to the classical form of Hinduism and the earliest development within Buddhism, especially the *dāna* tradition. The redefinition of the role of mediator and the staunch defense of the soteriological goals asserted in the practice of ancestor worship are enacted first, and defended more fervently later, in the construction of the new paradigm for ancestor worship, the *śrāddha*-rite. I argue that debate over the final end of man and the definition of a religious expert that informs religious practice in India in the Common Era are grounded in the redefinition of ancestral rites in the Gṛhyasūtras.

I

Ancestral Rites in the Early Vedas

THE OLDEST REFERENCE to ancestor worship in the Vedic literature occurs in the *R̥g Veda*, a text almost entirely dedicated to the liturgical poetry of the Soma cult. While the Ancestors do appear in several hymns, there is only one explicit reference to their veneration through ritual. In R̥V 10.16.10 the poet calls Agni to the *pitr̥yajñá*, the Sacrifice to the Ancestors. In this chapter I will outline the Vedic understanding of ancestor worship through two lenses: the conception of the Ancestors and a pair of terms intimately involved with the propitiation of the Ancestors.

I first review the Vedic conception of the *pitŕ̥*—literally father, but referring to both the direct ancestors of the Sacrificer and the earliest ancestors who found the path to the next world—in order to describe their role in the ritual life of the Vedic people. Then, to understand the later development of the ancestral rites, I also explore the use of two key terms: *pitr̥yajñá* and *svadhā́*. The term *pitr̥yajñá* occurs only once in the *R̥g Veda*,[1] and its referent is unclear. The term *svadhā́* can mean independence or one's own power as well as the call *svadhā́*;[2] the former sense occurs frequently in both the *R̥g Veda* and *Atharva Veda*, but the latter sense occurs rarely in the Saṃhitā literature, though it is later inexorably connected with the rituals to propitiate the ancestors.

The Ancestors

The Ancestors are semidivine beings who receive oblations and share in the sacred Soma that so animates the gods mythic actions. They bestow beneficial gifts, heroes, and wealth and ensure the success of those among the living who venerate them. They are both the deified dead and the earliest and ancient Ancestors of the human race, but the distinction between the two is not always clear. Nor is the distinction between Ancestor and god.

Most commonly, the Ancestors enjoy the position of the deified dead in Vedic mythology. They are once spoken of as gods (*ṚV* 10.56.4), and, as they do with the various other deities, the poets invoke them for protection (e.g., *ṚV* 3.55.2, 6.52.4, 6.75.10, 10.15.2, 5) and call upon them for aid (1.106.3). Like Varuṇa, they are asked not to punish sinners (10.15.6). Often hymns associate them with the accumulation of wealth, in connection with the gods broadly (1.91.1), or Indra specifically (7.18.1), or Sarasvatī in connection with both food and wealth (10.17.9). All sorts of wealth are granted by the Ancestors, like gold, horses, barley, and abundant heroes (9.69.8).

There is a strong association between the Ancestors and light. The poets tell us they found the light in darkness (7.76.4), dwell in the light (10.15.10, 10.107.1), and put the constellations in the sky, put day in night and night in day (10.68.11). Similarly, the Ancestors are understood to be connected with Truth (*ṛtá*). They are called strong through Truth (*ṛtāvṛ́ddha*) several times (1.106.3, 1.159.1, 10.16.11, 10.154.4) and elsewhere related to truth (e.g., 10.15.10). Their adherence to the moral order also qualifies them to partake in the oblations offered at rituals.

The Ancestors are said to weave the sacrifice at creation (10.130.1) and are intimately associated specifically with Soma in the sacrifice (10.130.6, 10.57.3–6). They are called soma-loving (*somyá*) often (6.75.10, 10.14.6, 10.15.1, 5, 8, 10.16.8) and invoked in hymns to Soma himself (e.g., 9.96.11, 10.57.3, 9.97.39) as well as in ritual offerings of Soma to other gods (8.48.12). Their role in the ritual is secured by this association with Soma and they are deified by having drunk the Soma. In one passage, the Ancestors receive oblations along with the gods (10.14.3); the two types of offerings are distinguished with the words *svā́hā*, which accompanies divine oblations, and *svadhā́*, which accompanies ancestral oblations. While the association with sacrifice appears throughout the *Ṛg Veda*, and the poets refer to the Ancestors receipt of those oblations often to praise them, they only actually receive those offerings in the context of the funerary hymns. The primary ritual engagement with the Ancestors is as the deified dead, who receive oblations in the context of ancestral rites, for example, *ṚV* 10.14.3; 10.15.4–5, 11–13; 10.16.11; 10.17.8.

In addition to their role in ritual and their granting of wealth, mentioned above, the Ancestors also grant offspring, often specifically sons, and make a place for the deceased in the next world. Their role in helping produce offspring is sometimes expressed explicitly—they place the seed (9.83.3)[3]—sometimes implicitly—they send down streams (*rétas*), which can refer to both libations and semen (10.64.14)[4]—and sometimes more generally (10.57.6). The Ancestors additionally have the responsibility for ushering the recently deceased into heaven. They mark the path to heaven (10.2.7, 10.14.2). Elsewhere they are said to provide this place (10.14.9, 10.17.3) or, along with Yama, they make a place for the deceased (10.18.13).

The Ancestors are the central object of veneration in at least one hymn (10.15) but they play a crucial role in all five funerary hymns (10.14–18) and play an increasingly central role in ritual as the Brahmanical authors give ancestral rites a more central role in the ritual cycle. They retain their status as the deified dead, but the manner of interacting with them gradually changes as the rites do. Constant though is their role as benefactors to the proper ritual performer, bestowing the benefits that continue their hereditary line. As the tradition develops, both the recently dead and the earliest and ancient ancestors of the human race are classified in increasingly complex mythologies.[5]

With a general sense of the Ancestors in the Saṃhitās, I now turn to what we know of their propitiation through ritual. Two technical terms will serve as a lens for understanding the traditions of ancestor worship referred to in the Vedas. I begin with the *pitṛyajñá*, the Sacrifice to the Ancestors.

Sacrifice to the Ancestors in the Ṛg Veda

I will show that the term *pitṛyajñá* refers to the initial offering to a deceased man as a part of the funeral ceremony. While this term comes to have a different referent and a broader semantic range in the later literature, the evidence in the Saṃhitā literature does not support this.

The term *pitṛyajñá* occurs in the *Ṛg Veda* only once, in the hymn to the Funeral Fire, 10.16. This hymn is employed in the cremation rite and represents the first offering to the deceased as an Ancestor. In the first two verses, the poet pleads with Agni to convey the deceased to heaven[6] without consuming him completely (*ṚV* 10.16.1–2). The following verses alternate between verses to aid the deceased in his transition and verses to enjoin Agni to properly effect the transfer of the deceased from this world to the next. Verses 9 through 12 are of a piece and offer some insight into the details of this ritual.

> 9 Flesh-eating Agni I send off in the distance. Carrying away defilements, let him go to those who have Yama as their king.
>
> Here let only this one, the other Jātavedas, carry the oblation to the gods, knowing what's ahead.

10 The flesh-eating Agni who entered your house, though he saw this one here, the other Jātavedas—

that god I take for the sacrifice to the forefathers. He will send the *gharma*(-drink) to the highest seat.

11 The flesh-conveying Agni who will sacrifice to the forefathers, who are strong through truth,

he will proclaim the oblations to the gods and the forefathers.

12 Eagerly we would install you; eagerly we would kindle you.

Eagerly convey the eager forefathers here, to eat the oblation. *ṚV* 10.16.9–12[7]

(Brereton and Jamison, forthcoming)

In verse 9 the poet sends Agni to heaven, just as Agni sent the deceased to heaven in the first verse. This is not a coincidence or even simply a verbal play; the verb *pra-hi,* convey, dismiss, dispatch, occurs in both verses and resonates with the first verse, a connection a native listener would recognize in hearing the hymn. The poet intends for this verse to resonate with the first by the repetition of the verb, *pra-hi*. We know from the first verse that Agni sends the deceased to the world of the Ancestors (*'them enaṃ prá hiṇutāt pitṝbhyaḥ*). Now the poet sends the fire to "those who have Yama as their king." The semantic link between these two verses implies that the poet has sent Agni to heaven, *with the dead man*.

Agni, the god and the ritual fire, is described here as being one of two, *ayám ítaram*; the poet emphasizes that in his different roles Agni takes on different personas. He distinguishes the two fires: Agni Kravyād, Flesh-Eating Agni, who prepares the body for sacrifice, and Agni in his persona as Jātavedas,[8] who ensures the success of the sacrifice. The parallel of the divine fire, Jātavedas, who takes oblations to the gods, and Agni Kravyād, who takes the sacrifice to the Ancestors, alleviates the negative aspect of the flesh-eating fire. The eagerness expressed in verse twelve confirms the auspicious character of the fire.

These verses give us some sense of the metaphysical workings of the process of dying. For example, the poets imagined no period of transition between the cremation and achieving heaven, a period that is assumed in the later conceptions of ancestor worship. And earlier verses, 4–8, also suggest some logistical elements of the ritual, for example, laying the caul of a cow on the deceased, but these refer to the funeral and not the ancestral rites that are performed for years after the death of a father. The next three verses, 10–12, however, offer a better opportunity for understanding what is meant by the term *pitṛyajñá*.

In verse 11 Agni Kravyavāhana, Flesh-Conveying Agni, sacrifices to the Ancestors and proclaims the sacrificial food to both the gods and the Ancestors. These three aspects together describe the role of Agni in a funeral and verses 10cd–12 culminate in the *pitṛyajñá*, the climax of the funeral. In sum, Agni successfully conveys the deceased to heaven and now the survivors honor him with oblations *as an Ancestor* in the *pitṛyajñá*.

Let us consider the hymn as a whole. The first eight verses encompass the cremation; the first half of verse 9 sends Agni to heaven with the deceased. The second half of verse 9 to verse 11 describe the ritual offerings: to the gods, to the Ancestors, and to both. Verse 12 invokes Agni to bring the Ancestors to the ritual for their offerings. Finally, verses 13 and 14 mark the quenching of the funeral fire. The *pitṛyajñá* is an offering to the deceased immediately after, or as a part of, the cremation. This may imply that periodic rituals to feed the ancestors were performed, but the only evidence available points to a ritual as part of the funeral. Despite Caland's assertion that the *pitṛyajñá* is a synonym for the cremation (Caland 1893, 152), the context suggests the *pitṛyajñá* is a specific aspect of the cremation, not a name for the whole rite.

Sāyaṇa indicates that this hymn is recited when a Vedic ritual practitioner dies (*dikṣitamaraṇe, āhitāgnimaraṇe*), and assumes that *pitṛyajñá* in this context is the same as the *pitṛyajña* described in *Āśvalāyana Śrautasūtra* (Müller 1890, 40, 43). Kane agrees in part, but adds that the funeral hymns of the *Ṛg Veda* are employed in rites immediately after death and are aimed at making the ancient Ancestors favorably disposed to the recently departed (*HoD* 4:201). Kane's second assertion hits the mark. The internal evidence shows that the hymn is a central part of the cremation ritual and was likely composed for that purpose. This hymn seems to be central to the practices immediately after death, but its funerary context suggests something more relevant. The Sacrificer praises the deceased as an Ancestor; his promotion from corpse to Ancestor seems more basic to the intent of this ritual. I assert that *pitṛyajñá* in the *Ṛg Veda* is a key component of the cremation ritual; it marks the transition from dead body to Ancestor. The deceased relative is promoted to Ancestor during the funeral.[9]

The only ritual of ancestor worship indicated by this term, then, is the initial offering to the newly promoted Ancestor as a part of the rite that made him an Ancestor, the cremation. In the later literature *pitṛyajña* comes to refer to the fuller rites of ancestor worship, but the context of the word in the Saṃhitā literature does not allow us to suppose that fuller meaning.

Another technical term central to the later tradition's conception of ancestor worship is a verbal call that accompanies offerings made to the Ancestors, *svadhā́*

Svadhā́ in the Vedic Literature

A review of the use of the term *svadhā́* in the Vedic literature shows that in the earliest literature the term occurs most often in its broadest meaning, independence or one's own power. The poets increasingly employ this word in a technical sense in the younger *Ṛg Veda* and *Atharva Veda*. This suggests at least an increasing importance of the ancestral rites and this terminology in the textual tradition, but, more importantly, it demonstrates the coalescence of a technical terminology around the ancestral rites. This indicates the gradual incorporation of ancestor worship into the Vedic textual tradition.

The term *svadhā́* has a rich semantic range in the Vedic literature. Its oldest and broadest meaning is independence, the power of self-determination. As the ancestral rites come to be more central to the tradition reflected in the texts it takes on new meanings. In this section I will outline the development of this technical term covering the oldest meaning, independence, and three addition senses: the call *svadhā́*, which later is the hallmark of the ancestral rites; synecdoche for the entire ritual of ancestor worship; and the oblation made to the Ancestors in that ritual. The term retains the older meanings, allowing the poets to play with meanings and imply multiple senses.

The term *svadhā́* occurs in the Saṃhitās most frequently in the common sense of power or will, implying the independence of the actor, or their own special power (*Eigenhiet*) (*KEWA* 3:559); quite frequently associated with a god or goddess. For example, "Pṛśni gave birth to the turbulent face of the unruly Maruts for great joy/battle. They, in shared delight, begat the formless (cloud) mass. Just after that they surveyed their vigorous self-power (*svadhā́*)" (*ṚV* 1.168.9, Brereton and Jamison, forthcoming).[10]

In this verse the Maruts perceive their inherent power, the power by which they create the clouds. In another example, this power is contrasted with magical power (*māyā́*). "With your craft [*māyā́*] you blew away the crafty, who willfully [*svadhā́bhir*] poured (offerings) on their shoulders.

You, mindful of men, broke Pipru's strongholds and aided Ṛjiśvan in the slaying of *dásyus*" (*ṚV* 1.51.5, Brereton and Jamison, forthcoming).[11] While *svadhā́* ordinarily shows one's independence in a positive light, this instance exhibits a counter example. Indra, the preeminent example of the independent deity, uses his magical power to defeat those who willfully (*svadhā́bhir*) violate the sacrifice. The irony in this verse nicely highlights the contrast of these two power words.

Frequently, the word *svadhā́* appears in the instrumental case with the verb *mad*, to rejoice, to exult, to be exhilarated, for example:

> When, Indra and Fire, at the rising of the sun in the middle of the heaven you bring yourselves to elation by your own power, from there, bulls—yes! drive here. Then drink of the pressed Soma. *ṚV* 1.108.12 (Brereton and Jamison, forthcoming)[12]

> I direct down the divine hotar-priests, the two that are first. The seven fortified, become exhilarated by their own will. Reciting the truth, they speak only the truth, as they, the protectors of commands, reflect upon their commands. *ṚV* 3.4.7 (Brereton and Jamison, forthcoming)[13]

In the *Ṛg Veda*, over half of the occurrences of *svadhā́* or some derivative, for example, *svadhā́vat*, refer to a deity; among those Indra is most frequent. The term appears almost as frequently with a slightly broader sense with the same implications, that is, by one's own power, referring to a broader range of actors. The term occurs in the *Atharva Veda* in this sense as well.

This meaning is not lost in the subsequent literature. In the *Śatapatha Brāhmaṇa* when the ritualist is instructed to recite a mantra to repel demons (*ásura*) that may covet the offerings, the term *svadhā́* is used in the sense more common in the Saṃhitā literature. "He lays (the firebrand) down (saying) "Whatever *asuras* go about loose by their own will (*svadháyā*) in various shapes, great bodied or small bodied, may Agni expel them from this world. Agni is the destroyer of demons, therefore he lays it down" (*ŚBM* 2.4.2.15).[14] In this case the author employs the word simply to indicate that the demons have the power to roam about, but at least one commentary reads this as "(attracted) by the *svadhā́* (offerings to the fathers)" (Eggeling 1882, 365 n1). That the translator had to add "attracted" in parentheses emphasizes the strained nature of this interpretation. We find another example in the same text at the beginning of the section on the *píṇḍapitṛyajña*.

In the mythic preamble to this rite the author lists the foods for each of the classes of beings: gods, ancestors, men, beasts, and *ásuras*.

> 1 He (Prajāpati) said to them, "Sacrifice is your food, (therefore) immortality is yours; vigor is yours. The sun is your light."... 2 To them (the Ancestors) he said, "Monthly you will eat, (therefore) *svadhā́* is yours and quickness of mind is yours. The moon is your light."... 3 To them (men) he said, "In the evening and the morning you will eat, (therefore) offspring is yours and mortality is yours. The fire (Agni) is your light." *ŚBM* 2.4.2.1–3[15]

The author continues with animals and *ásuras*, though he breaks from the nice parallel construction that marks the first three beings. The pattern is clear: 1. food, 2. defining characteristic, and 3. light. The primary aim of this section is to define the food and character of the beings, the latter being indicated by the manner of eating. Gods eat at the sacrifice, the Ancestors at the monthly ancestral rites, and men twice during the day. The gods are associated with the sun as the Ancestors are with the moon, and men, by their performance of sacrifice, with fire. The second item on each list defines the primary attribute of the being, their mode of existing; gods are immortal and men mortal. The Ancestors, then, are defined by *svadhā́*. The term is invoked here with two senses: *svadhā́* meaning independence or one's own power and *svadhā́* as employed in reference to the ancestral rites. This relates to the second meaning of this term, *svadhā́* as the verbal call used in ancestral rites.

The texts employ the term far less frequently in the Saṃhitā literature in the context of the deceased and the Ancestors than in its more general meaning of independence. Of the 103 occurrences in the *R̥g Veda* eight appear in the funeral hymns, 10.14–18.[16] Most of these refer to the verbal call, but the term does occur in its broader sense of independence.

In the first of the funeral hymns, 10.14, there is a verse with strong ritual implications. "Matali is strengthened by the poets, as is Yama by the Aṅgirases, and Bṛhaspati by the R̥kvans. Whom the gods strengthen and who strengthen the gods; some are exhilarated by the call *svā́hā* and others by the call *svadhā́*" (*R̥V* 10.14.3).[17] The poet draws connections between deities and classes of priests, between the gods and those who give them material support—the Sacrificer who supports the gods through ritual—and between the two ritual calls, *svā́hā* and *svadhā́*. These two mantras are employed in the rituals to the gods and to the Ancestors, respectively. Despite this recognition of a distinction, this hymn gives us little to understand the details of the distinction; another funeral hymn aids in clarifying this point.

In several instances the poet incidentally draws a distinction between the verbal call and the oblation itself. In *ṚV* 10.16, the poet invokes Agni in two of his roles: the fire "who carries the oblations to the gods," (*ṚV* 10.16.9),[18] and the fire employed "for the purpose of *pitṛyajñá*," (*ṚV* 10.16.10).[19] The next verse makes a distinction between oblations to the gods and to the Ancestors (*ṚV* 10.16.11).[20] One verse invokes the call and the next invokes the oblation, therefore the term *svadhā́* does not refer to the oblation itself, but to the verbal formula, *svadhā́*, used to address the Ancestors. In the context of the *pitṛyajñá*, the *Taittirīya Brāhmaṇa* is explicit about the import of the word *svadhā́*, "the call *svadhā́* is for the Ancestors" (*TB* 1.6.9.5).[21]

This distinction is seen in *ṚV* 10.15 as well. In this hymn to the Ancestors, the word *svadhā́* is addressed to the class of Ancestors known as the Barhiṣads and their enjoyment of Soma. "I found the benevolent Ancestors, and a son, and the step of Viṣṇu. The Ancestors seated on the *barhis* who, with the call *svadhā́*, enjoy the pressed (Soma), they come quickly for the drink" (*ṚV* 10.15.3).[22] This marks the verbal formula as accompanying the offerings of Soma. What is significant for understanding the meaning of *svadhā́* in this context is that the call *accompanies* the offering, that is, it is separate. The picture here, I suggest, is that the Ancestors are exhilarated to hear the call, because they know that offerings are to follow.[23] Geldner chooses to translate the word in this context as *nach Herzenslust*, but he emphasizes that a double meaning is likely here (Geldner 1951, 145n4c).

The poets regularly employ this word in such a way as to draw out its multiple meanings. One example invokes Yama and Varuṇa, "Go forth along those ancient paths on which our ancient Ancestors went; you will see the two kings, Yama and the god Varuṇa, exhilarated by the call *svadhā́*" (*ṚV* 10.14.7).[24] The gods Yama and Varuṇa revel in heaven, like other gods in the *Ṛg Veda*, for example in *ṚV* 1.108.12 discussed above. The context, however, suggests that these gods are specifically exhilarated because of the impending offerings, specifically offerings made in a funerary context.

Another example supports the notion that *svadhā́* is not limited to referring to the verbal call. In 10.16, Agni is enjoined to release the dead man, and the dead man is said to move under his own power. "Release (him) again, Agni, to the Ancestors. He who is offered to you goes by his own power (*svadhā́bhir*). Let him follow (his) remainder, clothing himself in life. May he come together with the body, Jātavedas" (*ṚV* 10.16.5).[25] With a new body—that is, with the transformation to Ancestor complete—the deceased is able to make his way to heaven by his own power, as the gods and the Ancestors do. The conjunction of *svadhā́* and the verb *car* also occurs in *ŚBM* 2.4.2.15 referring to the *ásuras* who threaten the ritual. The term *svadhā́* describes the supernatural beings ability of self-determination, what I have called independent power. These two examplesindicate that the term retains its broader semantic range, even in a funerary context. The poet likely intended this double meaning, emphasizing the special power of the Ancestors, Mayrhofer's *Eignekraft*, as well as their particular relationship with the verbal formula *svadhā́*.

While *svadhā́* as referent to ancestral rites is limited in the *Ṛg Veda* to the funeral hymns, the term occurs with this sense more often in the *Atharva Veda*. In fact, the term refers to ancestor worship not only in the funerary context, but in other contexts as well. In the funerary hymns of the *Atharva Veda* the term is employed much in the same way as in the *Ṛg Veda*, though this should not be surprising as many verses are borrowed directly from that text.[26]

A handful of the verses discussed in their Ṛg-vedic versions above appear again in the *Atharva Veda* funeral hymns; for example, *AVŚ* 18.1.45 is *ṚV* 10.15.3 and *AVŚ* 18.1.54 is *ṚV* 10.14.7. In total six verses that use *svadhā́* are drawn from the *Ṛg Veda* and their new context does not suggest a reinterpretation of these terms.[27] However, some of those verses which do not occur in the *Ṛg Veda* do raise interesting possibilities. Of the thirty-six occurrences of the word *svadhā́* in the funeral hymns of the *Atharva Veda* six are borrowed from the *Ṛg Veda*, and ten use *svadhā́* in its older sense of the call *svadhā́*.

An example of the latter appears in one funeral hymn, "68 May those cake-covered pots that the gods hold for you, accompanied by the call *svadhā́*, be rich in honey, and flowing with ghee. 69 May that grain, mixed with sesame and accompanied by the call *svadhā́*, that I scatter along be increasing and abundant. May king Yama approve them for you" (*AVŚ* 18.3.68–69).[28] As in the *Ṛg Veda*, the term here refers to the call made to accompany the offerings. In this context it would be hard to argue that it is indicative of another ritual.[29]

In another context *svadhā́* occurs in the sense of the call, but also indicates a shift toward expanding the semantic range. One verse in a hymn to the cow extols three virtuous acts—ancestor worship, sacrifice to the gods, and the gifting of a cow—acts that have held the religious imagination in India for millennia. "By the call *svadhā́* for the Ancestors; by sacrifice for the gods, by gifting a cow, the kingly (man) does not invoke the ire of his mother" (*AVŚ* 12.4.32).[30] The parallel construction of the verse indicates that the call *svadhā́* is put on par with sacrifice (See also *AVŚ* 15.14.13–14; *AVP* 5.31.5 and 6.10.5). Neither the verbal formulation nor the oblation in an ancestral rite are equal to a sacrifice to the gods; the poet employs the key ritual element of the ancestral rite, the verbal call, as a synecdoche for the entire ancestral rite. Because it is emblematic of ancestor worship, the term *svadhā́* has come to refer to the whole ritual.

The word *svadhā́*, then can refer to both the verbal call and the ritual itself. Two other examples play on this ambiguity and call to mind both the sense of the verbal call and the entire ritual. "I auspiciously cover you with the garment of mother Earth. What is auspicious among the living—that is in me; the *svadhā́* among the Ancestors—that is in you" (*AVŚ* 18.2.52).[31] The first hemistich, referring to the internment of the relics of cremation, reinforces the funerary context. The second half of the verse reiterates, for both the deceased and the survivors, that the former are dead and the latter living. The hymn invokes the dual benefits of the funeral; taking upon the living the benefits appropriate to the living, and consigning to the recently deceased the benefits that are due an Ancestor. The implication of the benefits suggests this could refer to the ritual more generally, not only the call itself.

The other verse relates to the notion that the rituals one performs in this life will build a heaven that awaits one's death. The *Śatapatha Brāhmaṇa* says "He is born into that world he made; therefore, they say 'A man is born into the world he made'" (*ŚBM* 6.2.2.27).[32] But in the example from the funeral hymns of the *Atharva Veda*, something changes. "May you be destined for the un-crowded wide world of the earth. May those *svadhā́s* that you performed while living be flowing with honey" (*AVŚ* 18.2.20).[33] The wish that the *svadhā́s* be flowing with honey calls to mind the call and the offering of rich oblations, that is, of the entire ritual. This rather strange verse implies that the *svadhā́s*, that is, the ancestral rites, that one performs while living will be awaiting that very person. It describes the ritual storehouse that one establishes in heaven through sacrifice (see Malamoud 1983, 31) with the term *svadhā́*. I found no other instance that used the word in this way; though it has a certain logic.[34] What is significant for my argument here is that the *svadhā́* is described as flowing with honey. This could work as *svadhā́vat* does, the oblation is flowing with honey and is accompanied by the call, but it seems likely that the term is here meant to imply the call and the oblation together, that is, the ritual as a whole.

Finally, in another verse from a non-funerary context *svadhā́* more clearly refers to the oblation itself. It occurs in a hymn that praises Agni in two of his aspects: Kravyād, Flesh-Eating Agni, and the householder's fire (*gā́rhapatya*). This distinction also occurs in the hymn to Agni in the *ṚV*, 10.16, and, in fact, the *Atharva Veda* hymn borrows from that very hymn as well as from *ṚV* 10.18, another funerary hymn. This verse uses the term *svadhā́* to refer to an oblation, "I separate these two from the sacrificial offering; I fashion these two with a *bráhman*. I make the *svadhā́* undecaying for the Ancestors; I join it with a long lifespan" (*AVŚ* 12.2.32).[35] The adjective, undecaying (*ajára*), cannot refer to the call *svadhā́*. This is the first instance I was able to find in which *svadhā́* refers to the offering. This meaning is a secondary implication from its use in the mantras, and, I assert, is the beginning of the semantic shift whose end is seen in the later literature, which considers *svadhā́* synonymous with the rituals of ancestor worship and the oblations offered therein. Unlike in the *Ṛg Veda*, *svadhā́* also occurs with this expanded semantic range occurs outside the funerary context in the *Atharva Veda*.

One example is found in a hymn to Virāj, the female creative principle. "She ascended; she went to the Ancestors. The Ancestors called to her, "O *svadhā́*, come!" King Yama was her calf; the vessel of silver was her vessel. Antaka Mārtyava milked her; he milked this *svadhā́*. The Ancestors live on that *svadhā́*; who knows thus becomes one to be depended upon" (*AVŚ* 8.10.23).[36] The poet here glorifies Virāj and describes the Ancestors calling to her to be milked. In this passage the term *svadhā́* clearly refers to the oblation itself and likely calls to mind the Brāhmaṇa passage that describes the ancestral rites as primarily concerned with feeding the Ancestors.

The review of the term *svadhā́* in the Vedic literature shows that the technical language for ancestor worship in the oldest texts is minimal and often only refers to the ancestral rites in particular contexts. This suggests the relatively minor importance of such rites in the oldest layers of the *Ṛg Veda*, though the absence of evidence is certainly not conclusive. The gradual increase in the explicit reference to the ancestral rites with this term indicate a growing importance for the rite in the minds of those that preserved these texts, and the increased use of *svadhā́* as a technical term referring to the ritual of ancestor worship. A similar shift can be seen, though less clearly due to the lack of use, with the term *pitr̥yajñá*. That is, the term *pitr̥yajñá* comes to greater use as the rituals focused on the Ancestors become more fully expressed. I discuss the development of that term in the Brāhmaṇas in the next chapter.

Conclusions and Speculation

In the *R̥g Veda* and *Atharva Veda* the term *svadhā́* most frequently refers to the self-determination of the person praised or described. This usage even occurs in the funerary context in both texts where the tradition and scholarly interpreters have generally, due to the context, read the term as necessarily referring to the ritual, or the oblations therein, of ancestor worship. In the *R̥g Veda* the term appears as an unambiguous referent to some sort of ancestor rite once, 10.14.3, where a distinction is made between *svā́hā* and *svadhā́*, though the use of this dichotomy, in fact of the verse itself, is a bit disconnected from the context of the rest of the hymn. Therefore, in the *R̥g Veda* we know offerings were made to the Ancestors, but we know little about the nature of these offerings outside the context of the funeral without the help of the later tradition.

In the *Atharva Veda*, the *svadhā́* most often carries the more general meaning of independence as well (e.g., *AVP* 5.6.3), though there is a greater frequency of instances where the term refers to the *svadhā́* call and as a synecdoche to the whole rite. Additionally, the term takes on a new use, referring to the oblation itself. Whether due to the nature of the texts—for example, that the *R̥g Veda* is primarily a Soma text—or due to an increased association of the word *svadhā́* with the ritual and oblations to the Ancestors, the term does carry that latter connotation more frequently in the *Atharva Veda*.

In a funerary context, in both texts, the poets employ the term most often as the call *svadhā́*, or, in the *Atharva Veda*, for the rite as a whole, but a number of times the term seems to have both the sense of the call *svadhā́* and one's independent power. This play, this ambiguity, is a hallmark of the R̥g-vedic poetry in general, and it acts to enrich the ancestral rites and serve to integrate them into the Vedic ritual system quite well.

The fact that the term is also used with this sense outside the funerary context indicates that ancestor worship has come to have a greater import in the general ritual tradition of the Vedic world. Unfortunately, while the *svā́hā/svadhā́* dichotomy appears in the *Atharva Veda* context as well, the sum of the occurrences of the term *svadhā́* in the *Atharva Veda* adds little detail to our understanding of the ancestral rites themselves during the Saṃhitā period.

I have shown that the ritual implied by the term *pitṛyajñá* in the *Ṛg Veda* refers to the brief offerings made to the deceased upon his promotion to heaven. That the poets fail to mention details of the ritual follows the dictates of the genre. The poetic praise of the divine does not require a detailed explanation of the ritual, in fact it probably prohibits such expressions, but the poets give us clues as to the nature of the ritual.

It is through ritual that one wins heaven and through ritual that the material concerns are secured there, "Meet with the Ancestors, with Yama, in the highest heaven with what is sacrificed and given. Having abandoned imperfections, come home again. Come together with a body, full of radiance" (*ṚV* 10.14.8).[37] The ritualist earns the next world through the performance of sacrifice and, as in *ṚV* 10.16, a new body awaits him. A similar concern about building a body for the deceased is expressed in the later *śrāddha*-rite, which explicitly constructs a new body for the next world.

Hymn 10.15 invokes several types of Ancestors by name, inviting them to come forward and protect the Sacrificer.[38] They are invited to eat and enjoy Soma (*ṚV* 10.15.3) and are repeatedly asked for protection, and the poet reinforces the offering, this time referring to the food as "dear treasures that are placed on *kuśá* grass" (*ṚV* 10.15.5).[39] Later the Ancestors are urged to eat with, "Eat the pure offerings on the sacred *kuśá* grass" (*ṚV* 10.15.11),[40] and the rice-balls are offered on the *kuśá* grass in the later tradition (e.g., *ŚBM* 2.4.2.18, *ĀpŚS* 1.9.1). The reward sought is made clear in the same verse: "then bestow wealth together with sons."[41] The final verse in this hymn connects the body sought in *ṚV* 10.14 with the ritual referred to here, "May you (Agni), along with them, create a body and this heaven, O resplendent one, according to your desire" (*ṚV* 10.15.14).[42] The ritual, of which this hymn was a component, aims to convey the deceased to heaven, complete with a body. While unlike the monthly *śrāddha*-rite of the domestic ritual tradition, this looks very similar to the *ekoddiṣṭa* and *sapiṇḍīkaraṇa śrāddha*-rite of the later period. That these rites are more closely related to the funeral than the monthly rites—and are even added to funeral rites in some Gṛhyasūtras—makes such comparisons natural. Nevertheless, it seems most likely that the transfer of the deceased to heaven was a function of the cremation rather than a separate ritual as it is in the later tradition.

Coupled with my reading of the term *pitṛyajñá* above, this reading of the goal of the ritual makes the ritual referent in the *Ṛg Veda* clear: these offerings are a part of the funeral/cremation in the Ṛg-vedic period. The *pitṛyajñá* involves offerings to the deceased upon their promotion to the status of Ancestor. One might draw the conclusion from this that there were indeed periodic offerings to the dead, otherwise a single oblation to the recently deceased may seem odd, but this is highly speculative and there is no direct evidence either way from which to draw a definitive conclusion.

The adoption of the funerary language by the later tradition indicates the influence of this ritual cycle on the later tradition. The authors of the later tradition, while integrating elements of ancestor worship, did so within the framework established by the older ritual texts, using the technical vocabulary, for example, *svadhā́* and *pitṛyjajñá*. This interpretation would support the notion that the literary tradition legitimizes an extra-textual practice, as mentioned above, but this does not permit reading later traditions into the older material. One could speculate that the ancestral rites that are described in the Brāhmaṇas existed in the Saṃhitā period, as others have done, but I am satisfied to simply assert that the funerary offerings, language, and rituals strongly influence the later tradition, and leave speculation on the nature of those older rites to others.

2

The Solemn Ancestral Rites

THE BRĀHMAṆAS AND Śrautasūtras provide us with a rich storehouse of information about the sacrificial cult of the Vedic culture. In this treasury of ritual details, the authors include a considerable about of information about ancestor worship in ancient South Asia.[1] The Brāhmaṇas offer both the earliest clear reference to the details of ancestor worship and mythic explanations of its rituals. They illustrate the logistics of the ritual as well as the dynamics of the relationship between the Ancestors and their descendants, which helps indicate what these rituals meant to those that recorded them. The Śrautasūtras outline the procedure of the rituals in great detail and the Brāhmaṇas and the Śrautasūtras frequently coincide in many details of the descriptions of the rituals discussed; thus I draw upon both genres to create a composite summary of the solemn ancestral rites.

This chapter has two aims: to describe the rituals of ancestor worship in Vedic context and to outline the broader historical development of ancestor worship. In order to accomplish the first goal, I will briefly outline the default ritual paradigm, then describe the ancestral rites and highlight the elements that distinguish ancestral rites from divine rites. With the second goal I am primarily concerned with establishing a relative dating of the two primary ancestral rites in the Vedic corpus, the *piṇḍapitṛyajña* and the *pitṛyajña*.[2] I argue that the *piṇḍapitṛyajña* is the older of the two rites and that the development of these rites evident in the textual sources further indicates a gradual incorporation of the ancestral rites into the Vedic theological discourse.

Because my aim is to describe the broader developments over time, the differences between theological schools do not receive extensive treatment.[3] The focus is on the most basic paradigm of the two rituals. This approach necessarily generates a "lowest common denominator" of the ritual, but a more detailed understanding of the difference between theological schools is unnecessary for understanding the historical development and socio-religious implications to be drawn from the discourse on the ancestral rites.

The ancestral rites are imbedded in the larger ritual cycles of which they are a part, and their descriptions generally assume an understanding of the basic ritual paradigm. Because the New and Full Moon Sacrifices (*darśapūrṇamāseṣṭi*) serve as the template for both of the primary forms of ancestral rites, I will briefly describe that model.

The primary ritual act of the New and Full Moon Sacrifices is an offering of a cake (*puroḍāśa*); at the full moon it is offered to Agni and Soma and at the new moon to Agni and Indra. If the Sacrificer is a Soma Sacrificer, he may also make a Milk Offering (*sāṃnāyya*) to Indra or Mahendra. Unless otherwise indicated the ritual and elements of the ritual are assumed to orient toward the east. This is the direction in which the gods dwell, therefore the ritual is oriented toward them. The Sacrificer, as a qualified Brahmin, wears a sacred cord as a mark of his station. He wears this cord over his left shoulder and under his right arm (*yajñopavītin*), the orientation appropriate for divine rites.

The preparations for the actual sacrifice[4] begin on the day preceding the ritual. At each action listed here an appropriate verse is recited to accompany that action. The rite begins with the performance of an Agnihotra. Fire is either brought from the householder's fire or a new fire is kindled, then the Adhvaryu makes some of the items uses in the ritual: the brush (*veda*), the poking stick (*upaveṣa*), purifiers (*pavitra*), and bundles of grass used in the ritual. Fuel for the fire is gathered and made ready for the ritual. After the evening Agnihotra oblation the fire is surrounded with grass, with the blades pointing either east or north, and the ritual implements are laid out. If the Milk Offering is to be made, then a branch is used to drive the calves that will provide the milk and they are milked.

On the day of the sacrifice, more preparations lead up to the main phase of the sacrifice. The four priests and the Sacrificer wash their hands and more grass is spread around the householder's and offertorial fires as seats for the Brahman priest and the Sacrificer. Water is purified and set down by the offertorial fire, and the various instruments are ritually prepared. To the west of the fires, they lay out the skin of a black antelope, and thereupon set up a mortar and pestle and grinding stones. The Adhvaryu retrieves the offering material, usually rice, and it is sprinkled with water to purify it, threshed, husked three times,[5] winnowed, and ground into flour. According to some traditions the wife pounds and grinds the grain. From the flour produced cakes are made and cooked upon pieces of pottery (*kapāla*) set up on one of the fires.

Then the wooden sword (*sphya*) is used to drawn three lines—from east to south into which water is poured—and dig out the altar (*vedi*). The altar should incline toward the east or the northeast. After the altar is traced with the wooden sword other ritual implements are laid out and cleaned. The wife is made to wear a girdle made out of grass and sit to her husband's right, the south, facing the north. The clarified butter to be used in the ritual is prepared and placed on the wooden sword-drawn lines, and the ritual space sprinkled with water. Then the Adhvaryu encloses the offertorial fire by laying three enclosing sticks (*paridhi*) around the offertorial fire; this demarcates the sacred space. The ladles and spoons are filled with clarified butter and placed on the grass. Finally, the cakes are smeared with clarified butter and placed on the altar. This concludes the preparations for the sacrifice.

The principal ritual phase is a series of offerings. Fifteen verses are recited as the fuel is offered into the fire, then a series of food offerings are made: two oblations of clarified butter—after which the Hotṛ is formally chosen—five fore-offerings (*prayāja*), and two butter-portion offerings (*ājyabhāga*) made to Agni and Soma. At each offering, the Adhvaryu calls for the Āgnīdhra saying "Make it heard!" (*āśrāvaya*) and the Āgnīdhra replies with "May it be heard!" (*astu śrauṣaṭ*). The Adhvaryu similarly commands the Hotṛ to recite by saying "Sacrifice!" (*yaja*) and saying the names of the deities invoked. At the end of the verse the Hotṛ says "Vaṣaṭ," which cues the Adhvaryu to make the oblation. The principal offerings are a cake for Agni, an offering of butter made to one of several deities, included Viṣṇu and Prajāpati, and a second cake, to Agni and Soma at the full moon and to Agni and Indra at the new moon (*KŚS* 3.3.24–25). The offering to Agni Sviṣṭakṛt (Agni Who Makes the Sacrifice Correct) concludes the primary offerings.

In the subsequent rites the cakes are divided among the priests. The Brahman gets one cutting (*prāśitra*) and four or five portions are cut off from all the offerings made; this offering, the *iḍā*, is invoked with a verse and shared by the four priests and the Sacrificer. The cake made for Agni and rice porridge (*odana*) made after the *iḍā* are divided among the four priests. The priests then perform the three after-offerings (*anuyāja*), and "good words" (*sūktavāka*) and an invocation of prosperity is recited by the Hotṛ. The various implements used in the ritual are then thrown into the fire and several final offerings bring the sacrifice to an end.

Employing that rite as the paradigm, the Vedic texts describe two primary types of ancestral rites: the *piṇḍapitṛyajña* and the *pitṛyajña*. I will begin with the *piṇḍapitṛyajña*, which occurs as a part of the New and Full Moon Sacrifices. Rather than review the ritual in full, I will briefly outline the ritual procedures which differ from the model New and Full Moon Sacrifices.

Rice-Ball Sacrifice to the Ancestors

The *piṇḍapitṛyajña*[6] is performed once a month in the afternoon of the new moon, and as in the normal rituals, there are preparations to be made. The priests follow the same paradigm, making alterations to accommodate the divinity of this rite, the Ancestors. The Sacrificer sits behind the householder's fire (*gārhapatya*), facing the south wearing his sacrificial cord over his right shoulder (*prācīnāvītin*). He prepares the ritual space as in the model ritual. After the Sacrificer's wife winnows rice grains the grains are husked once, not three times as in the model.[7] The Adhvaryu boils the rice over the southern fire, stirring counter clock-wise, and makes an offering of clarified butter into the rice. The Hotṛ then recites mantras to Agni and Soma, as in the model, and makes an offering for each into the fire.[8] After drawing the lines with the wooden sword the Sacrificer lays down a firebrand (*ulmuka*) at the south end of the lines to ward off demons (*asuras* and *rākṣasas*), who can tamper with the food offered to the Ancestors.[9] With an accompanying mantra he asks Agni to expel the demons. The offerings are made ready as in the model rite and the principal offerings can begin.

He makes the Ancestors wash themselves, as he would a guest about to eat; he takes a water pitcher and pours out the water saying "<Father's name>, wash yourself."[10] He then does the same with his grandfather and great-grandfather, using their names. He cuts the sacrificial grass with one stroke and spreads the grass along the line with their tops oriented toward the south.

Then he offers the rice-balls to the Ancestors on the grass with the phrase "<Father's name>, this is for you,"[11] repeating the process for his grandfather and great-grandfather. Enjoining them to enjoy the food with another mantra, he turns his back to allow them to eat.[12] After recognizing that the Ancestors have completed their meal with another mantra, he again pours water, washing the Ancestors as he did before, reinforcing the fact that they consumed the meal. After the offering of rice-balls, he offers collyrium (*āñjana*), ointment (*abhyañjana*), and a tuft of wool (*ūrṇāstakā*).[13]

In the Brāhmaṇas, he then pulls down the tuck of his sacrificial garment and pays them homage.[14] In the Śrautasūtras, this act of holding onto the fringe of his garment is transformed; a thread from his garment, or a piece of wool—or, if he is older, a body hair—is placed on the *piṇḍas* while the Ancestors are praised with a mantra (*VS* 2.32) entreating them for houses (See *ŚBM* 2.4.2.24≈*ŚBK* 1.6.1.28).[15]

With the primary offerings complete, the rice-balls, of which the Ancestors have partaken, are placed back in the dish containing the remains of the boiled rice, and the Sacrificer and the priests smell the rice; through smelling the rice they partake in the rice.[16] The rice-balls are disposed of in water or eaten by Brahmins.[17] He finally disposes of the sacrificial grass in the fire and throws away the firebrand, concluding the *piṇḍapitṛyajña*.[18]

I will now describe the *pitṛyajña* which belongs to the Sākamedha sacrifice—the third of the Four-monthly Sacrifices. Again, I will briefly review the procedures only in so far as they diverge from the model sacrifice.

Sacrifice to the Ancestors

The other solemn rite of ancestor worship occurs during the Sākamedha (*TB* 1.6.8–9). The *pitṛyajña* is performed in the autumn on the full moon of Kārttika (October-November) or Mārgaśīrṣa (November-December).[19] These factors suggest another *bandhu*-style association. The ritual begins on the new moon, so the moon is waning, that is, "dying," and the Ancestors are dead. Performing the rites during the waning of the moon would strengthen the ritual associations with the Ancestors.[20] Similarly, autumn is the waning of the year; therefore, the tradition may have associated the decline into winter with the Ancestors. In modern practice, the ideal time to perform the *śrāddha* at Gayā, according to tradition, is the Half-month for the Ancestors (*pitṛpakṣa*), which occurs following the new moon—that is, during the waning moon, in October.[21] Oldenberg sees the offerings to the Ancestors in the Four-Monthly Sacrifices as the "remains of an Indo-European winter all souls feast" (quoted in Keith 1967, cv). To posit a historical connection goes too far, but the associations with the waning of the year and the moon are consistent with Vedic ritual thinking.

The *pitṛyajña*[22] is performed on the second day of the Sākamedha. The Sacrificer—he performs this ritual without his wife (*ŚBK* 1.6.1.9)—stands in the south of the ritual space, north of the southern fire, wearing his sacred thread over his right shoulder. He makes offerings of cakes (*puroḍāśa*), a sacrificial milk-drink (*mantha*), and fried grain (*dhānā*) to the six types of Ancestors on pieces of pottery, which he has placed on the southern half of the householder's fire. The Adhvaryu priest grinds the rice while standing north of the fire and facing the south.[23]

He then establishes the altar (*vedi*), with its corners facing each of the cardinal directions, to the south of the southern fire. On the altar he establishes the offertorial fire, having brought fire from the southern fire, instead of from the householder's fire. Once the Adhvaryu has strewn the grass and enclosed the ritual space with the wooden sword-drawn lines to establish the ritual, the Adhvaryu switches his sacred thread to his left shoulder and makes two oblations, one to Soma and one to Agni.

After an invitation of the gods and the Ancestors, the priest makes another oblation into the fire. The participants then switch their sacred threads back to the right shoulder and invite the different classes of Ancestors to the ritual; each is then made an offering. One last oblation is made to Agni Kavyavāhana, as the deity who will carry the oblations to the Ancestors, instead of Agni Sviṣṭakṛt as in the model. Different texts vary in the details of the offerings and oblations made before the offering of rice-balls, but they all specify switching the sacred thread back and forth as is appropriate for the divine or ancestral portions of the ritual, for example, *KŚS* 5.9.21, 23, 27.[24]

Next he mixes portions taken from the cakes, milk-drink, and fried grain to make the rice-balls offered to the Ancestors. While circumambulating the altar in a counter-clockwise direction, either the Adhvaryu or the Sacrificer sprinkles water on it for the Ancestors to wash, then places the three rice-balls on three of the corners of the altar also in a counter-clockwise direction: first the father's on the northwest, then the grandfather's on the southwest, and the great-grandfather's on the southeast.[25] All the ritual actors move to the north of the ritual space, leaving the Ancestors to eat.[26] The *Taittirīya Brāhmaṇa* (1.6.9.8) indicates that they should hold their breath while the Ancestors partake in the offerings and this accords with the later tradition. A mantra declares that the Ancestors are satiated and the priest washes them again.[27] The rite concludes with a dismissal of the Ancestors[28] and all the ritual implements are disposed of in the fire, ending the ritual. The remnants of the offerings are eaten by priests or thrown into water.

Distinguishing Ancestral from Divine Rites

An appreciation of the differences between the divine and ancestral rites and between these two ancestral rites is central to my argument about a repeated, conscious effort to synthesize the ritual activities of the solemn cult and the practices associated with ancestor worship, particularly those connected to the death of a man who kept the sacrificial fires (*āhitāgni*). I review the differences between divine and ancestral rites not only to highlight the differences in form, but also to highlight evidence of the development of ancestor worship during its integration into the ritual tradition described in the texts. The differences between the two ancestral rites reveal clues to help understand which rite was integrated into the textual tradition first, thereby illuminating the development of ancestor worship through the Vedic period.

Many of the ritual details point to significant differences between rituals to the gods and rituals to the Ancestors. The correspondence between elements of the ritual and the human or divine realm that the priests create in the ritual establish identity and just as they can bring the Sacrificer benefit, they can bring danger. The priests must be careful about establishing such equivalences in a ritual involving dead participants, lest he allow death to enter his life. In this section I review five features that distinguish ancestral from divine rites: the manner of wearing the sacred cord, the orientation of the ritual and some of its elements, changes in the way rice is cleaned and grass is cut, changes to the call and response sequence that accompanies offerings in the ritual, and the addition of a new form of offering, the rice-ball.

In the divine ritual paradigm the priests and the Sacrificer wear their sacred cords over their left shoulder and under the right arm (*yajñopavītin*). This is contrasted in ancestral rites, in which the priests and Sacrificer wear their cords over their right shoulder and under the left arm (*prācīnāvītin*). In the preamble to the *piṇḍapitṛyajña*, the *Śatapatha Brāhmaṇa* indicates that the gods are wearing the sacred thread on the left shoulder and under the right arm (*yajñopavītin*) (*ŚBM* 2.4.2.1), and the Ancestors are wearing the sacred thread on the right shoulder and under the left arm (*prācīnāvītin*) (*ŚBM* 2.4.2.2). The Sacrificer—who is specifically enjoined to wear his thread in the latter fashion in *ŚBM* 2.4.2.9—wears his thread in a manner appropriate for each in divine and ancestral rituals. This is one of many reversals that indicate the difference between auspicious rites to the gods and those to the Ancestors, which, because of the association with the dead, are ambiguous in a way that divine rites are not.

This difference also relates to the orientation of ritual, which reflects the cosmological associations inscribed on the world itself. Each of the cardinal directions has a primary association. Most important of these are the east, which is associated with the gods, and the south, which is associated with the death, the dead, and especially the Ancestors (Smith 1994, 142–144). In the normal ritual paradigm the ritual itself and many of the elements orient toward the east, for example, when the Adhvaryu digs the altar it should be elevated to "face" the east—that is, sloping toward the east—or to the northeast.[29] This establishes a connection between the ritual space and the realm of the gods, in the east, or a connection to the east and the north, the realm associated with material success. In the *piṇḍapitṛyajña*, when grass is strewn, it is strewn with its points toward the south.[30] Similarly, offerings to the Ancestors are made in the southern part of the ritual space. In the ancestral rites, the Sacrificer faces the south, because that is where the Ancestors dwell; in the ritual to the gods, he faces the east, because that is where the gods dwell. The gaze is a form of contact (Gonda 1969), thus orienting oneself in a particular direction establishes a connection between the person in the ritual and the object of veneration.

Certain ritual actions also distinguish the ancestral rites from the divine rites. The offerings are made into the southern fire rather than the offertorial fire (*KŚS* 5.8.6). This difference also relates to the cosmological orientation; the fire is in the south, closest to the Ancestors. Offerings made to the Ancestors in the offertorial fire would contaminate the divine fire. The connections made in the ritual are real and powerful, thus the ritual actions must clearly distinguish between actions aimed at the Ancestors and those meant for the gods. In the preparation too, one must be careful with the associations generated.

In the normal ritual the utensils are placed on the sacrificial grass in pairs (*KŚS* 2.3.6–9), but in the *piṇḍapitṛyajña* they are placed one-by-one (*KŚS* 4.1.4). He also husks the rice only once (4.1.6), whereas is it done three times in the normal ritual paradigm (*KŚS* 2.4.22). The author of the *Śatapatha Brāhmaṇa* explains that the Ancestors passed away only once[31] thus the cleaning is to be done only once (*ŚBM* 2.4.2.9). We might also understand this difference to indicate the Ancestors' lower status, as compared to the gods, whose rice must be cleaned three times. In general, these differences serve to clearly demarcate between those rituals oriented toward the gods and those oriented toward the Ancestors.

Movement through space also generates these associations. When the rice-offering is stirred, it must be stirred in a counter-clockwise direction (*MŚS* 1.1.2.5). When circumambulating in any context associated with death, it must be done in a counter-clockwise direction (e.g., *ĀpŚS* 14.22.1), as opposed to the auspicious clock-wise direction.

This demarcation of differences even extends to the calls (*kāra*) used in the rituals. The call and response take on the form recognized as relating to the Ancestors, using the term *svadhā*, which has, by the time of the clearly laid out instructions of the Śrautasūtras, come to be the hallmark of ancestral rites. As early as the latest layers of the *Ṛg Veda* this term has distinguished ancestral from divine rites, the former accompanied by *svadhā*, the latter by *svāhā*. And in the solemn rites, the series of calls and responses outlined earlier in the model ritual are altered for both ancestral rites. The Adhvaryu call to the Āgnīdhra—"Make it heard!"—is replaced with "*ā svadhā*." The Āgnīdhra's response—"May it be heard!"—is replaced with "So be it! *Svadhā*!" (*astu svadhā*). The Adhvaryu orders the Hotṛ to recite the verses with "Soma accompanied by the Ancestors, *svadhā*!" (*somaṃ pitṛmantaṃ svadhā*) instead of the usual "Sacrifice!" and the names of the deities. And finally, instead of uttering "Vaṣaṭ" at the end of the verse to indicate that the Adhvaryu can make the offering the Hotṛ utters "*svadhā*! Reverence!" (*svadhā namaḥ*).[32]

The last difference changes the ritual is a different way. The alterations to the sacred cord, the ritual orientation, preparatory actions, and the call-and-response reorient the ritual within the normal Vedic ritual frame, but the addition of the rice-balls adds something new. This is a new type of offering, unique to the Ancestors, and it is central to both ancestral rites, despite the fact that the word *piṇḍa* only occurs in the name of the ancestral rite that is a part of the New Moon Sacrifices.

Both forms of ancestor worship share these elements intended to distinguish ancestral from divine rites, but they differ in many respects as well.

Distinguishing between Ancestral Rites

These differences, I argue, are important for understanding the manner in which different forms of ancestral offerings are made in the Vedic tradition and how these two rites came to be a part of the solemn ritual corpus. There are three key differences between these rites: the switching back and forth of the sacred thread during the ritual; the exclusion of offerings of collyrium, ointment, and a tuft of wool; and the offering of rice-balls on the altar instead of on grass. I argue that incorporation of ancestor worship into the solemn ritual literature is best understood as the introduction of extra-textual practices into the solemn ritual cycle in the form of the *piṇḍapitṛyajña* followed by the modification of this rite, to further integrate the ancestral rites into the Vedic ritual cycle, in the form of the *pitṛyajña*. The characteristics of each rite discussed will be integral to the following section about the relative dating of the two rites.

The *piṇḍapitṛyajña* requires the Sacrificer and priests to wear their sacrificial cords over the right shoulder for the entire rite, even if offerings are made to gods. For example, in the *Śatapatha Brāhmaṇa* (2.4.2.9–11) the Adhvaryu is instructed to place the sacred cord on his right shoulder, the manner usually used for ancestral ritual action, then make two offerings to deities, Soma and Agni. These offerings are a part of the normal ritual paradigm, but they are performed with the sacred cord in the ancestral orientation. The *Śatapatha Brāhmaṇa* indicates that offerings are made to Agni and Soma because Agni receives a share in all offerings—because he is the embodiment of the sacred fire—and Soma receives a share because he is the god of the Ancestors (*ŚBM* 2.4.2.12). That is, they receive oblations because they are intimately related to the Ancestors.[33] The tradition asserts that the deity's place in the *piṇḍapitṛyajña* arises from a specific relationship with the Ancestors, the connection between the Ancestors and Soma is quite old (see Chapter 1). These gods receive praise from the Sacrificer in the Ancestor-oriented mode of ritual; any potential tension is ameliorated by their association with the Ancestors.

In the *pitṛyajña*, however, the participants—Adhvaryu, Brahman, Āgnīdhra, Hotṛ, and Sacrificer—must repeatedly change back and forth between wearing it on the right shoulder and wearing it on the left shoulder (*prācīnāvītin* and *yajñopavītin*, respectively), the latter of which is appropriate for rituals to the gods. The ritualist moves back and forth between a divinely oriented mode of worship and an ancestrally oriented mode of worship, because—as the author of the *Taittirīya Brāhmaṇa* repeatedly informs us—the ritual is for both the Ancestors and the gods (*TB* 1.6.8.2; 1.6.8.5; 1.8.9.1). Despite the fact that offerings to gods do occur in the *piṇḍapitṛyajña*, such switches are not mentioned in the Brāhmaṇas. They do appear in some of the Śrautasūtra descriptions (e.g., *ĀpŚS* 1.8.3–4), but the fluidity of the ritual tradition by that point would allow for mutual influence between the two rites. For example, in his discussion of the *piṇḍapitṛyajña* Āśvalāyana (2.6.13) gives the option with regard to the offering to Agni Kavyavāhana: the offering may be made, having switched the sacred thread and using *agni kavyavāhanāya svāhā* instead of the customary *agni kavyavāhanāya svadhā namaḥ* (See also *BŚS* 3.10). This highlights the fluidity of the tradition well, because the sacrifice is given the option not only in the manner of wearing the sacred cord, but also in the use of either *svāhā*, the verbal formula used for gods, or *svadhā*, the formula for the Ancestors.

In general, in the *pitṛyajña*, the Adhvaryu switches his sacred thread when he makes an offering to a god and switches it back when a ritual action is again to be aimed at the Ancestors. It appears that the ritualists who composed this text worked hard to preserve the distinction between ancestral and divine rites. In addition, offerings made to gods without the clear connection to the Ancestors, for example, to Indra at *ŚBM* 2.6.1.38, must be done in the proper fashion, that is with the sacred cord in the divine orientation.

The second difference is the exclusion of the offerings of collyrium, ointment, and wool. There is little evidence to suggest the origins of these offerings, but they seem to fit a more fulsome conception of hospitality. The Ancestors are offered all the comforts of home: water to wash themselves, creams and ointments, and clothing. Their absence in the *pitṛyajña* suggests they were understood to be outside the normal Vedic ritual paradigm, that is, these ritual elements appear to come from the untextualized ritual tradition.

Finally, in the *piṇḍapitṛyajña* the rice-balls are offered on the sacred grass strewn south of the southern fire, whereas in the *pitṛyajña* they are offered on corners of the altar. The altar is central to the normal ritual paradigm, but the shift from offering onto the grass in the *piṇḍapitṛyajña* to offering on the altar in the *pitṛyajña* suggests that the former ritual was not conceived of as being within the normal ritual paradigm. Shastri's suggestion that the offerings being made on the altar recall the normal paradigm for ritual more clearly (1963, 99) supports this view.

The *piṇḍapitṛyajña* seems to follow a different paradigm, a paradigm of ancestor veneration drawn from the extra-textual tradition. I do not intend to imagine a non-Vedic tradition being assimilated into the Vedic ritual tradition, but merely the integration of the Vedic ancestral rites and the Soma-centered cult expressed in the textual tradition. My reading of these rituals suggests that the *piṇḍapitṛyajña* entered the monthly New Moon Sacrifices gradually, incorporating several traditional practices including the offerings to the ancestors beyond the rice-balls. That rite was incorporated into the Four-Monthly Sacrifices and underwent some alterations to make it better fit the normal Vedic paradigm, becoming the *pitṛyajña*.

Putting this evidence in the context of two scholarly treatments of ancient ancestor worship in India, I will argue that the *piṇḍapitṛyajña* represents the older rite and the *pitṛyajña* illustrates a subsequent, and more fully integrative, incorporation of the untextualized, likely domestic, practice of ancestor worship into the Vedic ritual literature.

The Integration of Ancestral Rites

The evidence in support of and counter to this view are of three types: referential, linguistic, and structural/conceptual. In reviewing each, I refer to the conclusions found in the two significant works on the history of ancestor worship in ancient India, Caland's *Altinjdischer Ahnencult* and Shastri's *Origin and Development of the Rituals of Ancestor Worship in India.*

In the category of referential evidence Caland asserts that the presence of the *pitṛyajña* and absence of the *piṇḍapitṛyajña* in the oldest Brāhmaṇas suggests that the *pitṛyajña* is the older rite (Caland 1893, 152).[34] Unfortunately he is far from clear about the texts to which he refers. He must not be referring to the *Aitareya Brāhmaṇa*, since neither ancestral rite finds mention there, though there is mention of an ancestral offering during the evening pressing of the Soma Sacrifice (*AB* 3.337.19). However, Caland is correct in so far as the *pitṛyajña* appears in the *Kauṣītaki Brāhmaṇa* (5.6), whereas the *piṇḍapitṛyajña* does not, but this is an argument from silence. In fact, the *Taittirīya Saṃhitā* describes the ancestral offerings integrated into the Sākamedha sacrifices, (1.8.5), and while that author does not use the term *piṇḍapitṛyajña*, he also describes offerings to the Ancestors as a part of the New and Full Moon Sacrifices (*TS* 2.5.3, 2.5.6). The references to each of these rites in the early Vedic literature suggest a dynamic period of development undergone unevenly across theological schools.

Caland also asserts that the mantras employed in the rites serve as evidence. He says, "Alle die vielen beim pitryajna gebrauchten mantras sind in der RS Vorhanden, nur einen ausgenommen; von den mantras des pindapitryajna dagegen finden sich kaum zwei in deiser samhita" (Caland 1893, 153), and concludes that the *pitṛyajña* must be older. Caland's assertion fails on multiple accounts. First, many of the mantras used in the rituals appear to be secondary to the ritual itself. This precludes using older mantras to argue for the age of the rituals. Second, our limited access to the mantras available to the authors of these works makes assertions about relative age impossible. An example will make these critiques more clear.

The nature of the hymns included in the performance of the *pitṛyajña* indicates their secondary nature. The *Taittirīya Saṃhitā*, for example, includes nine mantras. The first and the fifth seem integrated into the rite, for example, the first says "This is for you O Father..."[35] (*TS* 1.8.5.1) and continues thus for the grandfather and great-grandfather. Another declares that the Ancestors have eaten and are exhilarated (*TS* 1.8.5.2). But other mantras are not as integral to the ritual itself. Of the remaining mantras, two are borrowed from *ṚV* 10.82, a hymn to Indra, and three are borrowed from *ṚV* 10.57, a hymn in which Indra, Soma, and the Ancestors play a central role. The last is a general plea to be released from sin (*enas*). Oldenberg and Keith agree that the verses borrowed from the *Ṛg Veda* are secondary to the original ritual (Oldenberg quoted in Keith 1967, 117n2; Keith 1967, 117n4). The association of these verses with the Ancestors is clear—most invoke the Ancestors directly—but they are not integral to the ritual of offering to the Ancestors, they invoke the Ancestors' connection to Soma and their power to offer benefits to their living descendants.

In sum, those mantras that are clearly integrated into the ritual have no Ṛg-vedic precedent, and those that are not integral come from the *Ṛg Veda*. Theologically, the secondary verses create associations that draw the Ancestors' attention to the Sacrificer and invoke them in their beneficent forms. They also invest the ritual with Vedic authority and make the ritual more integral in the sacrificial cult centered on the *Ṛg Veda* as liturgy. However, neither of these qualities speak to the relative age of the rites. We cannot assume that those verses not found in the *Ṛg Veda* are younger than those found in that text. Further, we do not know when these verses were added to the rituals, so we cannot draw chronological conclusions from their inclusion. We simply do not know the extent of the verses available to the authors of these texts.

Material in the Śrautasūtras also supports the view that the *pitṛyajña* derives from the *piṇḍapitṛyajña*. As already seen, the *piṇḍapitṛyajña* is a shorter, less complicated rite, whereas the *pitṛyajña* is a more involved ritual, even in the Brāhmaṇas. While this comparison does not give us historical clues as to the relative ages of the rituals, it does indicate a conception in the tradition of which ritual is the more basic expression of the underlying practice, that is, ancestor worship. For the authors of the Śrautasūtras, the *pitṛyajña* draws on the *piṇḍapitṛyajña* as the basic paradigm. It is clear from *Āpastamba Śrautasūtra* 8.16.13 that one portion of the *pitṛyajña* of the Sākamedha follows the *piṇḍapitṛyajña*.[36] Other Śrautasūtras also allude to the *piṇḍapitṛyajña* as the model for the offering of rice-balls found in the *pitṛyajña*, though the references are more oblique (*ĀśŚS* 2.19.26 and *KŚS* 5.9.13). In short, at least part of the tradition understood the *piṇḍapitṛyjajña* to be the more fundamental rite.

Caland also offers linguistic evidence, suggesting that the name, specifically the "addition" of *piṇḍa*, indicates that the *piṇḍapitṛyajña* is of more recent origin. While it may at first blush seem to make sense that *piṇḍa* was added to an older name, the nature of the ritual precludes such an interpretation. Every instance of the *pitṛyajña* after the rite mentioned in the *Ṛg Veda* and the *Atharva Veda*—and Caland himself recognizes that that term refers to something else entirely—employs rice-balls. Only speculation supports the existence of an older ancestral rite without the offering of rice-balls, especially with no evidence to support this claim.

Beyond the comparison of the two names, the use of these terms in the later Saṃhitā and Brāhmaṇa literature indicates that this was a period of development, in which terminology had not been standardized. The *Taittirīya Saṃhitā* describes the *pitṛyajña*, but does not use the term *pitṛyajña*. That word appear in a list of the types of Sākamedhas elsewhere (3.2.2), and, as mentioned earlier, the author of this text describes offerings to the Ancestors as a part of the New and Full Moon Sacrifices, but fails to use the *piṇḍapitṛyajña*. The *Maitrāyaṇī Saṃhitā* treats the ancestral offerings in the Sākamedha sacrifices (1.10.3), but also does not use the term *pitṛyajñá* to describe the rite. By contrast, in another description the word is used several times (1.10.17). The *Aitareya Brāhmaṇa's* description of the ancestral offerings during the Soma Sacrifice refers to the rite with the term *pitṛyajña*—not *piṇḍadāna*, as the later tradition does (3.37.19). This evidence suggests that these two rites—and the terminology used to refer to them—are being integrated into the textual Vedic ritual tradition at uneven paces in the different theological schools.

Finally, a structural/conceptual interpretation of the two rituals further suggests that the *piṇḍapitṛyajña* predates the *pitṛyajña*. Caland asserts that the three immediate Ancestors were not an original part of the rite and it was dedicated instead to the Celestial Ancestors, for example, Barhiṣad Ancestors, Ancestors Seated on the *barhis* Grass, and Agniṣvātta Ancestors, Ancestors Tasted by Agni. The evidence from the *Ṛg Veda* suggests otherwise: the only occurrence of the term *pitṛyajñá* in the *Ṛg Veda* is in the funeral hymn, 10.16, and involves the promotion of the deceased father to the status of Ancestor. In addition, at least one of the Ancestors names, Agniṣvātta, suggests, that they were conceived of as real ancestors, if far removed; they are the Ancestors who have gone through the transformation described in *ṚV* 10.16, that is, they were "tasted", that is, consumed, by Agni in the funeral fire. This descriptor for the Ancestors appears almost exclusively in a funerary context.[37] While the later tradition develops elaborate notions of which Celestial Ancestor is ancestor to which group of beings (*HoD* 4:340ff.; Prasad 1995, 8; e.g., *MDhŚ* 3.192–201), this context, and the term's meaning—literally, "tasted by Agni"—indicate a different possibility. The *Śatapatha Brāhmaṇa* corroborates this (2.6.1.7).[38] In his commentary on *ṚV* 10.15 Sāyaṇa's describes them as "those eaten by Agni."[39] In the light of this evidence, it seems unlikely that the regular performance of the *pitṛyajña* excluded the most recently deceased Ancestor from consideration.[40]

The mythic explanations of the two rituals offer some clue to the purpose of the ritual. The *Śatapatha Brāhmaṇa* discusses the *piṇḍapitṛyajña* in the context of feeding the Ancestors (*ŚBM* 2.4.2.1–8), while it places the *pitṛyajña* in the context of the gods' restoration of the Ancestors through ritual (*ŚBM* 2.6.1.1). The purpose of the *piṇḍapitṛyajña*, according to the *Śatapatha Brāhmaṇa*, is to feed the Ancestors (*ŚBM* 2.4.2.7–8). On the other hand, the Sacrificer performs the *pitṛyajña* not only to feed the Ancestors, but also to move his Ancestors to a better world, fend off demons, and absolve himself of whatever sin he may have committed (*ŚBM* 2.6.1.3).

These differences run deeper than contextualizing two different rituals in two different mythic cycles. First, the mythic cycle of the *piṇḍapitṛyajña* is more basic to the conception of one's responsibility to one's ancestors, that is, feeding them. Second, the *pitṛyajña* adds ritual benefits more frequently associated with ritual in general to the basic aim of the *piṇḍapitṛyajña*; in short, it appears to be a composite rite based on the *piṇḍapitṛyajña* as older core ritual or a preexisting rite that influences the former's construction.[41] Unless one presumes a simplification of an older rite—which is possible, though certainly less likely—this suggests that the *piṇḍapitṛyajña* is the older of these two rituals. This view accords with Shastri's view of the differences of the two rituals, "This sacrifice is essentially the same as the Piṇḍa Pitṛ yajna, the only difference being that a very strong garb of sacrifice has been introduced here which makes it very complicated in appearance" (1963, 103–104).

Caland and Shastri disagree, with Caland offering scant and ambiguous evidence and Shastri offering an opinion with little evidence. Caland says, "Daraus schliesse ich, dass als Vedische ceremonie der Pitṛyajña älter ist als der Piṇḍapitṛyajña" (1893, 153). And Shastri concludes his discussion of the *piṇḍapitṛyajña* with: "This form of 'father-worship' seems to be the first step of development in the department of Rituals of ancestor worship" (1963, 99). While some of the evidence muddies the water, and some can be interpreted to support either position, the majority of the evidence supports the notion that the *piṇḍapitṛyajña* is the older rite and the *pitṛyajña* represents a subsequent effort to integrate the ancestral rites into the Vedic ritual tradition.

The solemn ritual texts record a synthesis of the ritual structure basic to the sacrificial religion and the practices observed upon and after the death of a man consecrated in that religious tradition. The tradition gradually integrates elements of an extra-textual tradition of feeding the dead into their theological discourse on sacrifice, simultaneously invigorating the archaic Vedic ritual cycle and lending legitimacy to the previously untextualized practices related to ancestor worship. The *piṇḍapitṛyajña* employs some elements of the basic Vedic model of sacrifice, but also shows the absence of certain key elements of Vedic ritual and the inclusion of ritual elements that are not common in Vedic ritual. The *pitṛyajña*, on the other hand, is a more fully integrated rite, a more fully developed integration of Vedic sacrifice and hither-to untextualized practice. The veneration of the Ancestors in the Four-Monthly Sacrifices was structured in ways more akin to the divine rite than the *piṇḍapitṛyajña*. These rites represent two phases of the incorporation of the practices of ancestor worship into the Vedic sacrificial model. Whereas the *piṇḍapitṛyajña* is a hybrid ritual, the *pitṛyajña* is a more fully Vedicized ancestral rite.

This repeated process of integration and synthesis characterizes the development of religion in a general sense, but in this context it represents the perpetual efforts of the educated religious class that composed theological treatises to integrate religious practice and in the process secure for themselves the privilege to define the tradition and ensure a place for the ritual experts of their tradition in the practice of ancestor veneration. By incorporating the ancestral rites into the Vedic ritual cycle, which require Vedic priests, the authors sought to extend the cycle of ritual dependence to include ancestor worship. This process of synthesis and integration continues during the process of recording the domestic ritual practices in the *Gṛhyasūtras*, as do the discursive efforts to legitimate and codify the ancestral rites and authorize and increase the ritual dependence upon the Brahmanical ritual experts.

3

The Domestic Rice-Ball Sacrifice to the Ancestors

THE GṚHYASŪTRAS MARK a significant moment in the history of ancestor worship in India; they codify the domestic ritual tradition alluded to in the older ritual literature. The domestic tradition of ancestor worship, like the solemn ritual tradition, dates back to a time far earlier than its textualization. References to domestic rituals in the Brāhmaṇas attest to a lively domestic ritual life (Gonda 1977b, 547; Oldenberg 1967, xv–xxii), but Oldenberg successfully demonstrates that no sustained literature on the household ritual predated the Gṛhyasūtras (Oldenberg 1967, xviii). Both the large-scale Vedic expression of ancestral rites found in the solemn ritual texts and the domestic practice, hitherto untextualized, thrived within the same larger tradition. However, Gṛhyasūtras do not merely record the domestic tradition, nor is it a simple appropriation of "popular" practices. The texts demonstrate significant influence from both the solemn rites and the domestic tradition and an intentional synthesis that draws upon both ritual traditions.

Understanding the influences and the synthesis involved is difficult, because the chronological relationship between the individual Gṛhyasūtras is extremely complicated. Gonda (1977b, 477–479) describes various issues that go into establishing even a relative dating, including copying, revisions (sometimes complete), and the myriad of details that point to borrowings not only within theological schools, but between them. For example, Caland has shown that the *Jaimini Gṛhyasūtra*, a text in the *Jaiminīya* school of the *Sāma Veda* tradition, includes a significant amount of material borrowed from the *Baudhāyana Gṛhyasūtra*, a text in the Taittirīya school of the *Yajur Veda* tradition (1922, xi). If we add to this diversity within the theological schools—for example between the Gṛhyasūtras of Pāraskara, Āpastamba, and Bharadvāja all of which belong to the Vājasaneyi school of the *Yajur Veda* tradition, the picture gets rather messy. Oldenberg suggests some structural elements that will help divide the domestic ritual manuals into earlier and later (1967 2:xxxix),[1] but he also points out several places where entire chapters are added to the *Śāṅkhāyana Gṛhyasūtra* (1967, 1:9–11). In the end, however, there is no convincing relative dating that would suffice to make judgments about the development of the domestic ritual tradition. The development seen in the Gṛhyasūtras happened in uneven ways in and between the theological schools. I will show the development in relation to the previous and subsequent texts and not attempt to construct a very specific relative chronology.

The Gṛhyasūtras record two threads in the development of ancestral rites. One preserves, in a modified form, the Vedic rite of ancestor worship. The other describes a significantly different domestic rite of ancestor worship. The former ritual occurs as one part of the Ninth-Day Ancestral Offerings (*anvaṣṭakya*). The name *anvaṣṭakya* refers to the rites "following the *aṣṭakā*." The title Eighth-Day Offerings (*aṣṭakā*) refers to both the eighth day after the new moon and to the seasonal rituals performed on the eighth day after the new moon in the winter and cool seasons.[2] Authors describe it by reference to the *piṇḍapitṛyajña* of the solemn ritual, though the ritual differs in some ways from the solemn rite. The latter ritual, most often called *śrāddha*, looks remarkably similar to the rite described in the Purāṇas and practiced among contemporary Hindus. The later expressions of the *śrāddha*-rite are in fact based on the domestic ritual texts, but just as the *piṇḍapitṛyajña* undergoes changes from the early Vedic period of the Brāhmaṇas and Śrautasūtras to the Gṛhyasūtras, so does the *śrāddha*-rite from its first expression in the Gṛhyasūtras to the Purāṇas.[3]

Both the Ninth-Day Ancestral Offerings and the *śrāddha*-rite owe something to the basic paradigm for ancestor worship that stretches back to the Brāhmaṇas, but both also bear evidence of the introduction of elements that are not present in the Vedic material, elements from the domestic practice of ancestor worship. There is no clear linear development in the textual production of the Brahmanical tradition; we cannot say definitively that the Śrautasūtras followed the Upaniṣads, which in turn followed the Brāhmaṇas, or that the Gṛhyasūtras followed the Śrautasūtras. It is clear from the intimate connection of the domestic ritual manuals to the mantras associated with each theological school and dependence of a majority of the Gṛhyasūtras on the corresponding Śrautasūtras (Oldenberg1967, xxx) that the domestic ritual manuals were composed after the earliest Śrautasūtras. However, exceptions to the chronological priority of the Śrautasūtras,[4] the assertion of common authorship to at least the Gṛhyasūtra and the

Dharmasūtra of Āpastamba (Olivelle, 2000, 4), and the development seen in the Gṛhyasūtras themselves indicate that the Gṛhyasūtras are composed over a relatively short period of time and that the composition of the Gṛhyasūtras more generally overlapped with the composition of some of the Śrautasūtras. These new elements could not then have arisen in some imagined time "between" the Śrautasūtras and the Gṛhyasūtras; there was no such gap in textual production. These differences must have developed outside the literary tradition, in the untextualized tradition of domestic ritual practice. It is during the composition of the Gṛhyasūtras that the solemn rituals of ancestor worship and the domestic tradition of ancestral offerings are integrated and innovated upon.

Several innovations apparent in the domestic ritual manuals radically alter the traditional conception of ancestor worship and establish a new paradigm for ancestor worship that shapes the subsequent Hindu tradition. This and the next chapter will describe these four developments, contextualize them in the ritual literature, and demonstrate that they are central to the discursive reconstruction of the ancestral rites that occurs in the *Gṛhyasūtras*. Two significant developments are visible in both the Ninth-Day Ancestral Offerings and the *śrāddha*-rite and probably arise from the previously untextualized practice of ancestor worship: the introduction of meat offerings and the introduction of Brahmins as guests who are fed and legitimize the rite. The second two developments indicate that the Brahmins defining the ancestral rites in the domestic ritual manuals used the advent of this genre to construct for themselves a specific role as ritual expert. In the process of recording and legitimating the domestic ritual formed in the synthesis of solemn and domestic ancestral rites, they also legitimate the role for a ritual expert that is integral to the ancestral rites. These two developments are: the assertion that the Brahmin invited to the rite is understood to represent the Ancestors in the ritual, accepting offerings on their behalf, and the establishment of the *śrāddha*-rite as the paradigmatic mode of ancestor worship.

I describe the Ninth-Day Ancestral Offerings then discuss the first two developments in this chapter and in the next chapter I describe the *śrāddha-rite* and the other two developments.

The Ninth-Day Ancestral Offerings

The solemn rite of *piṇḍapitṛyajña* finds expression in the domestic ritual manuals as the Ninth-Day Ancestral Offerings. In general the *piṇḍapitṛyajña* accords with the older solemn ritual model on many counts, often authors simply refer to that rite, but one dramatic change consistent across *śākhā* is the inclusion of a meat offering.

Since *Gobhila Gṛhyasūtra* records the particulars of the ritual in great detail, his work serves as a good example (*GGS* 4.2–3). The householder begins with his sacred thread over his left shoulder, the usual manner for divine offerings, and his wife assists him in the performance of the rite. He first apportions the ritual space to the south-east of the house, and orients the space in that same direction by making its long side in that direction. The domestic ritual shares with the solemn ritual the effort to establish associations through orientation and placement. This ritual is oriented to the south-east to associate it with both the gods and the Ancestors. Similarly the performer faces the southwest during the ritual making a connection to the south, in which the Ancestors dwell, and to the west, which is associated with the offspring, regeneration, fecundity, procreation and material wealth (Smith 1994, 144). He then establishes the fire and places the mortar within that space. The solemn ritual emphasis on associating the singular with the ancestors persists, and as in those rites the householder takes up the rice for offering in one grasp, threshes the rice only once, and, later, cuts the grass in one stroke. In addition, the authors emphasize that the left hand is for offerings to the Ancestors; the rice is taken up with the left hand and husked with the left hand on top and offerings are made with the left hand throughout the rite.

He then prepares the offering materials by cutting a lump of meat from the thigh used on the previous day in the Eighth-Day Offerings to be mixed in with the rice-ball. On the same fire he cooks up an oblation of rice grains and of meat, stirring them in a counter-clockwise direction (*prasavyam*).[5] He then pours butter on them and removes them from the fire toward the south.

With the offerings prepared, he turns to organizing the sacrificial space and the necessary implements. In the southern part of the sacrificial space he digs three furrows (*karṣū*) and reestablishes the fire to the east of the eastern-most furrow. He then strews one handful of *darbha* grass—cut off in one stroke—around the fire and over the furrows and spreads out a layer of *kuśa* grass to the west of the furrows with it tips pointed to the south. On the *kuśa* grass he places a mat and the sacrificial instruments. The Sacrificer's wife places a stone on the *barhis* grass and grinds fragrant powder and collyrium; with these she anoints three blades of *darbha* grass. He also brings sesame oil and a piece of linen from the fringe of his garment.

He invites an odd number of Brahmins to represent the Ancestors and seats them, facing north, on a seat of *darbha* grass he has made for them.[6] Having offered water and sesame to the Brahmins he says his father's name and recites, "This sesame water is for you! And for those who follow you here and for those whom you follow. For you, *svadhā*!"[7] Then he purifies himself by touching water and repeats the offering for his grandfather and great-grandfather. This whole cycle is repeated with an offering of perfume.

Before offering the oblations into the fire, he indicates his actions to the Brahmins, thereby asking permission, saying, "Shall I offer it in the fire." When they assent with, "Offer it," he cuts off a portion from each oblation, offering the first with "*svāhā* to Soma accompanied by the Ancestors!" and the second with "*svāhā* to Agni, who bears the ancestral offerings!"[8]

After these initial divine offerings are made into the fire, the householder switches to the offerings to be made to his Ancestors, by switching his sacred thread to his right shoulder.[9] In addition, we are told the householder is to proceed silently, though the use of mantras continues. He then takes a blade of *darbha* grass with his left hand a draws a line from north to south with a mantra to expel the demons (*asura*). Again with his left hand, he takes up a firebrand and places it on the south side of the furrows, with a mantra to drive away demons (*rākṣasa*).

He then invites the Ancestors to the sacrificial space with a mantra, "Come here Ancestors who are worthy of Soma!"[10] As in the solemn rite he affords his Ancestors a chance to wash before eating. He takes up a water pots with his left hand and pours from right to left on the *darbha* grass in each furrow with the name of each ancestor, "<Name> wash yourself, those who follow you, and those whom you follow. To you *svadhā*!"[11] and touches water between each ancestor to purify himself.

Now, with the left hand, he cuts off one-third of the mixture of oblations and make a rice-ball; that he places in the eastern most furrow with his father's name and "<Name> this rice-ball is for you, those who follow you, and those whom you follow. To you *svadhā*!"[12] He again purifies himself and repeats the rice-ball offerings in each subsequent furrow to each subsequent ancestor.[13] Just as in the solemn rite, after putting the rice-ball down on the grass and encouraging his Ancestors to enjoy themselves, he turns away and holds his breath. Before releasing his breath he turns back and says, "The Ancestors have exhilarated themselves, having rushed in like a bull, each to his own share!"[14] He then takes up each of the anointed *darbha* blade with his left hand and places it on each of the rice-balls in turn, dedicating the collyrium on it to each of his Ancestors. He repeats this cycle, offering unguent and perfume in turn.[15]

Looking at his home he says, "Give us houses, O Ancestors!" Looking at the rice-balls he says, "May we give you an abode!"[16] He then takes a thread and places it on each rice-ball in each furrow, from right to left, with the name of each Ancestor with the mantra "<Name> this garment is yours, of those who follow you, and of those whom you follow. To you *svadhā*!"[17] purifying himself between each ancestor.

Taking up the water vessel again with his left hand, he sprinkles around the rice-balls in a counter-clockwise manner. If he desires a son, then he has his wife eat the middle rice-ball. If not, the Brahmins who receive the remnants consume it. He then extinguishes the fire-brand and cleans the sacrificial vessels by sprinkling them with water, ending the ritual. The rice-ball can be disposed of in four ways: throw them in water, throw them in the fire, feed them to a Brahmin, or feed them to a cow.

Though all the Gṛhyasūtras address this rite, this detailed description is not common in the genre; the Ninth-Day Ancestral Offerings receive uneven treatment in the different Gṛhyasūtras. For example, Śāṅkhāyana only pauses briefly at the end of his brief description of the Eighth-Day Offerings to mention the Ninth-Day Ancestral Offerings, merely stating that it follows the procedure of the *piṇḍapitṛyajña* (*piṇḍapitṛyajñavat*) (*ŚGS* 3.13.7). He need not mention the details; they would be known to anyone who knew the Śrautasūtra.

Pāraskara also describes the Ninth-Day Ancestral Offerings in one *sūtra*, "On the next day, on the Ninth-Day Ancestral Offerings, of each, (he sacrifices) in the enclosure with the left rib and thigh, as in the *piṇḍapitṛyajña*" (*PGS* 3.3.10).[18] He gives us more detail, indicating the enclosure created in the ritual and the inclusion of meat offerings, but he too feels no need to review the procedure at length. He does, however, append two *sūtras* indicating that the Sacrificer should also make offerings to his female ancestors[19] with liquor, water, collyrium, unguents, and garlands. He also grants the option of offering to pupils and teachers who have no children.

Āśvalāyana's account represents a slightly more complex description of the *piṇḍapitṛyajña* (*ĀśGS* 2.5.1–9). He reviews the procedure in one unusually long *sūtra*, but his description, however short, accords in the basics with Gobhila's account. Like Pāraskara, Āśvalāyana offers the option of making offerings to one's female ancestors (*ĀśGS* 2.5.5). He also states an option with regard to the placement of the rice-balls. Some, he says, offer the rice-balls in the furrows dug as part of the ritual (2.5.6), as seen in the *Gobhila Gṛhyasūtra*. But Āśvalāyana presents this as an alternative, not as the usual practice, as Gobhila does. Āśvalāyana too refers to the *piṇḍapitṛyajña* as the basic paradigm, that is, offering on grass as in the Śrautasūtras. In short, Āśvalāyana's description of the *piṇḍapitṛyajña* accords with the older solemn ritual model on many counts, but one dramatic change we see in Āśvalāyana's account is the inclusion of a meat offering. These differing opinions and changes in the procedure for ancestor worship also indicate the fluid nature of the domestic rites during the composition of the Gṛhyasūtras.

Rice-Ball Sacrifice to the Ancestors: Conservative and Innovative

This review of the Ninth-Day Ancestral Offerings enables a discussion of the development of the *piṇḍapitṛyajña*, its conservative nature, and the significant innovations that appear in the Gṛhyasūtras. The above summary of the *piṇḍapitṛyajña* of the Gṛhyasūtras reveals two things: the ritual is heavily indebted to the ancestral rites described in the Śrautasūtras, often simply referring to those texts for details, and the rite has undergone significant alteration.

The conservative trend anchors the domestic ritual cycles described in the Gṛhyasūtras in the ancient tradition of solemn ritual and authorizes those rites as a legitimate part of the Vedic ritual tradition. The innovative aspects of those rites incorporate the extra-textual practice and secure for the Brahmin ritual experts a central place in the religious life of the ritual actor. In their description of the ritual life the authors create a cycle of dependency; the performance of ritual depends upon the employment of ritual experts described, and authorized, by the texts. I will describe the conservative nature of the ancestral rites, then the innovative nature in order to show the development from the *śrauta* to the *gṛhya* ritual models. The last two innovations—the most significant—will serve my argument about the repeated integration and synthesis that characterizes the development of the ancestral rites in these texts.

The tradition is consistent in referring to the *piṇḍapitṛyajña* as the model for the Ninth-Day Ancestral Offerings, but there is evidence that both solemn rites shaped the domestic rite. The *piṇḍapitṛyajña* occurs monthly, on the new moon—the first night that the moon is invisible—while the *pitṛyajña* occurs seasonally, on the full moon in the month of Kārttika (October-November) or Mārgaśīrṣa (November-December). The Ninth-Day Ancestral Offerings occur seasonally on the ninth day after the full moon in the months of Mārgaśīrṣa, Pauṣa (December-January), Māgha (January-February), and Phālguna (February-March). While the procedure of the Ninth-Day Ancestral Offerings is clearly drawn from the *piṇḍapitṛyajña*, the conception of ancestor worship as a seasonal event is associated with the *pitṛyajña*. The *piṇḍapitṛyajña* and the *pitṛyajña* occur on the new and full moons respectively, but the Ninth-Day Ancestral Offerings occurs, as its name indicates, on the ninth day of the moon in particular months. The solemn ancestral rites appear to have influenced each other, and the authors of the Gṛhyasūtras made specific choices in their synthesis of these two ritual cycles.

This evidence suggests the Gṛhyasūtras are actively drawing upon multiple conceptions of ancestor worship; they do not simply perpetuate the *piṇḍapitṛyajña* as a part of the new moon ritual cycle. The textualization of there rituals represents the further integration of the ancestral rites into the Vedic ritual tradition.

There is precedent for ritual on the eighth day of the new moon (*ŚBM* 6.2.2.23), but it is not associated with the Ancestors. However, one of the two major ancestral rites does coincide with the domestic seasonal offerings. The *pitṛyajña* and the Ninth-Day Ancestral Offerings occur in the autumn. They both occur during the waning moon during the waning of the year, as discussed above in relation to the *pitṛyajña*.

This synthesis of the two ancestral rites described within the textual tradition also has a procedural impact. Gobhila is explicit about the need to switch from the divine mode of sacrifice to the ancestral mode (4.3.1). This switching of the sacred thread occurs as a part of the solemn *pitṛyajña*; it does not occur in the *piṇḍapitṛyajña*. All domestic ritual authorities agree on the fact that the Ninth-Day Ancestral Offering is modeled on the *piṇḍapitṛyajña*, but this convention usually associated with the other rite has crept into this rite.

A comparison of this ritual with the solemn rite of *piṇḍapitṛyajña* reveals a strong conservative tradition.[20] The description above should make clear that the domestic rite is in large part a slimmed down version of the solemn rite. The key actions mention to distinguish ancestral from divine offerings persist. For example, the association of the specific actions with the number one, repeated throughout the solemn ancestral rites occurs here as well. The grass is to be cut in one stroke;[21] utensils are to be laid out singly rather than in pairs;[22] and the rice is husked only once.[23] Offerings to Soma and Agni Kavyavāhana still stand at the opening of the ritual proper. The primary offerings made to the Ancestors—rice balls, collyrium, unguent, and thread—are the same. The mantras about houses invoke the Ancestors as those who give houses.[24] The use of the left hand or turning or stirring to the left is another feature common to both solemn and domestic rites.[25] Finally, other specific ritual actions point to continuity, such as the laying of the firebrand to expel demons[26] and the instruction to feed the second rice-ball to his wife should the householder desire children.[27] The householder turns away from the rice-balls to afford the Ancestors privacy[28] and most of the mantras used in the rituals are those used from the oldest period.[29]

More telling even than a review of such specific continuities is the manner in which authors include the rite in the text. In nearly all the Gṛhyasūtras, the details of the ritual are either abbreviated or omitted; instead the authors refer to the *piṇḍapitṛyajña*, assuming their audience is familiar with the solemn rite. Better than any other evidence, this indicates that this domestic rite is largely continuous with the solemn rite. But clearly there were differences, otherwise there would be no need for the domestic manuals.

I first discuss several minor changes to the ritual then turn to two that have more significant impact on the performance of ancestor worship and indicate the nature of the development of this rite in the Brahmanical discourse. There are changes to specific elements of the ritual—for example, sesame was associated with ancestral offerings since at least the *Atharva Veda* (*AVŚ* 18.3.68–69, quoted above)—and in the Dharmasūtras, only slightly younger than the Gṛhyasūtras, the sale of sesame is equated with selling one's Ancestors.[30] The integration then of an offering of sesame water into the domestic rite is neither a dramatic innovation nor a great surprise. The addition of an offering of perfume, also new, does not alter the flow of the ritual tremendously, and might even be considered in keeping with the offerings of collyrium and unguent and symbolic housing and clothing, which symbolize hospitality.

In addition to these changes to the elements of the ritual, there is a significant change to the selection of the ritual space and the architecture of the ritual space itself. The choice of locations for a ritual follows the dictates of the solemn and ritual traditions. The solemn tradition grew out of a nomadic past and was portable by nature. In contrast the domestic ritual tradition presumes a relatively permanent home. It makes sense then that the location for the rite is determined in relation to their place of residence, that is, to the south-east. East is the absolute orientation, that is toward the gods. South is the direction associated with death. The relative movement from one's home toward the east and south positions the ritual in the cosmos relative to the absolute, the gods, and the mundane, the home.

Within the ritual space itself, the domestic rite introduces the creation of three furrows, unto which grass is strewn and the rice-balls are offered. In the solemn rite the Adhvaryu digs a single line with the wooden sword, sprinkles it with water, and strew it with grass; this acts as the altar for the ritual.[31] The furrows dug in the domestic rite are more substantial; they "they should measure the span from thumb to forefinger and four finger widths wide and just as deep."[32] In the ritual they serve the purpose of giving each of the three Ancestors—father, grandfather, and great-grandfather—their own space. The nature of that space, that is, a rather deep furrow, and the division of the offerings into those three furrows, does not appear to come from the ritual tradition described in the solemn ritual manuals. This feature must originate in the untextualized domestic practice of ancestral rites.

The last two innovations are the most significant for understanding process of synthesis and innovation I have described. The incorporation of meat to the offerings made to the Ancestors and the new role of professional guest to be filled by a Brahmin in the domestic rite described in the Gṛhyasūtras alter the rite described in the solemn ritual tradition. These elements fundamentally alter the nature of the ancestral rites and the domestic ritual model created in this synthesis becomes the paradigm for the later tradition. While the addition of meat changes the offerings and presages the later obsession with the type of offering made, the new role for the Brahmin in the domestic rite indicates at least some of the motive of the ritual innovation. The Brahmins inscribe themselves into the ritual lives of ancient India. The ritual now depends upon their participation. I first describe the inclusion of meat offerings to the ancestral rites.

All the Gṛhyasūtras includes a meat offering in the Ninth-Day Ancestral Offerings. *Āśvalāyana Gṛhyasūtra* 2.5.2 mentions the preparation of meat offerings. Pāraskara states this at the beginning of the Eighth-Day Offerings: "The (offerings) are cakes, meat, and vegetables, respectively"

(*PGS* 3.3.3).[33] Śāṅkhāyana mentions offering the omentum (*ŚGS* 3.13.2).[34] In the *Gobhila Gṛhyasūtra* the author explicitly states that the sacrifice has one mess of rice and one of meat (*GGS* 4.2.14).[35]

Since the Ninth-Day Ancestral Offerings are modeled on, indeed are a continuation of the *piṇḍapitṛyajña*, but that rite has no meat offering in its solemn mode, we can deduce that the introduction of meat into the rite has its origins in the previously untextualized tradition of domestic ancestor worship, that is, the untraceable practice that first finds expression in the Gṛhyasūtras. The inclusion of meat in the offering was a part of the synthesis of the solemn and domestic rituals traditions. The addition of meat offerings probably served to integrate ancestral worship with the rituals of the Eighth-Day Offerings, the focal point of which is the slaughter of a cow. Meat offered to the Ancestors is taken from the left thigh of the sacrificial animal used in that rite.

In addition, the meat is intended to make the offerings to the Brahmins a complete meal. This would dovetail nicely with the conception of *śrāddha*-rite as feeding the Ancestors and the term *śraddhā* often connected with the *śrāddha*-rite. The word *śraddhā*, conveys both a confidence in the efficacy of the ritual and of the power of hospitality.[36] The meat offering is integral with the changing conception of the *śrāddha*-rite. While meat offerings are absent in the earlier tradition, it becomes a central concern of the *dharma* literature for the performance of a successful *śrāddha*-rite. In short, the inclusion of meat offerings in the ancestral rites is a key aspect of the textualization of the rituals and evidences the synthesis of solemn and domestic modes of ancestor worship.

The last innovation, the new role created for a Brahmin to act as professional guest, illustrates the authors' intent to establish themselves as the ritual experts indispensable to the performance of the ancestral rites. While the advent of the domestic ritual manuals as a genre of literature probably had several causes—including a new increased interest in the domestic rites and an increased desire to define the proper ritual procedures—the construction of this new ritual expert was certainly one of the more significant. The evidence reviewed so far shows that the authors took this chance to innovate upon the inherited traditions. The authors reconceptualized the role of ritual expert, inscribing themselves onto the domestic rites, especially ancestor worship, just as the authors of the older literature inscribed the Vedic priest into the ancestral rites during the integration of those rites into the texts of the solemn ritual tradition. They included themselves in the role of a new religious experts and claimed for themselves a new mode of authority. The Gṛhyasūtras illustrate both the continued role for the Vedic priests and the creation of a new religious expert, the professional guest. The marginalization of the Vedic priest in the domestic ritual cycle was a part of the authors' efforts to claim new modes of authority through the establishment of a new religious expert.

In the solemn rites, the role of religious expert in the Vedic literature is clear: the four Vedic priests enact the ritual on behalf of the Sacrificer. In the domestic ritual, however, while the Vedic priests retain some of their responsibilities, the householder performs most of the ritual actions and allocates to his wife a few other functions. The Brahmin who is invited as guest, however, becomes increasingly central to the domestic ritual. His inclusion in the domestic ritual cycles is another example of the competition between different Brahmanical groups, and non-Brahmanical religious experts, for the patronage of the ritual practitioner, the householder. The descriptions of the Brahmins role and the central place that role took in the conception of domestic ritual in general highlight the importance of authorizing, textually, this new role.

Inviting and feeding a Brahmin of quality became integral to most domestic rituals. In his outline of the basic ritual paradigm Śāṅkhāyana tells us that feeding of Brahmins is a customary part of performing the domestic rituals, "At the conclusion of rites (there is) the feeding of Brahmins" (*ŚGS* 1.2.1).[37] Further, the authors integrate this new role for the Brahmin into their classifications of ritual, thereby codifying it. Āśvalāyana defines three kinds of Small Sacrifices (*pākayajña*), a general term for domestic rituals.[38] "There are three Small Sacrifices: *huta*, which are offered into the fire; *prahuta*, which are not offered into the fire; and what is offered into the Brahmin at a Brahmin Feeding" (*ĀśGS* 1.1.2).[39] Āśvalāyana names the first two, *huta* and *ahuta*, but fails to name the last, merely describing the offering that is giving food to a Brahmin. Śāṅkhāyana lists four types: *huta*, *ahuta*, *prahuta*, and *prāśita* (*ŚGS* 1.5.1).[40] Later he defines them, as Āśvalāyana did, though reordering the referents, "A *huta* (is made) by performing an oblation in an Agnihotra; an *ahuta* (is made) by performing a *bali* offering. A *prahuta* (is made) by performing an Ancestor offering; a *prāśita* is offered into a Brahmin" (*ŚGS* 1.10.7).[41] Despite the different categorization of the types of small sacrifices, the Gṛhyasūtra authors agree that giving food to a Brahmin is an integral part of domestic ritual life. And indeed the feeding of Brahmins is mentioned quite frequently in the Gṛhyasūtras.

In fact, I found only one statement that suggests Brahmins are not to be fed at the end of any particular ritual. At the end of his description of the Ninth-Day Ancestral Offerings, Hiraṇyakeśin says, "He does not here engage in the giving of food or gifts" (*HGS* 2.5.15.12).[42] Its explicit omission, along with the *sūtras* enjoining it mentioned above, indicates that the feeding of Brahmins is integral to the domestic ritual.

The new Brahmanical ritual expert role is not limited to that of a professional guest. The authors of the Gṛhyasūtras indicate two new aspects of the Brahmins role: the Brahmins authorize the householder's ritual offerings and the householder implores the Brahmin to declare the day meritorious and proclaim the success of the ritual. Gobhila instructs the householder in this way, "When he is about to sacrifice he addresses the Brahmins saying 'Shall I offer it in the fire?' When they have replied 'Offer it,' he should cut off a portion of the two oblations into the drinking vessel and offer an oblation with the stirring stick..." (*GGS* 4.2.38–39).[43] Āśvalāyana describes the exact same exchange in his outline of the *śrāddha*-rite: the householder asks for permission (*anujñāpayati*) to make the offerings and the Brahmins give their consent or permission (*pratyabhyanujñā*) (*ĀśGS* 4.7.18–19). The success of the ritual depends upon their consent from the very beginning, but it does not end there.

At the end of the ritual, the Brahmin is again called upon to validate the ritual. Hiraṇyakeśin says "Having served food to Brahmins and caused them to say 'This is a meritorious day! Blessings! Prosperity!' They rest that night" (*HGS* 2.7.17.13).[44] The Brahmin's proclamation ensures the success of the ritual. The role of professional guest is simply not to invest the ritual with their revered presence, but to authorize and endorse the ritual success. The integral nature of this ritual expert and the codification of their role authorized their place in the ritual cycle of dependence.

The authors have legitimized the Brahmin guest as the ritual expert, whose active participation, though minimal, is required for the ceremony. The authors authorize, textually, a new role as ritual expert that is central to the domestic ritual practice of all twice-born men, those initiated in the tradition and thereby able to perform Vedic domestic rites. That this new role is available only to Brahmins learned in the tradition in which these texts are written indicates an important aspect of the motivation for the composition of the Gṛhyasūtras. The domestic ritual manuals seek to establish the learned Brahmin as the proper ritual expert within a competitive religious marketplace. They legitimate their own religious expert in contrast to both the older Vedic priest and the other religious experts of other religious traditions. A discussion of the full import of this new role requires a discussion of the *śrāddha*-rite, the descriptions of which more fully demonstrate the construction and import of this new role. I discuss both in the next chapter.

4

*The Śrāddha-Rite**

IN ADDITION TO the Ninth-Day Ancestral Offerings, the Gṛhyasūtras also describe a new form of ancestral rite, the *śrāddha*-rite. The prescriptions for this ritual in the Gṛhyasūtras form the basis for the entire subsequent tradition of ancestor worship in Hinduism. The most significant development within the ritual procedure is the new role established for the Brahmin, that is, the Brahmin stands in for the ancestors, to receive oblations on their behalf.[1] In addition, the domestic *piṇḍapitṛyajña* is gradually supplanted—by means of the dynamic redefinition of the ancestral rites—by the *śrāddha*-rite as the paradigmatic mode of ancestor worship.

In this chapter I describe the *śrāddha*-rite then highlight elements of the ritual that illustrate the last two innovations of the four I began to outline in the last chapter: the enhanced role that the Brahmin guest takes in the *śrāddha*-rite and the shift in conception of the paradigmatic rite of ancestral offerings, namely from the *piṇḍapitṛyajña* of the solemn rites to the *śrāddha*-rite in the later Gṛhyasūtras. These developments in the tradition of ancestor worship fit into my larger argument about the gradual integration and synthesis of the ancestral rites and demonstrate the Brahmin theologians' efforts to construct a new ritual expert. The following evidence shows that, as in the Saṃhitā literature of the earlier tradition, the establishment of a clear tradition of ancestor worship with definitive rites—and procedures for those rites—was a slow and contested process. The construction of this new ritual expert role and the establishment of the *śrāddha*-rite take place at uneven paces across the *śākhās*, but by the advent of the new genre of literature, the Dharmasūtras, the new paradigm was an accepted part of the proper life of the ritual actor. I begin with the ideal, then demonstrate the complicated nature of the

* An earlier version of parts of this chapter appeared as "Gayā-Bodhgayā: The Origins of a Pilgrimage Complex" in *RoSA* 4.1 (2010) 9–25; (c) Equinox Publishing Ltd 2010.

evidence with a mind to describing the process whereby this ideal came to prominence.

Ideally, the *śrāddha*-rite takes four primary forms: the *pārvaṇa*, the *ekoddiṣṭa*, the *sapiṇḍīkaraṇa*, and the *ābhyudayika*. The *pārvaṇa śrāddha*-rite (new moon *śrāddha*-rite) describes regular monthly ancestor worship, focused on the offering of *piṇḍas* to the Ancestors and modeled, broadly, on the *piṇḍapitṛyajña*. The name derives from the day of the new moon (*parvaṇa*). The *ekoddiṣṭa śrāddha*-rite (*śrāddha*-rite directed to one person) sustains the deceased father in the first year after his death, between the states of living father and Ancestor, that is, as a ghost. By performing the *sapiṇḍīkaraṇa* (*śrāddha*-rite that creates the bond of kinship) the deceased man's son promotes his father from this liminal state to the position of Ancestor. In the process, he promotes each subsequent Ancestor to the position of his predecessor, and the eldest Ancestor, his father's great-grandfather, to the class of anonymous Ancestors beyond the three involved in the *śrāddha*-rite.[2] A householder performs an *ābhyudayika śrāddha*-rite (the prosperity *śrāddha*-rite) on any auspicious occasion, such as a wedding or the birth of a son, to invoke the positive, beneficial aspect of the ancestors.[3]

Śāṅkhāyana enumerates each of these four types of *śrāddha*-rite in a separate chapter.[4] He first describes the monthly *śrāddha*-rite, elsewhere called the *pārvaṇa śrāddha* (*ŚGS* 4.1.1–13). In keeping with the *sūtra* style described earlier, Śāṅkhāyana relies on the older solemn ritual model. Reference is made to the *piṇḍapitṛyajña* and derivations from that rite are briefly outlined.

Like the solemn *piṇḍapitṛyajña*, the *śrāddha*-rite should be performed monthly. The monthly offerings sustain the Ancestors; this underscores the main purpose of the rite as well, that is, to feed the ancestors. Brahmins are invited to the ritual and said to represent the Ancestors (*pitṛvat*). They receive the water to wash themselves, food offerings, and the rice-balls on behalf of the Ancestors. As in the Ninth-Day Ancestral Offerings, the householder also offers rice-balls to the wives of his Ancestors. The three other *śrāddha*-rites described in this Gṛhyasūtra, however, serve different purposes.

The *ekoddiṣṭa śrāddha*-rite is performed by the surviving son of the deceased ritual during the year following his father's death, sustaining him until his integration into the pantheon of the Ancestors. Śāṅkhāyana's description is limited to the ways in which this rite differs from the ordinary *śrāddha*-rite, a point that emphasizes the paradigmatic status of the *pārvaṇa śrāddha*-rite in the mind of this and other authors, that is, the author merely outlines the alterations made to the *pārvaṇa* for the *ekoddiṣṭa*.

Not surprisingly the most significant change involves the number of ritual objects and offerings. Since the ritual aims to sustain only one person, instead of the usual three, the Sacrificer makes only one purifier (*pavitra*) used in the water pot, only one offering of water as to a guest (*arghya*), and only one rice-ball. He does not invite the Ancestors to the ritual, nor the Viśvadevas—the class of anonymous ancestors beyond the three honored in the monthly *śrāddha*-rite—since the ritual is aimed at the deceased alone. While he still expresses his concern about the offering satisfying the deceased, the mantras differ. This shift highlights the new emphasis with respect to the aim of this *śrāddha*-rite. Replacing the mantra: "Inexhaustible" (*akṣayya*) with: "May he approach the Ancestors" (*upatiṣṭhatām ity akṣayyasthāne*) changes the focus of the ritual. Whereas the normal mantra expresses the hope that the offering to the Ancestors will last forever, this ritual aims to elevate the deceased to the status of Ancestor, so the mantra must reflect this hope. The duration also differs; this *śrāddha*-rite is performed for one year following death. This leads to the ritual transformation of the deceased into an Ancestor.[5]

The *sapiṇḍīkaraṇa śrāddha*-rite transforms the deceased father into an Ancestor. The great-grandfather is promoted to Viśvadeva and each subsequent Ancestor advances one step. As with the *ekoddiṣṭa*, Śāṅkhāyana restricts himself to addressing the differences in the ritual, mentioning almost no ritual detail. The *sapiṇḍīkaraṇa* also shares with the *ekoddiṣṭa* a concern over numbers, by which we see the ritual process that integrates the father with the Ancestors.

The *sapiṇḍīkaraṇa* normally occurs one year after death,[6] though Śāṅkhāyana allows for its performance on an auspicious occasion.[7] The primary difference, as with the *ekoddiṣṭa* is the number of items used, in this case, four. The householder fills four pots with water and creates four rice-balls, one for each of his Ancestors—in this case his father's father, grandfather, and great-grandfather—and one for his deceased father. During the ritual he joins the water in the deceased's water pot with the water pots of the Ancestors and the rice-balls of the deceased with the three of the Ancestors (ŚGS 5.9.4–5). The joining of the physical substances of the offerings, water and rice-balls, integrates his deceased father into the class of Ancestors—this also advances each Ancestor one step so each new generation venerates the three previous generations. By doing this, the deceased becomes an Ancestor, to receive the offerings of the *pārvaṇa śrāddha* thereafter.[8]

The last form of *śrāddha*-rite—the *ābhyudayika śrāddha*-rite—has little to do with the death of one's father; it calls on the Ancestors in their role as progenitors and dispensers of wealth, a theme clearly expressed in both the Vedic materials. A householder performs the *ābhyudayika śrāddha*-rite on auspicious occasions and the alterations to the ritual paradigm reinforce the shift from a ritual associated with death to one promoting life.

> 1 Now the *ābhyudayika*. 2 (This ritual is performed) on the fortnight of the waxing moon on a meritorious day, 3 after he has performed the sacrifice to the Mothers. 4 He should invite an even number of (Brahmins) who are conversant in the Vedas. 5–6 He performs the rite in the earlier part of the day in a clockwise direction. 7 He utters (mantra, but) omits the mantras dedicated to the Ancestors.
>
> 8 The *darbha* grass is straight, 9 (and he uses) barley instead of sesame. 10 The rice-balls are mixed with coagulated milk, jujubes, and un-husked barley corns. 11 At the invitation he says "I will invite the Nāndīmukha Ancestors." 12 In the place of "Imperishable" he says "May the Nāndīmukha Ancestors be delighted." 13 At the recitation he says "I will make the Nāndīmukha Ancestors speak." 14 The question about their being satisfied is "Is it palatable?" 15 The rest is the same for it is consistent (with the other *śrāddha*-rites). *ŚGS* 4.4.1–15[9]

Whereas the *pārvaṇa śrāddha*-rite, the paradigm for the other three types, is performed during the waning moon, this *śrāddha*-rite occurs during the waxing moon (*ĀpGS* 8.21.10). The Ancestors' association with death makes clear the connection to the waning, that is, dying, moon. Thus the reversal of the *ābhyudayika śrāddha*-rite seeks to invoke the increasing, that is, waxing, moon. Relatedly, the tradition also refers to this type of *śrāddha*-rite as the *vṛddhi śrāddha*-rite (*śrāddha*-rite of increase) (e.g., *ĀśGS* 2.5.1–15). Other changes reflect this reversal from death and inauspicious associations to positive, auspicious associations: inviting an even number of Brahmins, instead of the usual uneven number (See also *GGS* 4.3.35); the change from the afternoon, the normal time for performance of the *śrāddha*-rite to the forenoon; and performing the ritual in a clockwise (*pradakṣiṇa*) rather than counter-clockwise direction (*ĀśGS* 4.7.12). In the oldest rituals, clockwise is the proper manner of circumambulation in rituals to the gods; it presents the performer's right side to the object of veneration. It invokes an auspicious, connective relation to the object of veneration. The manner of circumambulation for ancestral rites inverses this. Whereas in the normal ritual the Sacrificer seeks to connect with the divine, in the ancestral rites one must keep death at bay, by circumambulating in a counter-clockwise direction, minimizing contact with the Ancestors, with death. In the *ābhyudayika*, the auspicious aspect of the Ancestors is emphasized, and thereby the ritual establishes a connection in the manner of circumambulation.

Through this connection the ritual seeks to emphasize the role of the Ancestors as benefactors. First, those elements of the *pārvaṇa śrāddha*-rite that highlight the Ancestors' benevolence remain unchanged. Second, the name Nāndīmukha Ancestors (glad-faced Ancestors) suggests their benevolent aspect. The invocation of the Ancestors in this way describes the state of mind with which the worshipper implores his Ancestors to approach the ritual.

All these alterations to the performance of the *śrāddha*-rite should be understood as systematic changes that occur in the shift from the paradigmatic *śrāddha*-rite—which necessarily involves an association with the Ancestors as dead people—to the *śrāddha*-rite that seeks to invoke their beneficent aspect. That is, the shift is better understood as one more way to modify a ritual usually associated with death to one that celebrates life.[10] Finally, the shift of mantras highlights the shift in emphasis with respect to the aim of this *śrāddha*-rite, as seen in the mantra substitution in the *ekoddiṣṭa śrāddha*-rite. The shift from "Inexhaustible" (*akṣayyam*) to "May the Glad-faced Ancestors be delighted" (*ŚGS* 4.4.12) changes the focus of the ritual. Since the aim of this ritual is not the regular feeding of the Ancestors, as seen already, but an invocation of their ability to benefit the ritualist, the mantra that replaces this older mantra aims to please the Ancestors. Not only does the mantra state the householder's hope that they are pleased, but it also emphasizes that they should be cheerful; in fact the term *nāndī* suggests satisfaction, gladdening. By invoking this aspect of the Ancestors, and deemphasizing their inauspicious aspects, the householder celebrates significant moments in his life, invoking the Ancestors' benevolence and deemphasizing their association with death.[11]

What must be understood is that the well-developed rituals portrayed here belie the contested nature of the ancestral rites in the Gṛhyasūtras in general and of the *śrāddha*-rite specifically. In this section I address the two innovations mentioned earlier as they are expressed in the domestic ritual manuals. In the discursive formation of the Brahmanical view of ancestor worship the *śrāddha*-rite exhibit two factors absent in the Ninth-Day Ancestral Offerings that followed the *piṇḍapitṛyajña* relatively closely. Whereas the latter rite exhibited both the inclusion of meat offerings and the introduction of new religious experts, the *śrāddha*-rite continues the meat offerings and reinforces the role occupied by the new religious expert.

Central to the domestic ritual is the invitation of Brahmins to be fed at the ritual, as shown earlier with respect to domestic ritual more broadly. Significant specifically for a study of the *śrāddha*-rite is the role of this Brahmin as stand-in for the Ancestors, that is, as a proxy for the offerings to the deceased ancestors. The incorporation of this new role occurs alongside the gradual normalization of *śrāddha*-rite, that is, the construction of *śrāddha*-rite as the paradigmatic rite of ancestor worship. These two changes support my argument that the domestic ritual manuals are intentional efforts on the part of Brahmanical authors to integrate two different traditions of ancestor worship—the Vedic mode expressed in the solemn *piṇḍapitṛyajña* and the domestic tradition that was under construction in the Gṛhyasūtras—and define a new religiosity, a new religious mode oriented around the new ritual expert constructed in that effort.

The new role created for the Brahmin occurs in both forms of ancestor veneration in the Gṛhyasūtras, but the increased importance given the Brahmin as professional guest rather than Vedic priest, outlined earlier, finds a more significant expression in the context of the *śrāddha*-rite. This importance of feeding Brahmins takes on particular import for a study of ancestor worship; that is, the Brahmin stands in for the deceased.

Brahmin as Stand-in for the Ancestors

Āśvalāyana and Śāṅkhāyana both tell us that the Brahmin stands in for the deceased father during the *śrāddha*-rite.

> He should cause Brahmins who are endowed with fame, character, and (good) behavior, or with one (of these), who were informed at the proper time, have bathed, are purified to their feet, and have sipped water to sit down as the Ancestors, with their faces to the north, one for one, two for two, or three for three. *ĀśGS* 4.7.2[12]

> He should invite an uneven number of Brahmins, at least three, conversant in the Vedas, as the Ancestors. *ŚGS* 4.1.2[13]

Both authors use the term *pitṛvat* (as the Ancestors) to indicate that Brahmins stand in for, literally sit in the place of, the Ancestors, acting as their proxy for the oblations that the Sacrificer makes in the *śrāddha*-rite. The following passages illustrate how the Brahmins physically stand in for the Ancestors.

> 3 Having strewn an uneven number of water vessels with sesame seeds, 4 he should pour (the water) on the Brahmins' hands, assigning it (to them) with "This for you <name>!" 5 Then they are adorned. 6 Having saluted them and offered the food in the fire, 7 he should feed them, assigning it (to them) with "This is for you <name>!" *ŚGS* 4.1.3–7[14]

The Sacrificer washes the Brahmins as he washed the Ancestors in the solemn rite, and feeds them, as he fed the Ancestors in the solemn rite. The Brahmins not only symbolically represent the Ancestors, they actually receive the offerings made to the Ancestors, on their behalf; they mediate the exchange between son and father, between householder and ancestor.

Āśvalāyana's language expresses the Brahmins' role as physical stand-in less explicitly, but it is clear nonetheless that the Brahmin receives the offerings of the Ancestors and interact with the ritualist on behalf of the Ancestors. The Sacrificer interacts with the Brahmins as if they were the Ancestors, "7 Having given water (to the Brahmins), 8 Having presented (them) with doubly-bent *darbha* grass as a seat, 9 Having presented (them) with water" (*ĀśGS* 4.7.7–9).[15] Later, the householder asks for permission to make the offerings, then does so. He has the option of offering into the fire, as is usual, or in the hands of the Brahmins (*ĀśGS* 4.7.20–21).[16]

Quoting a Brāhmaṇa to add authority to the declaration, Āśvalāyana reiterates the notion that the Brahmins convey the offerings to the Ancestors, "It says in a Brāhmaṇa, 'The gods have Agni as their mouth, the Ancestors have the hand as their mouth'" (*ĀśGS* 4.7.22).[17] As Agni mediates between the Sacrificer and the gods, the Brahmin mediates between the ritualist and the Ancestors, between the householder and his Ancestors. When the Brahmin accepts the food, it is on behalf of the Ancestors.

Hiraṇyakeśin, during the preparation of food to be offered to the Brahmins, instructs the Sacrificer to touch the food while uttering a mantra.

> Then he touches the food (saying) "The earth is your vessel; heaven is your cover. I offer you into the mouth of *brahman*; I sacrifice you

into the in-breath and the out-breath of learned Brahmins. You are undecaying! May you not decay for the Ancestors there in the other world. The earth is constant; Agni is his witness, so that what is given is not neglected." *HGS* 2.4.11.4[18]

This mantra reiterates the notion that the offerings are being made to the Brahmins on the behalf of the Ancestors. Brahmins have come to replace the fire as the mediator between the householder and his Ancestors. This notion appears explicitly in the Dharmasūtra of Āpastamba; in the mythic introduction to the ancestral offerings, he says, "In this (rite) the Ancestors are the deity, but Brahmins stand in for the offertorial (fire)" (*ĀpDhS* 2.16.3).[19]

These authors express the Brahmins' role as mediator in two ways. Some authors express this role with the term *pitṛvat*, as the Ancestors; the Brahmins act as proxy for the Ancestors, accepting their offerings and conveying to them the benefit thereof. Others merely describe the Brahmin accepting offerings. They stand in for the fire, acting as Agni does to convey the oblations to the gods. A Brahmin with the proper qualities is able to take on such a role; the failure of a Brahmin of poor moral character to take on this role is discussed in greater detail in later literature (see Chapter 7).

The Brahmins' role as stand-in for the Ancestors is a feature of all four types of *śrāddha*-rite in the Gṛhyasūtras and is so throughout the development that is apparent in the Gṛhyasūtras. That development began sometime before the composition of the *Śāṅkhāyana Gṛhyasūtra*, however, it is clear that the construction of the *śrāddha*-rite was not complete by the time of the earliest of the Gṛhyasūtras' composition. Different Gṛhyasūtras capture different moments in the development and codification of the *śrāddha*-rite and its types.

Shifting Paradigms: Reconstructing Ancestor Worship

One outcome of this process of contestation and synthesis is the establishment of the *śrāddha*-rite as the paradigmatic form of ancestor worship. By the time of the Dharmasūtras, the *śrāddha*-rite is no longer contested, it is accepted as the standard form. A review of the different descriptions of the *śrāddha*-rite in the Gṛhyasūtras reveals some of the process whereby these four clear types outlined by Śāṅkhāyana became the norm for the subsequent tradition and *śrāddha*-rite was constructed as the paradigmatic rite of ancestor veneration. The extant Gṛhyasūtras do not agree completely on terminology, categorization, or even, arguably, a basic conception of the *śrāddha*-rite. This diversity could be a function of diversity among theological schools, temporal differences, other influences hidden by the nature of the genre in which the evidence is found, or, as is more likely, a combination of these; however, it does indicate that *śrāddha*-rite is a contested category in the Gṛhyasūtras. Out of the diverse efforts to define the ancestral rites that appear in the domestic ritual manuals, the theologians construct a reimagined ancestral ritual cycle centered not on the solemn model of *piṇḍapitṛyajña*, but on the *śrāddha*-rite that emerges from the discursive efforts evident in the Gṛhyasūtras.

This section will outline five factors in the treatment of the ancestral rites in the domestic ritual manuals that will illustrate the diversity of expression and show the development from a domestic ritual largely reflective of the older solemn ritual model to a new model that comes to be called the *śrāddha*-rite. These factors are: 1. use of the term *śrāddha*, 2. inclusion of multiple types of *śrāddha*-rite, 3. the amount of detail included in the description, 4. the decision to include the *śrāddha*-rite in its own section, and 5. the priority of the *śrāddha*-rite over the Ninth-Day Ancestral Offerings. Since the treatments in the texts are not linear, my treatment of them will not be either, though my discussion is organized around these elements in this order. The first two factors relate to the terminology used by the different authors of the Gṛhyasūtras and offer some insight into the discursive construction of the *śrāddha*-rite.

As the terms *piṇḍapitṛyajña* and *pitṛyajña* distinguished between the two ancestor worship rituals of the earlier tradition, distinct terminology distinguishes between different modes of ancestor worship in the Gṛhyasūtras. The domestic ritual manuals consistently use *piṇḍapitṛyajña* to refer to the seasonal ancestral offerings of the Ninth-Day Ancestral Offerings and *śrāddha* to refer to the monthly offerings of food to the Ancestors. This is not to say that these terms are consistently used, but when they are used, they almost always refer to their respective rituals.

The authors most frequently invoke the *piṇḍapitṛyajña* as the paradigm upon which the performance of the Ninth-Day Ancestral Offerings is based. Śāṅkhāyana, for example, says, "On the next day is the Ninth-Day Ancestral Offerings, performed in accordance with the *piṇḍapitṛyajña*" (*ŚGS* 3.13.7).[20] Likewise, Āśvalāyana indicates the procedure for the Ninth-Day Ancestral Offerings is done "according to the procedure for the *piṇḍapitṛyajña*" (*ĀśGS* 2.5.3).[21] The term most often refers to the Ninth-Day

Table 4.1 Reference to different types of *śrāddha*-rite in the Gṛhyasūtras. Filled dots indicate the text describes that ritual with that term. Empty dots indicate that the text describes that ritual without that term.

	ŚGS	*ĀśGS* 2.5	*ĀśGS* 4.7	*BGS*	*PGS*	*ĀpGS*	*HGS*	*BhGS*	*GGS*	*JGS*
śrāddha	○	○	●	●	○	●	●	●	●	●
pārvaṇa	○	○	●	○	○	○	○	○	○	○
ekoddiṣṭa	●		●	●	○					○
sapiṇḍīkaraṇa	●			●	○			●		
ābhyudayika	●	○	●	●				○		○
śrāddha 1st						●	●	●		●

Ancestral Offerings, but is used, at least once, as the referent ritual for the *śrāddha*-rite. At the end of the description of the *pārvaṇa śrāddha*-rite, Śāṅkhāyana concludes with this *sūtra*, "The rite of offering food into the fire and the rest is described in detail by the *piṇḍapitṛyajña*" (*ŚGS* 4.1.13).[22] Initially, the authors of the domestic ritual manuals employed the *piṇḍapitṛyajña* as the model for ancestor worship, be it in the Ninth-Day Ancestral Offerings or the *śrāddha*-rite, though certainly the former is more common. That is true, however, because the term *śrāddha* does not enter the ritual vocabulary until later in the authors' efforts to define the domestic ancestral rites.[23] Table 4.1 gives some sense of the nature and the complexity of the *śrāddha*-rite in the Gṛhyasūtras and guides the present discussion.[24] My argument aligns these data and show the ways in which the Brahmanical authors worked to reinvent the ancestral rites.[25]

The fact that two authors do not use the term *śrāddha*-rite in their description of that ritual may help illuminate the history of the term itself. For the sake of clarity I give the first lines of each chapter from Śāṅkhāyana's introduction to the four types of *śrāddha*-rite:

> He should offer to the Ancestors monthly. *ŚGS* 4.1.1[26]
> Now the *ekoddiṣṭa*. *ŚGS* 4.2.1[27]
> Now the *sapiṇḍīkaraṇa*. *ŚGS* 4.3.1[28]
> Now the *ābhyudayika*. *ŚGS* 4.4.1[29]

All but the first announce the ritual to be described by name. The first section, however, simply describes the ritual. While this certainly refers to the ritual other texts call the *pārvaṇa śrāddha*, as Nārāyaṇa and Oldenberg both indicate in their commentaries (Rai 1995, 150; Oldenberg 1967, Part I 106 n.1), the author fails to use that word. While Śāṅkhāyana does not use the term *śrāddha* anywhere in the section describing the *śrāddha*-rite, he does use it elsewhere.

The term *śrāddha* occurs in the *Śāṅkhāyana Gṛhyasūtra* only three times and always in the same context, the interruption of Vedic recitation (*ŚGS* 4.7.5; 4.7.55; 6.1.7). Oldenberg argues that the whole chapter in which the last occurs is a later addition (Oldenberg 1967, Part I, 11). Unfortunately, the other two are members of a list, which makes dating extremely difficult. The only other author who fails to use the word *śrāddha* in his description of that ritual is Pāraskara, yet he too uses the term *śrāddha* in the section on the interruption of Vedic recitation (*PGS* 2.11.2). Unlike Śāṅkhāyana, Pāraskara's description of the *śrāddha*-rite is not very extensive. It amounts to eight cryptic *sūtras* emended to the funerary rites.

It is highly unlikely that the authors of the sections of Śāṅkhāyana and Pāraskara that describe the *śrāddha*-rite knew the term *śrāddha* yet failed to use it. The *sūtra* genre values brevity over almost every other quality of a text, including sometimes clarity. It seems unlikely then, that the author would use two words, *pitṛbhyo dadyād*, when one would do, *śrāddha*. This is clearly seen in the other authors' work on the *śrāddha*-rite as well. Gobhila for example introduces the section on *śrāddha*-rite in this way, "This *śrāddha* (is performed) on the night of the new moon" (*GGS* 4.4.2).[30] The details of both the *Śāṅkhāyana Gṛhyasūtra*, which includes a separate section for each of the four types of *śrāddha*-rite, and the *Pāraskara Gṛhyasūtra*, which mentions far less detail, but is clearly aware of at least three kinds of *śrāddha*-rite, suggest that they knew the ritual we now call *śrāddha*-rite. Similarly, Āśvalāyana uses the term in one context, but does not in another (*ĀśGS* 2.5 and 4.7). Their failure to use the term in the description of that rite suggests that the term had not gained currency in either their time or their cultural sphere.

The second element is the categorization of the *śrāddha*-rite into four types. The complexity of the Gṛhyasūtra treatment of *śrāddha*-rite, seen schematically in Table 4.1 appears in the differing conceptions of the *śrāddha*-rite types in each of the Gṛhyasūtras as well. The illusion of consistency and formal organization created by the review of Śāṅkhāyana's sections on the different types of *śrāddha*-rite contradicts the heterogeneous expressions of the *śrāddha*-rite found in the Gṛhyasūtras. Śāṅkhāyana describes four types of *śrāddha*-rite in some detail without using the term *śrāddha*, Āśvalāyana mentions three types at the beginning of his section on the *śrāddha*-rite, but never distinguishes between any of the practical aspects of their procedure in his description (*ĀśGS* 4.7.1). Gobhila mentions the monthly *śrāddha*-rite, but no other type of *śrāddha*-rite. Pāraskara describes the *śrāddha*-rite, but does not use the term *śrāddha* or any of the names for different types of *śrāddha*-rite, though, as I will show, one does find hints of other types.

Despite lacking the clear-cut distinctions that Śāṅkhāyana makes between the different types of *śrāddha*-rite, other authors do differentiate between the elements of ritual that are associated with different types of *śrāddha*-rite in the later tradition. The manner of the distinction, however, is often obscured by the style of this genre. This derives, to one degree or another, from the fact that the author assumes his audience already has considerable understanding of the ritual tradition. The authors of the domestic ritual manuals assumed that his audience would understand his abbreviated references to the different types of *śrāddha*-rite. Explanation requires some examples.

As indicated by Table 4.1, Pāraskara discusses these different *śrāddha*-rites, but fails to label them as such. He does not deal with the *śrāddha*-rite in four different sections, as Śāṅkhāyana does (*ŚGS* 4.1–4) or even in its own separate section, as Āśvalāyana does (*ĀśGS* 4.7). Instead he addresses the different forms in a few rather cryptic *sūtras* in the section that addresses the rituals surrounding the death of a relative. Only ten *sūtras* in all deal with offerings to the dead.

> 27 Having given a rice-ball to the deceased, taking his name at the washing, the giving, and the second washing, 28 that night they should put milk and water in an earthen vessel in an open space, (saying) "Bathe here, O departed one." *PGS* 3.10.27–28[31]
>
> 48 On the eleventh (day), having fed an uneven number of Brahmins (a meal) with meat, 49 some kill a cow in the name of the departed. 50 When he makes the rice-balls the departed becomes first of the Ancestors, if he has sons. 51 A fourth (rice-ball) is prohibited. 52 Some (give the rice-ball) separately for a year. 53 There is a rule, however, from *śruti*: "There is no fourth rice-ball." 54 Every day he gives him food, to a Brahmin a pot of water also. 55 Some offer rice balls too. *PGS* 3.10.48–55[32]

The first two *sūtras*, situated as they are in the middle of a discussion of death pollution practices, clearly refer to some practice to propitiate the deceased. *Sūtra* 48 refers to the *ekoddiṣṭa śrāddha*-rite performed eleven days after the death of the father and the commentary confirms this (Gauda 2001, 175). The term *piṇḍakaraṇa* in *sūtra* 50 is a bit ambiguous, but the outcome of this rite, namely the deceased father becoming first of the Ancestors, indicates that Pāraskara refers to the *sapiṇḍīkaraṇa*. This ritual promotes the father to the station of Ancestor from that of ghost (*preta*, literally departed). The next *sūtra* indicates that there cannot be four *piṇḍas*, that is, the father must be integrated into the Ancestors, and there can only be three Ancestors when this is accomplished. This further confirms that the author refers to the *sapiṇḍīkaraṇa*.

Pāraskara then gives the opinion of other teachers, "Some (give rice-balls) separately for a year," then quickly reminds his audience that there can be no fourth rice-ball according to tradition. Authors in this genre, commonly record the opinion of other theologians, and this further supporting the notion that the details of the ritual are still contested.

The first four elements are visible in Āśvalāyana's treatment of the ancestral rites. He outlines the *śrāddha*-rite in two places, and both refer to different types of *śrāddha*-rite in similarly cryptic passages. The first is extremely brief:

> 10 And so he should offer to the Ancestors every month, with uneven (numbers). 11 He should feed at least nine (Brahmins), 12 or an uneven (number). 13 An even (number) at a *vṛddhi* (*śrāddha*-rite) or an auspicious occasion, 14 (but) an uneven (number) at other (*śrāddha*-rites). 15 This ritual is performed in a clockwise direction and sesame is replaced with barley. (*ĀśGS* 2.5.10–15)[33]

Like Pāraskara, Āśvalāyana packs a considerable about of information into these five *sūtras*. The monthly performance and the uneven number of Brahmins indicate that the first two *sūtras* refer to the monthly *pārvaṇa śrāddha*-rite. He then indicates the *vṛddhi śrāddha*-rite, elsewhere called the *ābhyudayika*. This *śrāddha*-rite happens on auspicious occasions and requires an even number of Brahmin invitees (Compare *ŚGS* 4.4). Āśvalāyana clearly knows that his audience understands the details of this *śrāddha*-rite and merely refers to the number of Brahmins as short hand to indicate the rite.

Āśvalāyana's second treatment of the *śrāddha*-rite runs to thirty-one *sūtras* and shows the third and fourth elements, an increase in the details of the ritual and the inclusion of the rite in its own section. This passage includes far more detail, including details on the quality of Brahmins to be invited (4.7.2), mantras, and specifics on ritual gestures. A comparison of the two sections suggests that the second (4.7) is a later, more mature description than the first (2.5.10–15). The first passage occurs at the end of the discussion of the Ninth-Day Ancestral Offerings, makes brief mention of the details of the ritual, and refers to only two of the four *śrāddha*-rites, and fails to use the term *śrāddha*. The second is a section dedicated to this ritual cycle, describes the rituals in great detail, refers to three of the types of *śrāddha*-rite, and uses the term *śrāddha* as well as the name for the three individual types mentioned.[34]

The similarity of the this passage to the treatment in the *Pāraskara Gṛhyasūtra*, where the term *śrāddha* finds no mention, suggests that Āśvalāyana records an older and a newer description of the monthly ancestral rites, one from a period when the term *śrāddha* had not gained currency, another after the name *śrāddha* and the labels for the different types had gained currency.[35] In addition, that the *śrāddha*-rite, in Āśvalāyana's mind, deserves a separate treatment, suggests the authors are affording it more autonomy as a ritual in its own right, rather than as an aspect of a larger ritual series, as is the case in the Śrautasūtras and the other Gṛhyasūtras.

These examples demonstrate the developing nature of *śrāddha*-rite during the composition of the Gṛhyasūtras. Āśvalāyana captures two moments in the Brahmanical authors efforts' to legitimate and normalize the *śrāddha*-rite, that is, to actively codify the ancestral rites. His second description of the rite includes the term *śrāddha*, includes most of the four types, lays out far more detail, and affords the rite its own space in the organizational structure of the text. Evidence of a development of the *śrāddha* as the paradigmatic form of ancestor worship, my fifth element, is found in the *Āpastamba* and *Hiraṇyakeśin Gṛhyasūtras*.

Āpastamba—and Hiraṇyakeśin, who draws heavily on Āpastamba—preserves a different manner of recording the *śrāddha*-rite.[36] Instead of dealing with the *śrāddha*-rite after the Eighth-Day Offerings, as most Gṛhyasūtras do, he deals with *śrāddha*-rite in its own section—as Āśvalāyana does in the second treatment of that ritual, which I argue is younger. Āpastamba, however, not only treats *śrāddha*-rite first (*ĀpGS* 8.21–22), he incorporates the Ninth-Day Ancestral Offerings as a subsidiary rite, a special instance of the *śrāddha*-rite (*ĀpGS* 8.22.8–12).[37]

> 9 Some prescribe the offering of rice-balls on the day after the Eighth-Day Offerings. 10 Now an alternative to that: He offers

> coagulated milk with his hands joined in reverence, and, in the same manner, the cake. 11 Then he sets aside as much meat as is needed, and, on the next day (he performs) the Ninth-Day Ancestral Offerings. 12 The procedure for this is explained in detail by the (section on) the monthly *śrāddha*-rite. *ĀpGS* 8.22.9–12[38]

In Āpastamba's opinion the *śrāddha*-rite held the place of prominence among ancestral rites. Either he composed his Gṛhyasūtra during a period in the development of the *śrāddha*-rite when that rite had become the paradigm of ancestor worship, or he is making this assertion discursively by reorganizing the text with the older Ninth-Day Ancestral Offerings as the sub-rite. No longer is the *piṇḍapitṛyajña* the model for both the Ninth-Day Ancestral Offerings and the *śrāddha*-rite; the *śrāddha*-rite now is the archetype of ancestor worship.

It is difficult to draw conclusions about the chronological relationships of these texts at all, let alone based merely on the expressions of ancestor worship generally and the four-fold *śrāddha*-rite specifically, but these passages and the variety in which the ancestral rites are discussed are suggestive. If a single author, or small group of editors, is responsible for the Śrauta-, Gṛhya-, and Dharma-Sūtra of Āpastamba and Olivelle is correct in dating him to the beginning of the third century B.C.E. (Olivelle 2000, 10), then Āpastamba was probably late among the Gṛhyasūtras. Whether Āpastamba is reacting to a trend or shaping it by means of his text is unclear, but this marks a significant reversal of the treatment of the Ninth-Day Ancestral Offerings and the newer *śrāddha*-rite and harkens a new centrality of the domestic *śrāddha*-rite over and against the solemn rituals of ancestor worship.

The Brahmins' construction of the *śrāddha*-rite is uneven and the details of this process are unclear. The clear cut distinctions in Śāṅkhāyana indicate an effort to develop a more mature, distinct classification of the elements seen in the less developed treatments of the ancestral rites that come to be labeled *śrāddha*, yet the term *śrāddha* is absent. Āśvalāyana uses this term, but does not mention all the types. Āpastamba gives priority to the *śrāddha*-rite, but mentions only one type. Even if dating these texts with greater precision were possible, the evidence suggests that the construction of the *śrāddha*-rite as a relatively consistent ritual cycle, with four forms, happened in uneven ways among the different Brahmanical communities. Table 4.1 clearly illustrates, and I have argued, that the treatment of the *śrāddha*-rite in most of the early Gṛhyasūtras varies tremendously.

This is indicative of a rite under contestation; the authors of the domestic ritual manuals discursive construct ancestor worship; they define the *śrāddha*-rite, establish the four types, gradually normalize the technical terminology, establish the *śrāddha*-rite as the paradigmatic rite, and create the new role for the Brahmin, the ritual expert as guest.

However, it seems clear that the Brahmins drew upon Vedic models of sacrifice and actively appropriated domestic modes of ancestor veneration to construct an ancestral ritual cycle based on the monthly offering of food to the Ancestors: the *śrāddha*-rite. The tendency toward monthly propitiation of the Ancestors is likely to be quite old, but the domestic ritual manuals' emphasis on the monthly performance of ritual also probably derived from their own investment in the ritual tradition. They made their livelihood attending rituals, including the ancestral rites and the domestic ritual manuals establish a cycle of ritual dependency with the Brahmin guest as the key to success. The regular performance of such rituals became central to the maintenance of a livelihood as a ritual expert.

In that reconstruction of the new ritual cycle they reimagined ancestor worship and redefined their own role as religious experts. Rather than performing the rituals as the Vedic priests did, they attended, received gifts, and authorized the ritual activities of the householder. Synthesizing and innovating upon two modes of ancestor worship—the solemn and the domestic—the Brahmins responsible for the Gṛhyasūtras created a new model of ancestor worship, one which is still operative in India today.

5

Ancestral Rites in the Buddhist Literature

LIKE THEIR BRAHMANICAL counterparts, the authors of the Buddhist texts drew upon common conceptions of religiosity—worship of the divine, hospitality, and ancestor worship—in their descriptions of the proper religious life. Of central concern for the present chapter is the Buddhist reflection on the relation of religious practitioners with their ancestors. Several passages in the Pāli Canon indicate that the authors accepted the practice of ancestor worship as part of the householder life, but gradually the paradigm of ancestor worship is subsumed under the broader practice of religious gifting. I will demonstrate that the Buddhist authors synthesized the widespread practices aimed at and ideas about the proper appeasement of the dead, strongly influenced by the Brahmanical reflection on the ritual for some time, and the moral/soteriological worldview and practices of Early Buddhism into a single discourse, stronger and more marketable to the householder of ancient South Asia.

This chapter will outline the early development of the relationship between the Buddhist householder and his departed relatives, from passages in the Sutta portion of the Pāli Canon that refer to a ritual practice indistinguishable from the Hindu *śrāddha*-rite to the cultural memory of *śrāddha*-rite that informs the religious gifts made through the Buddha in the *Petavatthu*, a collection of ghost stories.

This literature retains some material that may be contemporaneous with the construction of the domestic ritual manuals, but this cannot be presumed for the collection in general. However, the literature does reflect an engagement with the domestic ritual practice described in the Gṛhyasūtras, an interaction that highlights the competition for resources seen within the Brahmanical literature. These texts represent a reaction to the discursive efforts of the authors of the domestic ritual manuals. Just as the Brahmins who composed the domestic ritual manuals constructed their own conception of domestic ritual practice by reflecting on both solemn and domestic and textualized and untextualized traditions, the Buddhist authors construct a mode of religious behavior that reflects on the domestic religious practices constructed in the Gṛhyasūtras and the broader religious behaviors practiced by those in the *śramaṇa* movements. I will show that the cultural memory of the *śrāddha*-rite as it is described in the domestic ritual manuals has a powerful influence on the Buddhist reflections on ancestor worship. This cultural memory influences the form and function of the practice of religious giving throughout Buddhism (Holt 1981, Langer 2007, Egge 2002).

The Buddhist Śrāddha-Rite

Most of the references to ancestor worship in the Pāli Canon are not explicit discussions of the *śrāddha*-rite; they are aspects of brief descriptions of the duties and obligations of the average householder seeking advice from the Buddha or one of his disciples. In several places in the Sutta literature, the authors refer to the Five Offerings (*pañcabali*), a set of five ritual obligations roughly analogous to the Five Great Sacrifices (*pañcamahāyajña*) described in the Brahmanical texts. In the *Aṅguttara Nikāya*—in a discussion of the reasons for acquiring wealth—the Five offerings are characterized as basic to the *dhamma* (Pāli for *dharma*) of a householder. "And again, a householder, a gentlemen disciple, with wealth attained by work and zeal, gathered by the strength of his arms, earned by the sweat of his brow, acquired in accordance with *dhamma* becomes the performer of the Five Offerings: the offering to relatives, the offering to guests, the offering to the previously deceased, offering to the king, and the offering to the gods. This is the fourth reason for wealth" (*A* iii.45).[1] These passages invariably include the obligation to make offerings to his ancestors (*pubbapetabali*, elsewhere *pubbapetakaraṇīya*). Ancestor worship, in a general sense, occupies a central place in the Buddhist conception of the proper ritual life of the householder. More useful than dwelling on this general conception of ancestor worship as an ordinary part of the householder's regular ritual practice is a review of several direct references to *śrāddha*-rite in the *sutta* literature.[2]

In a dialogue with the Brahmin Ambaṭṭha in the *Aṅguttara Nikāya* the Buddha makes a passing reference to the *śrāddha*-rite (in the Pāli, *saddha*). In this well-known dialogue, the Buddha tries to dissuade the Brahmin from his entrenched view about caste. In his leading inquiry into the workings of those born from inter-caste relationships, the Buddha asks whether the offspring would be allowed to engage in certain religious activities, "But would the Brahmans allow him to eat food in a *śrāddha*-rite, or a milk-boiled rice offering, or a sacrifice, or a meal offered to a guest" (*D* i.97)?[3] The challenge to Ambaṭṭha revolves around the ability of the person produced by mixed parentage to act as a Brahmin should, that is, would he be qualified to accept food at a ritual. All four rites mentioned—ancestral offerings, milk-boiled rice offerings (*thālipāka*), divine offerings, and food given in hospitality—are central to the Indian notion of ritual obligation and have deep Vedic roots. In addition to indicating that the Buddhist authors accept this broad notion of religious responsibility, this passage indicates that the author identifies the *śrāddha*-rite with ancestor worship more generally. More significant for understanding these Buddhist reflections on the ritual life in context is the fact that the word used, *saddha*, is a Brahmanical technical term. The Buddhist authors of the Pāli Canon commonly draw upon the Brahmanical technical terminology (Egge 2002, 19–21) and their description of ancestor worship follows suit.

A second passage indicates a stronger advocacy of that ritual responsibility. When asked by Udāyin if he praises sacrifice, the Buddha replies with this verse.

> Restrained practitioners of *brahmacariya* approach a sacrifice
> That is ritually prepared, without killing, and done at the proper time.
> Those for whom the veil has been removed in this life, who have overcome death,
> Awakened ones, knowers of merit praise the sacrifice.
> Properly making an offering in sacrifice or in a *śrāddha* rite,
> A person of devoted mind sacrifices in a good field, among *brahmacārins*.
> What is done among those worthy of offerings is well-offered, well-sacrificed, and well-obtained;
> The sacrifice is abundant and the gods are pleased.
> Having sacrificed in this way, the wise, faithful, mentally liberated,
> Intelligent one arises in an undisturbed, happy world. *A* ii.43–44 (Egge 2002, 24)[4]

The Buddha reiterates his advocacy of ritual, provided the rituals are done without killing and in the proper frame of mind. Most significant for my purposes here is that the Buddha recognizes the performance of *śrāddha*-rite as a legitimate form of ritual activity for Buddhists.

Elsewhere in the *Aṅguttara Nikāya,* the Buddha engages a different Brahmin in a more telling conversation about *śrāddha*-rite, specifically addressing concerns the Brahmin has about the efficacy of the rite. Jāṇussoṇi the Brahmin comes to visit the Buddha and asks him about the *śrāddha*-rite.

> We, O Gotama, the Brahmins, give gifts; (we) perform the *śrāddha*-rites: saying "May this gift benefit the kinsmen and blood relations who have departed. May the kinsmen and blood relations who have departed eat this gift." Does this gift, O Gotama, benefit the kinsmen and blood relations who have departed? Do the kinsmen and blood relations who have departed eat this gift? *A* v.269[5]

Jāṇussoṇi asks the Buddha to reflect on a common householder practice, a practice often considered an exclusively Brahmanical practice by scholars. The Buddha informs him that the receipt of the offering depends upon the offering being made to the proper persons in the proper place. After reviewing the after-life destination of several classes of dead, all but the last of which are not the proper place for the offerings made in the *śrāddha*-rite, the Buddha identifies the proper place as the realm of the departed (*petti visaya*). The Buddha says:

> After death he is born in the realm of the departed. He is nourished by whatever nourishes the creatures of that realm. What friends, co-workers, kinsmen, and blood relations present to him, by that, there, he is nourished. By that he abides there. This, O Brahmin, is the proper place, where what is given to one who stands benefits him. *A* v.270[6]

The realm of the departed, then, is the only place where the offering made in *śrāddha*-rite actually feeds the deceased. Only the deceased (*peta*) receive the food offered in the *śrāddha*-rite, a fact verified by the Buddha himself.

> [Jāṇussoṇi:] If, O Gotama, that kinsman or blood relation who died does not arrive at the proper place, who eats that gift?

> [The Buddha:] Other kinsmen and blood relations who arrive at the proper place, they eat that gift.
>
> [Jāṇussoṇi:] If, O Gotama, that kinsman or blood relation who died does not arrive at that place and the other kinsmen and blood relations who died do not arrive at the proper place, who eats that gift?
>
> [The Buddha:] This is a nonplace, O Brahmin, it is impossible that that place would be long without deceased kinsmen and blood relations. Further, the giver is not without fruit. *A* v.270[7]

The Buddha understood Jāṇussoṇi's concern about the lack of a recipient for his offering to indicate a fear that would receive no benefit from making the gift; this notion is made more explicitly in *A* v.271. His concern comes from the conception of merit derived from giving. Sufficient for the current discussion is the fact that the Buddha validates the *śrāddha*-rite offerings, indicating that they are only effective for the deceased.

Jāṇussoṇi then asks about the possibility of the realm of the departed becoming empty. The Buddha assures him this will never happen, but proceeds to speculate on how that might happen. In short, the *sutta* becomes a discourse on giving, with the Buddha explaining the balancing of bad deeds with good, specifically giving. Significantly, none of those who offset their immoral lives with religious giving end up in the realm of the departed. The moral seems clear: gifting insures you will not go to the realm of the departed after death. In fact, the world set aside for *petas* would be empty if everyone engaged in the proper gifting to ascetics and Brahmins! The Buddhist authors are synthesizing the common practice of ancestor worship into their discourse on proper religious practice, specifically religious giving.

As is typical of Pāli Canon style, Jāṇussoṇi comments on how wonderful this is; in his praise he interprets the Buddha's words affirming that it is proper to perform the *śrāddha*-rite, "Wonderful, O Gotama, amazing, O Gotama, as far as this, O Gotama, it is proper to give gifts, it is proper to perform the *śrāddha*-rite, where indeed the giver is not without fruit" (*A* v.273).[8] The Buddha confirms this and eases Jāṇussoṇi's fear that the gift will not be beneficial for him, "This is so, Brahmin, this is so, Brahmin, the giver is not without fruit" (*A* v.273).[9] The *sutta* concludes with the formulaic conversion speech.

The significance of this passage for understanding the Buddhist reflection on the *śrāddha*-rite lies not in the Buddha's affirmation of the practice of the *śrāddha*-rite, nor in the subtle recentering of religious practice on gifting, though both are important; rather it lies in the manner in which he synthesizes the tradition of ancestor worship into the Buddhist *dhamma.* The Buddha accepts the *śrāddha*-rite as it operates in the wider tradition as appropriate for a householder; only then does he work to make its practice more relevant to his ideology. First he interprets Jāṇussoṇi's question broadly, shifting the question of whether the *śrāddha*-rite really reaches one's ancestors to a discussion about the place (*ṭhāna*) of those who have departed and been reborn. That shift changes the point of the conversation from ritual logistics to morality and the benefit of gifting. In this, the author of this *sutta* builds on the older Vedic model of sacrifice—through which one secures the material comforts in the next world—and effects a shift from the rather specific topic of giving to one's ancestors to gifting more generally. Emphasis on such a message was the impetus for the compilation of the *peta* stories, the *Petavatthu.*

The Petavatthu: Ancestral Offerings to Ghosts

Like the *Jāṇussoṇisutta*, the *Petavatthu*, literally "*Ghost Stories*", tells us a lot about the conception of the relationship between the living and the deceased, which is crucial for understanding the Buddhist appropriation and adaptation of *śrāddha*-rite. In addition, the details that are missing from the *Jāṇussoṇisutta* illustrate associations between the Buddhist and Brahmanical discourse on the common cultural practice of ancestor worship.

This concern over the welfare of the deceased—*peta* in Pāli, *preta* in Sanskrit, or Ancestor—another hallmark of the *śrāddha*-rite, is expressed loudly and clearly in the *Petavatthu*. Masefield indicates that the aim of both the *Petavatthu* and the *Vimānavatthu*, the *Mansion Stories*, is "stressing the urgent need to make merit and the means whereby such merit is to be generated" (Dhammapāla 1989, xix). The primary mode of making merit seen in these texts, in reality almost its sole concern, is almsgiving. While the context of most of the stories is generosity in general and giving to the Saṅgha in particular, the nature of the stories clearly illustrates the influence of the *śrāddha*-rite.[10]

Most of the *peta* stories describe the good and bad deeds that a person did in their life, then describes the rewards and punishments they receive in the next life. Frequently the figure in the tale suffers some fate due to bad *karma* and is rewarded for some good deed, or suffers due to some *karma*, but that suffering is mitigated by some act of charity. Masefield goes to great lengths to detail the possible combinations of the effects of bad *karma* and earning merit (Dhammapāla 1989, xxxv–xxviii). But, as we saw in the *Jāṇussoṇisutta* (*A* v.271), the authors of the *Aṅguttara Nikāya* were already aware of the multiple factors which go into determining one's fate. Amidst these moral tales are gems that highlight the influence that a tradition of ghost propitiation and Brahmanical discourse on *śrāddha*-rite had on the Buddhist discourse.

The *Petavatthu* exists today imbedded in its commentary, the *Elucidation of the Intrinsic Meaning: So named the Commentary on the Peta-Stories (Paramatthadīpanī nāma Petavatthu-aṭṭhakathā)* of Dhammapāla. The *Petavatthu* is a collection of verses attributed to the Buddha, but each story exists, imbedded within the commentary, in three parts: 1. an introduction story that explains the context of the verses, 2. the verses, and 3. a commentary on the verses. Dhammapāla attributes the first two to the Buddha himself and his commentary is largely concerned with the meaning of the words in the verses. Unfortunately, it does not expound upon the underlying doctrine as much as a modern student of religion would hope (Dhammapāla 1980, viii). Due to the divided nature of the text I first address the verses then the larger, collective text.

As in the *Aṅguttara Nikāya*, the first story portrays the Buddha advocating ancestor propitiation. In a tale entitled "Ghost Story of the Biscuit Doll" (*piṭṭhadhītalikapetavatthu*) (*Pv* 1.4), the Buddha enjoins one of his followers to give generously to those who have previously died.

> 10 To whomever the unselfish person should give a gift, be it those previously departed or the household deities,
>
> 11 or the four great kings, the renowned guardians of the world, Kuvera, Dhataraṭṭha, Virūpakkha, and Virūḷhaka, they indeed are honored; and the donors are not without fruit.
>
> 12 Certainly no weeping, sorrow, or any other lamentation is to the benefit of the departed (though their) relatives continue in this way.[11]
>
> 13 But this donation, firmly established in the Saṅgha, will immediately serve to benefit them for a long time. *Pv* 1.4.10–13[12]

The poet praises the act of giving gifts to the deceased (*peta*), and to the guardians of the world. He indicates that those who give are praiseworthy and should expect some benefit for their good deeds. The last idea reiterates the Buddha's lesson from the *Aṅguttara Nikāya*. Further the poet is more explicit—and specific—about the recipient of the gift, the Saṅgha.

In *A* v.271, the Buddha indicates that the gifts one gives that have an effect in the next life are to be given to mendicants or Brahmins (*samaṇassa vā brāhmaṇassa vā*). By the time of the composition of the *Petavatthu* the authors are most insistent about the Saṅgha being the most fruitful ground for giving. This demonstrates the continual concern with marketing the Saṅgha, reminding those who heard these tales that in the competitive religious marketplace, the Buddhist Saṅgha is the best recipient for one's gifts.

Further, the connection to the *śrāddha*-rite is clear. The verb *dā* and the term *dāna* frequently indicates the gift given to an ancestor in the *śrāddha*-rite in the Brahmanical literature (e.g., *ŚGS* 4.1.1, quoted earlier) and in the opening to the *Jāṇussoṇi Sutta* the author equates giving gifts,[13] with performing the *śrāddha*-rite[14] (*A* v.269). The author again asserts that giving and performing *śrāddha*-rite are synonymous at the end of the *sutta* when Jāṇussoṇi says to the Buddha that doing so is proper (*A* v.273). The phrase "and the donors are not without fruit"[15] would certainly remind an educated reader of the *Jāṇussoṇi Sutta*, which deals explicitly with the *śrāddha*-rite. The third verse addresses the concerns of a mourning family directly, indicating a context of death and its associated rituals, that is, the *śrāddha*-rite. The term *dakkhiṇā* (from Sanskrit *dakṣiṇā*) has a double resonance in this context. It would call to mind the efficacy of the ritual, which is ineffective without the *dakṣiṇā*, the sacrificial fee (Olivelle 1996, xliv). In addition, it would bring to mind the soteriological import of the *dakṣiṇā*. According to the *Śatapatha Brāhmaṇa*, when the sacrifice goes to the world of the gods, the *dakṣiṇā* follows, with the Sacrificer holding on (*ŚBM* 1.9.3.1 and 4.3.4.6).

Even if one were to argue that the verses predate the introductory prose,[16] the verses clearly refer to the *śrāddha*-rite, but the introductory material, which enhances this connection, further illuminates the contemporary conception of the *śrāddha*-rite.

We are told that the Buddha is staying in the Jeta Grove in Sāvatthī and that the tale concerns an instance of almsgiving (*dāna*) done by the householder Anāthapiṇḍika.[17] The householder's young granddaughter was given a biscuit doll (*piṭṭhadhītalika*) by her nurse and she comes to look upon the doll as her own daughter; but one day, playing carelessly, she drops it and it breaks. She cries out, "My daughter is dead!"[18] and none of the servants are able to console her.

At that moment the Buddha happened to be in the home of householder, seated next to him. The nurse brought the girl into the presence of the householder, who promptly asked why the girl was crying. The nurse relayed the events and the householder took the girl into his lap and told her, "I will give alms on behalf of your daughter."[19] He then turned to the Buddha and informed him he would be giving alms for his great-granddaughter, the biscuit doll, and invited him to attend. The Buddha consented with silence. When, the following day, they had finished their meal, the Buddha "spoke these verses expressing his appreciation."[20] Masefield suggests, "It seems that following an almsgiving the recipient(s) would generally, before leaving, evoke such an emotion in the donor from the practice of almsgiving or simply expressing the wish that the results desired by the donor be attained." He adds that the second possibility is supported by a later tradition which explicitly states so (1989, liv n45). Two similarities with the brahmanical *śrāddha*-rite are apparent here. Structurally, the recipient expressing the wish that the results may be attained follows the Brahmin's role in stating the success of the ritual seen in the Gṛhyasūtras earlier. In addition, the recitation of sacred verses at the end of the ritual is also customary at the end of a *śrāddha*-rite (e.g., *BDhS* 2.14.2–5.)

In his commentary on verse 10, Dhammapāla glosses the term *pubbapeta* with *pitaro*, Ancestors. Dhammapāla, then, sees the *petas* not as a general class of deceased kinsmen and blood relations, but as Ancestors. It appears that Anāthapiṇḍika performed a *śrāddha*-rite, with the Buddha as his guest and this is not an isolated example.

Another tale, "Ghosts Outside the Walls" (*tirokuḍḍapetavatthu*) (*Pv* 1.5), gives us much more detail and makes the Buddhist reflection on the *śrāddha*-rite clearer.

> 14 They stand outside the walls and at the junctions and crossroads; they stand at the door posts, returned to their own house.
>
> 15 (Even) when plentiful food and drink, foods both hard and soft, are served, no one remembers those being because of their actions.
>
> 16 In this way, those among their relatives that possess pity give pure, excellent food, at the proper time,
>
> 17 "Let this be for out relatives! Let our relatives be happy!" They assembled there, and those assembled ghost-relatives respectfully rejoiced over the plentiful food and drink (saying),
>
> 18 "Long live our relatives, by whom we have acquired (this). We have been revered, and the donors are not without fruit."

19 Because there is no farming there, and cattle herding is not to be found here, nor is there here such a thing as trade or buying and selling with gold; the ghosts who have passed on to that place, are nourished by what is given here.

20 Just as water fallen on elevated land flows to the low ground, so does what is given here benefit the ghosts.

21 Just as a full rain cloud fills the ocean, so does what is given here benefit the ghosts.

22 Recalling things they did, "He gave to me. He did for me. He was a friend and a relative, a companion to me," let him give donations to the ghosts.

23 Certainly no weeping, sorrow, or any other lamentation is to the benefit of the departed (though their) relatives continue in this way.

24 But this donation, firmly established in the Saṅgha, will immediately serve to benefit them for a long time.

25 Now, this duty to one's relatives has been declared and the ghosts have been revered excellently; and strength has been dedicated to the monks and the merit you produced was no little bit. *Pv* 1.5.14–25[21]

This passage offers us some insight into the Buddhist conception of ghosts and reminds us that often the most relevant ghosts were one's Ancestors (see also Holt 1981, 26n47). In the first five verses a narrative unfolds revealing the identity of the ghosts as relatives. They are haunting the spots usually associated with ghosts, but significantly they also haunt their own homes. In addition, the mantra in the fourth verse is reminiscent of key elements of the *śrāddha*-rite. The call "Let this be for our relatives! May our relatives be happy!"[22] reminds one of the mantra in the Gṛhyasūtras, "This rice-ball is for you! And for those who follow you and for those whom you follow, For you *svadhā*!" (*GGS* 4.3.8).[23] The mantra in the fifth verse correlates to the brahmanical view that one of the benefits of performing the *śrāddha*-rite is long-life (e.g., *MkP* 32.38). Verses 23 and 24 are identical to the end of the "Ghost Story of the Biscuit Doll" and evoke the same connections to the *śrāddha*-rite discussed in the previous section. The final verse invokes giving to the deceased as the duty to one's relatives (*ñātidhamma*). Performing the *śrāddha*-rite belongs to a class of duties incumbent upon every householder, that is, divine worship, hospitality, and so forth; the Buddhist author simply employs this common conception of the householder life to argue for a Buddhist worldview, as seen in the discussion of the Five Offerings.

The introductory material for this tale contextualizes these highly suggestive verses, filling in the broader outlines of the story with considerable detail. Ninety-two eons ago, in a city named Kāsipurī, there was a king named Jayasena. His queen bore a son named Phussa who achieved enlightenment in that lifetime. His father, the king, became quite possessive, thinking, "My son it is who performed the Great Renunciation and has become a Buddha. Mine alone is the Buddha, mine the Dhamma, mine the Saṅgha" (*PvA* 19, Dhammapāla 1980, 23)[24] and he alone attended upon the Buddha and the Saṅgha, denying all others access. Phussa's three brothers sought to attend upon him, and by earning a boon from their father, were granted three months to wait upon him. They chose to do so during the rain retreat and had a dwelling (*vihāra*, possibly a monastery) built and arrangements made. The princes' treasurer was a married householder of faith and devotion; he and his agent at the rain retreat organized the almsgiving with due care. Some officials at the retreat, however, were corrupt and obstructed the alms, stole some of the offerings for themselves, and set fire to the refectory. After the rain retreat was complete, the Buddha returned to the king's presence. Later the Buddha died, achieving final liberation (*parinibbāna*).

In due time the princes, their treasurer, his agent and the corrupt officials in their employ died. The latter were all born together in heaven. The corrupt people were born into hell. Ninety-two eons passed as they enjoyed and suffered their fates respectively and during the time of Kassapa, the corrupt people were born among the *petas*. They witnessed others receiving alms from their relatives with the mantra—seen in verse 16—and asked Kassapa how they could attain such satisfaction. Kassapa informed them that they would not receive alms until a time in the future, during the life of the next enlightened one, Gotama. He further informed them that the king Bimbisāra, who was their relative ninety-two eons ago, would give alms to the Buddha and dedicate it to them, whereby they would achieve satisfaction.

After one Buddha interval, during the time of Gotama Buddha, the three sons of the king, their agent, and their treasurer were reborn. The three princes renounced and became the three matted-hair ascetics of Gayāsīsa.[25] Their agent became king Bimbisāra; their treasurer became a wealthy merchant, Visākha; the remainder of their company became the king's entourage.

One day king Bimbisāra invited the Buddha to a meal; the Buddha accepted and came with Sakka (Indra), who was disguised as a Brahmin youth. The ghosts witnessed the meal and anticipated the king dedicating the alms to them, but the king was preoccupied with the arrangements for the Buddha and did not dedicate the meal to them. Distressed, the ghosts lost hope and that night moving about the king's residence wailing in distress. The king was afraid and went to the Buddha, relaying his fear and asking about a course of action. The Buddha allayed his fear and explained the situation. When the king asked the Buddha if such gifts would be received if given, the Buddha said they would. The king immediately issued a second invitation for that same day, promising to dedicate that meal to the ghosts.

At the meal the king offered water to the Buddha, dedicating it to the ghosts, and there arose for them lotus ponds covered with lotuses and blue lilies and their distress and thirst was alleviated. The king gave rice gruel and hard and soft foods; the ghosts received heavenly versions of the same and were refreshed (*piṇitindriyā*). Finally, the king gave clothing and lodging; heavenly clothing and palaces appeared for the ghosts. The Buddha finished his meal and offered the verses in appreciation for the meal.

Most significant in this story, for its relationship to the *śrāddha*-rite, is the emphasis placed on the relationship of the ghosts who are forced to wait for satisfaction to the king who will eventually dedicate an offering to them. Kassapa informs them that they must await a relative of theirs who will be born in the time of the next Buddha, Gotama. They are punished in hell for eons, then reborn as ghosts. While the basis of this story differs from the brahmanical conception of the ghost (*preta*) as a temporary stage between death and integration into the world of the Ancestors (*pitṛloka*), the reliance on relatives suggests this conception of alms for the dead derives from the older model of the *śrāddha*-rite. When the offending people are reborn as ghosts, in the time of Kassapa, they hear offerings made to relatives (*ñāti*), "Let this be for our relatives," as in the verses. Kassapa informs them that they will, eventually, receive offerings from one who was a relative in the past. The connection between the giver (*dāyaka*) and the recipient is a relationship between relatives. This further supports the view that this form of almsgiving has its roots in the *śrāddha*-rite.

The Buddhists have broadened the application, making giving in general a moral duty, but they have failed to strip the paradigm of its original import and flavor, that of ancestor worship. That the *Petavatthu* aims to valorize giving more generally and that most examples are not as clearly connected to the *śrāddha*-rite model indicates the development of the religious tradition away from the original model, but the survival of these *śrāddha*-rite motifs indicates the influence of ancestor worship.

One linguistic survival also supports this thesis. The king offered food to the Buddha, dedicating it to the ghosts, and they received heavenly food and "when they ate these their faculties were refreshed."[26] The word *pīṇitindriyā*, with senses refreshed, derives from the Sanskrit root *prī*, to please, gladden, satisfy and its association with the ancestral rites is quite old. The term is used to express the fulfillment of those who receive offerings, but it shows up consistently in the ancestral rites from the time of the Brāhmaṇas (*TB* 1.3.10.4–5; *KB* 5.8.32). In the Ābhyudayika *śrāddha*-rite, as seen in the *Śāṅkhāyana Gṛhyasūtra*, the mantra "May the Nāndīmukha Ancestors be delighted (*prīyantāṃ*)" (*ŚGS* 4.4.12)[27] is substituted for the mantra used in the *pārvaṇa śrāddha*-rite. *Āśvalāyana Gṛhyasūtra* 4.7.11 implores the funeral oblation, accompanied by the call *svadhā*, to satisfy the Ancestors and these worlds, "Offered in the traditional way with the call *svadhā*, make the Ancestors and these worlds pleasing to us. *svadhā*! Reverence!"[28] This verb, used in the narrative description of the ghosts enjoying their offerings, echoes the mantras that enjoined the *śrāddha*-rite offerings to satisfy the Ancestors.

In addition, the nature of the offerings provides an insight into the degree to which these stories reflect a memory of the *śrāddha*-rite. In this story the ghosts receive first water, then food, clothes, and a dwelling. The most basic offering made to the Ancestors is water; the first offering made in the *Gobhila Gṛhyasūtra* is of water (*GGS* 4.3.6); and in Manu a simple water offering can substitute for the usual ancestral ritual. "Even if a Brahmin (merely) bathes and satisfies the Ancestors with water, he obtains the whole fruit of the *pitṛyajña* ritual" (*MDhŚ* 3.283).[29] The rice-ball is literally made of food and serves as food for the Ancestors; the *Śatapatha Brāhmaṇa* indicates the monthly offering will be the Ancestors' food (*ŚBM* 2.4.2.2).

In the earliest ancestor worship clothing too is offered, at least symbolically, to the Ancestors. *Baudhāyana Śrautasūtra* enjoins an offering of cloth (*BŚS* 3.11). In *Gobhila Gṛhyasūtra* 4.3.24 the performer of the *śrāddha*-rite places a linen thread in the rice-ball of each of his three ancestors, representing an offering of clothing.

The association of houses with the Ancestors is similarly old. The *Śatapatha Brāhmaṇa* instructs the Sacrificer to ask the Ancestors for a house, since they are the guardians of houses. "(He says) 'Give us houses, O Ancestors,' for the Ancestors are the masters of houses. This is the entreating benediction of this rite" (*ŚBM* 2.4.2.24).[30] The *Vājasaneyi Saṃhitā* includes a mantra to ask the Ancestors for houses, "Give us houses, O Ancestors!" (*VS* 2.32g).[31] Some of the Gṛhyasūtras employ this very verse (e.g., *GGS* 4.3.22–23) and this connection survived in the Buddhist tradition. Though more loosely connected than offerings of water, food, and clothing, there is a clear association between ancestors and homes, and this indicates the cultural echo of the *śrāddha*-rite for the authors of this tale.

Without a doubt, offering food to the dead draws one's mind to ancestor worship, but the fact that food offerings appear in a vast majority of the ghost stories—whether they include such *śrāddha*-rite-like elements as these two stories or not—indicates that the *śrāddha*-rite model persisted in the Buddhist imagination. One may argue that food offerings are common, so this alone fails to convince, but the triad of food, clothing, and housing—a combination with strong and ancient connections to ancestor rites—appears in several stories, indicating that these ghost offerings draw on an old cultural inheritance of ancestral offerings derived in several ways from the *śrāddha*-rite.

The Buddhist reflections on the common practice of ancestor worship drew upon the cultural memory of ancestral rites, specifically the model established in the Brahmanical *śrāddha*-rite, in their discourse on the *dhamma*, the proper religious practice. We know that at least the parts of the Pāli Canon that use the term *saddha* discussed here post-date the Brahmanical construction of the *śrāddha*-rite described in the Gṛhyasūtras. The integration of the householder rites of ancestor worship seen in the *Jāṇussoṇi Sutta* into the Buddhist conception of the proper *dhamma* indicates the acceptance of ancestral rites. Buddhist authors sought to synthesis the widespread attitudes toward the proper appeasement of the dead, strongly influenced by the Brahmanical reflection on the ritual for some time, with the moral/soteriological attitude of Early Buddhism into a single discourse, stronger and more marketable to the householder of ancient South Asia.

The next chapter examines the soteriology of both traditions to understand what role they played in the development of ancestor worship and the development of this new religious expert.

6

Soteriology

THE DISCUSSION THUS far has focused on the procedure and discursive construction of the *śrāddha*-rite. While I have not focused on the impetus for the practice of ancestor worship, one must understand the discourse focused on soteriology in the Brahmanical literature that informs the performance of the *śrāddha*-rite to fully appreciate the gradual integration of diverse ideologies and practices relevant to ancestor veneration. The Brahmanical material composed subsequent to the establishment of the *śrāddha*-rite as the paradigmatic ancestral rite focuses not on the explanation or description of the details of the rite, but instead on the meta-issues of the practice of ancestor veneration. Most important of these is the construction of a single, cohesive ritualist soteriology that stands in successful opposition to the ascetically-oriented model aimed at liberation from rebirth. The tensions between the ritualist and the renouncer model of religious practice revolve around the soteriological aims of the actor. Central to the efforts of the authors in both traditions to market themselves as the more fit, that is efficacious, ritual expert are the soteriological aims of the religious actor, the householder seeking to perform ritual. Ritualists defend the heaven attained through ritual from the Brahmins who advocated renunciation and the goal of liberation. The Buddhists advance a different soteriology, but defend their claim to the role of religious expert as vehemently. These tensions are instrumental in the religious development for the first millennium of the Common Era, particularly in the composition of treatises expounding upon *dharma*.

The Śrāddha-Rite in the Dharma Literature

In the *dharma* literature, the Dharmasūtras and Dharmaśāstras, the *śrāddha*-rite takes on new importance in the fulfillment of the householder's *dharma*. The early *dharma* authors accept its importance, but Manu makes ancestor worship central to the fulfillment of one's *dharma*.

Of the two types of ancestor worship discussed in the Gṛhyasūtras, the *piṇḍapitṛyajña* and the *śrāddha*-rite, the former does not appear in any of the four Dharmasūtras. In addition, the Eighth-day Offerings and Ninth-day Ancestral Offerings ceremonies only finds mention in the Dharmasūtras a handful of times: in a list of different rituals (*GDhS* 8.18), among rules regarding the suspension of Vedic recitation (*GDhS* 16.38; *BDhS* 1.21.4; *VDhS* 13.22), and as a special case of the *śrāddha*-rite (*BDhS* 2.15.9; *VDhS* 11.43). That these rites appear in these contexts offers further evidence for the argument made earlier, vis-à-vis the acceptance of the *śrāddha*-rite as the paradigmatic rite of ancestor worship. That is to say, the *dharma* authors have accepted that the Eighth-day Offerings are a subclass of the *śrāddha*-rite. In contrast to the older rites, the *śrāddha*-rite receives a great deal of attention.

The Dharmasūtras give few details about the rituals, focusing instead on the meta-issues, for example, what type of Brahmin is to be invited, what type of meat is to be offered, and so forth. Most focus on the *pārvaṇa śrāddha*-rite and omit discussions of the other types of *śrāddha*-rite. Three authors mention specifically that one should perform the rite monthly (*ĀpDhS* 2.16.4–5, *GDhS* 15.1–4, *VDhS* 11.16). Āpastamba's mention is typical, "(The *śrāddha*-rite) is to be performed every month" (*ĀpDhS* 2.16.4–5).[1]

The *pārvaṇa śrāddha*-rite is the only *śrāddha*-rite that occurs on a monthly schedule, but beyond the indication of its frequency the generic procedural references support two readings: either 1. the author discusses the *pārvaṇa śrāddha*-rite because it is the paradigm, leaving the other types of *śrāddha*-rite performances to the accumulated knowledge of tradition, or 2. he speaks to the *śrāddha*-rite more generally, simply refraining from making any reference to a specific *śrāddha*-rite, because his concerns apply to all forms of *śrāddha*-rites. These interpretations seem equally likely. Gautama and Baudhāyana both indicate that an uneven number of Brahmins should be invited (*GDhS* 15.7; *BDhS* 2.14.6), indicative of the *pārvaṇa, ekoddiṣṭa,* and *sapiṇḍīkaraṇa,* but Āpastamba and Vasiṣṭha fail to mention whether the number of Brahmins should be even or uneven. What is significant for my review of the *śrāddha*-rite in the Brahmanical literature, is that by the time of the Dharmasūtras, the *śrāddha*-rite is an integral part of the proper religious life and requires little detailed explanation.

The few details about procedural aspects of the *śrāddha*-rite that do occur in the Dharmasūtras agree with the Gṛhyasūtra account of the ritual. Vasiṣṭha's section on ancestor worship, however, makes it clear that the Dharmasūtras had less of a concern about ritual details. His thoughts on the *śrāddha*-rite seem to be limited to a few *sūtras* on the time and quality of Brahmins to be invited and several verses expressing general wisdom about the *śrāddha*-rite—twenty-two loosely connected verses which address some aspect of the *śrāddha*-rite—rather than a sustained argument or narrative.

The treatment of the *śrāddha*-rite in the Dharmaśāstras indicates the rise of new concerns with respect to the ritual's performance. Manu best demonstrates these concerns and, in doing so, becomes the definitive statement of the householder's ritual obligations with respect to his Ancestors and establishes the centrality of the ancestral rites to the proper *dharma*.

Manu's introduction to ancestor worship differs from that of the Dharmasūtras in several respects and indicates more clearly the newer concerns of the *dharma* tradition with respect to the *śrāddha*-rite. Manu defines ancestor veneration in two ways. In two verses of a fifty-three verse section he defines the *pitṛyajña* as one aspect of the duties of the householder described the Five Great Sacrifices. Immediately after this discourse, Manu dedicates 163 verses to explicating the *śrāddha*-rite. The form of ancestor worship mentioned in his overview of the Five Great Sacrifices is quite brief:

> 82 He should make ancestral offering every day with food or water, or even with milk, roots, and fruits, gladdening his ancestors thereby. 83 He should feed at least a single Brahmin for the benefit of his ancestors as part of the five great sacrifices; at this he should never feed even a single Brahmin in connection with the offerings to the All-gods. *MDhŚ* 3.82–83 (Olivelle 2005, 112)[2]

The ancestral rite he describes here is the daily offerings to the Ancestors made as a part of the obligations defined by the doctrine of the Five Great Sacrifices. The offerings made to the Ancestors as a part of the Five Great Sacrifices, like the other "sacrifices", are condensed versions of the older Vedic ritual obligations, and they differ from the offerings made in the *śrāddha*-rite (Smith 1989, 196–7; *HoD* 2(1):697–698).

Manu begins his longer description of the *śrāddha*-rite—and the concerns that are associated with its proper execution—by transitioning from the *pitṛyajña* of the Five Great Sacrifices to the monthly ancestral offerings, the *śrāddha*-rite. "122 Having performed the *pitṛyajña*, a Brahmin who possesses the sacred fire should perform the *śrāddha*-rite including offerings of rice-balls monthly on the new moon. 123 The wise call the monthly *śrāddha*-rite to the Ancestors the *anvāhārya*; it is to be done diligently with the meat that has been proclaimed" (*MDhŚ* 3.122–123).[3] Manu employs specific terminology to make the distinction between the abbreviated ritual obligations of the Five Great Sacrifices and the *śrāddha*-rite very clear. The former is performed daily and amounts to little more than offering water and feeding a Brahmin. The latter is a more involved ritual cycle and requires significantly more discussion.

The only exception to the clean distinction between these two ancestral rites occurs in Manu's second definition of the Five Great Sacrifices. At 3.81 Manu defines the *pitṛyajña* with *śrāddha*. This indicates Manu's efforts to align two conceptions of ancestor worship. In general, Manu consolidates the ritual obligations of the householder, synthesizing the disparate voices of his intellectual heritage into singular vision of the householder's ritual obligations (Smith 1989, 196–199). Further, the amount of space dedicated to the *śrāddha*-rite indicates that Manu exhibits a great concern over this form of ancestor worship and that he considers it central to the householder's efforts to fulfill their *dharma*. Just as Manu constructed a single vision of the householder's ritual obligations, he unifies two arguments about the attainment of heaven through ritual and in the process constructs a single consistent soteriology capable of withstanding the challenges of the liberation-oriented soteriology of the renouncer tradition.[4]

Two Soteriologies

The authors of the *dharma* literature inherit two soteriologies, each with a different goal: an eternal heaven and liberation from rebirth, advocated by the ritualist and renunciate traditions respectively, though the differences and incompatibility of these two soteriologies are often glossed over in treatments of Indian religion. Since I am primarily concerned with the ritualist soteriology, my discussion of reincarnation and the liberation soteriology is brief.

The soteriology of the renunciate tradition, often associated with Hinduism more generally, asserts that our permanent Self (*ātman*) is perpetually reincarnated in a physical form, not always human, on one of several planes of existence that make up the universe (*saṃsāra*), according to an immutable moral law that governs our transmigration according to our actions (*karma*). This notion of the perpetual transmigration of the Self precludes the existence of any permanent abode for that Self; the only nontemporary state is release from this unending cycle (*mokṣa*, *mukti*). The rituals of ancestor worship—the *piṇḍapitṛyajña*, the *pitṛyajña*, and the *śrāddha*-rite—all hold the promise of an eternal stay in heaven (*svàr*, *svargá*, *pitṛloká*, etc.) in the literature of the period of this study. The renunciate ideology precludes the assumptions of the ritualist soteriology—specifically a perpetual stay in heaven—though performance of the ancestral rituals persist long after the acceptance of the philosophical notions of transmigration and its concomitant assumptions. Bodewitz has ably argued that the first expression of the ideology of reincarnation, that is, rebirth here on earth due to *karma*, occurs in the *Kauṣītaki Upaniṣad* (Bodewitz 1996a, 56), which Olivelle dates as pre-Buddhist, probably around the sixth or fifth centuries B.C.E. (Olivelle 1996 xxxvii). Although it is not entirely clear how widespread this ideology was at this time, it almost certainly predates all the Gṛhyasūtras and is known to the authors of the Dharmasūtras, as I presently show.

The ideology of liberation and freedom from rebirth threatens the centrality of the ritual life, of the householder life, and this contestation is one of the central issues in the householder-renouncer debate that shapes the development of all Indian religions. At stake is the livelihood of those who market themselves as the religious expert best able to guide the religious practitioner to the ultimate end of human life. The treatment of ancestor worship in the early *dharma* literature can be understood as a reaction to the liberation-oriented renunciate soteriology (e.g., *ĀpDhS* 2.23.3–12, discussed in the section entitled "The Ritualist Soteriology"; see also Bronkhorst 2007, 90–91), and Manu synthesizes material from the oldest texts expressing an eternal heaven with the reactions found in the Dharmasūtras to forge a unitary heaven-oriented ritualist soteriology capable of withstanding the threat posed by the renunciate ideology and the practices derived from it, that is, the patronage of ascetics and renouncers.

The conception of an eternal heaven is found in the oldest text available to us, the *Ṛg Veda* (See also Bodewitz 1999). "Where there is perpetual light, in which world the light is placed, place me in that imperishable, undecaying world, O Pavamāna. Flow for Indra, O Soma" (*ṚV* 9.113.7).[5] The poet uses two words to convey the eternality of heaven: *amṛta*, imperishable or immortal, and *akṣita*, undecaying. The term *ajasra*, perpetual, in the first clause, which describes the light in heaven, reinforces the notion that heaven is without end.

The ritual soteriology that advances such a conception of heaven, specifically the notion that the ancestral rites win an eternal heaven, goes back to the oldest forms of ancestor worship. In the context of the *pitṛyajña* the *Maitrāyaṇī Saṃhitā* refers to the battle against Vṛtra, indicating that the ritual is for the attainment of immortality in heaven. "Having created creatures, having gotten rid of danger by sacrifice, and having slain Vṛtra, the gods desired immortality. The world of heaven is immortality. The year is the world of heaven. When one (performs) the twelve oblations, by that he gains immortality" (*MS* 1.10.17).[6] The author connects the *pitṛyajña* to the gods' acquisition of immorality: by continued performance of the *pitṛyajña*, men too can attain immortality, that is, immortal life in heaven. Several passages which refer to the year (*saṃvatsara*) in the other Brahmanical descriptions of the *pitṛyajña* reinforce this association. The year is a trope that invokes the notion of completion and Thite's analysis of sacrifice in the Brāhmaṇas shows that the "possibility of 'year-gaining'" is simply one of many strategies to "elevate" the particular ritual (Thite 1975, 42). There are several such strategies, each of which is employed, in Thite's view, to escalate the value of the particular ritual dealt with at the moment.

A similar effort to escalate the value of ancestor worship is evident in a review of the benefits sought through a performance of the ancestral rites. The solemn rites offered many benefits to the Sacrificer and those benefits appear to multiply for each rite (Thite 1975, 54 and passim). While the trend of increased multivalent benefit arising from ritual performance occurred across the ritual spectrum, the trend is augmented in the realm of ancestor worship by two other factors: the increasing importance of ancestral offerings and the eclipsing of the solemn ritual model by the domestic ritual model. The importance of performing the ancestral rites was reinforced and legitimated by an increased association with all the benefits won through the performance of solemn rituals. This is seen very clearly in *Baudhāyana Dharmasūtra*, "The ancestral rite conveys long life, heaven, fame and prosperity" (*BDhS* 2.14.1).[7] The three most common benefits derived from the solemn ritual are now available through the performance of the *śrāddha*-rite. The ascription of these benefits to the *śrāddha*-rite was one strategy in investing those rites with the authority of the older Vedic model of sacrifice. The perception of continuity in the ancestral rites, despite the changes undergone in the reinterpretation of the Gṛhyasūtras, meant these rites were themselves considered a part of the Vedic corpus with the authority that carried. Assigning the ancestral rites a central place in the theological discussion of the householder's ritual responsibilities gave those rites the authority within the *dharma* tradition. These factors combined to reinforce the conception of the *śrāddha*-rite as the authoritative model of ancestor veneration and the conception of the heaven-oriented soteriology as the ultimate goal of the religious life.

The first texts to include references to both soteriologies, though usually not in the same context, were the Dharmasūtras. While we know that the authors inherit two soteriological aims, heaven- and liberation-oriented, I could only find one *sūtra* in which both ideologies occur; it appears in both the *Baudhāyana Dharmasūtra* and the *Vasiṣṭha Dharmasūtra*. "If a man uses sesame for any purpose other than eating, anointing, and giving as a gift, reborn as a worm, he will plunge into a pile of dog shit together with his ancestors" (*BDhS* 2.2.26, Olivelle 2000, 249).[8] That the man who misuses sesame is *reborn along with his ancestors* reveals a certain amount tension between the notion of the Ancestors residing in heaven and the reincarnation implied by the sinners' punishment, but the authors do not attempt a soteriological synthesis.

The two ideologies seem to be included for the sake of completeness, the authors of the Dharmasūtras are far from impartial about which they find proper; they advocate the householder's ritualist soteriology. Āpastamba, for example, is most explicit. After quoting "verses from a Purāṇa," which indicate that living a celibate lifestyle leads to immortality (*ĀpDhS* 2.23.4–5), he says, "11 With regard to the statement about 'cremation grounds', on the other hand, that passage enjoins the funerary rites at the death of those who have performed many sacrifices. 12 Therefore, the Vedas declare, they obtain an eternal reward designated by the term 'heaven'" (*ĀpDhS* 2.23.11–12, Olivelle 2000, 107–8).[9]

The *dharma* authors advocate the ritual-oriented life of a householder as the ideal lifestyle. Gautama goes so far as to say that the householder life is the only order of life (*āśrama*). After a discussion of the four orders of life, which some say are options,[10] and a description of the four orders of life—householder, student, mendicant, and anchorite,[11] he says: "There is, however, only a single order of life, the Teachers maintain, because the householder's state alone is prescribed in express vedic texts" (*GDhS* 3.36, Olivelle 2000, 129).[12] His opinion derives from the Vedic precedents for the performance of ritual. Baudhāyana agrees that the householder is the only order of life, but cites the failure to produce offspring in the other orders of life as the reason (*BDhS* 2.11.27). All the Dharmasūtra authors share the opinion that ritual is central to the religious life. Because of this mindset, the soteriology of the renouncers finds only a marginal place in their works.[13]

Interestingly, the *dharma* writers advocate an eternal heaven while simultaneously asserting that one should continue to perform the monthly *śrāddha*-rite. This, as I see it, could derive from three mind-sets. First, the heaven and food will be eternal because of the continuous performance, that is, if sons keep performing the *śrāddha*-rite eternally, the Ancestors remain in heaven, fed, eternally. Second, there exists a cognitive dissonance between the eternality of the offering and the continued performance of the ritual that fails to rise to the level of paradox. Third, the belief in the eternality of heaven is, to use the language of Richard Gombrich (1971), a cognitive religious idea and the perpetuation of ancestral rites is an affective religious idea. And, finally, the mention of an eternal heaven is just hyperbole. These speculations, in my view, are in order of likelihood. Later, in the Epics and Purāṇas, this tension is resolved by the assertion that performing the *śrāddha*-rite at specific places—Gayā, for example—relieves the performer of the responsibility to perform the rite again and secures eternal heaven for the recipient of the offering. Despite the later developments, the earlier *dharma* literature most often advocates an eternal heaven.

The continued assertion of the older notion of an eternal heaven, however, is not the only voice. In the Dharmasūtras we see, for the first time, concern over the Ancestors remaining in the world of the Ancestors, an idea previously only seen in the late Vedic arguments over redeath (*punarmṛtyu*) (see Bodewitz 1996b). Contrary to the assumption that the stay in heaven is a permanent one, there arises in the Dharmasūtras a list of oblations that sustain the Ancestors for a variety of durations, including eternally.

In a novel innovation, two authors address how long the oblations will serve the Ancestors. Āpastamba's enumerates different meats to be included in the *śrāddha*-rite, the offering of which grant increasingly longer benefits for the Ancestors.

> 23 The things used in this (rite) are: sesame and beans, rice and barley, water, and roots and fruits. 24 When such food is greasy the Ancestors' gratification is much greater and longer lasting, 25 as when one gives things acquired in according with *dharma* to a worthy person.[14] 26 With beef, (the Ancestors') gratification is for a year, 27 and more with the meat of a buffalo. 28 This (injunction)

> explains that the meat of domestic and wild animals is fit for oblations. 2.17.1 On the skin of a rhinoceros with rhinoceros meat (their gratification lasts) for an infinite time; 2 likewise with the meat of the Śatabali fish, 3 and of the Vārdhrāṇasa crane. *ĀpDhS* 2.16.23–17.3[15]

Āpastamba indicates the normal materials used in the ritual, sesame seeds, rice etc. He also tells us that offerings made in the *śrāddha*-rite last longer if they are greasy, that is, if they include meat. The other offerings prolong the duration of the benefit of the offering, that is, prolong the benefit of the ritual for the Ancestors beyond the month of the basic offerings. It is the meat that gratifies the Ancestors, and it is the type of meat that induces longer results. The meat of a cow satisfies the Ancestors for one year, that of a buffalo even longer. The flesh of a rhinoceros, the Śatabali fish, and the Vārdhrāṇasa crane will serve the Ancestors without end (*anantya*). Āpastamba's full list appears in Table 6.1.

Since we know from the Gṛhyasūtras that meat was a part of the *śrāddha*-rite offerings since at least that time, the inclusion of meat is not an innovation for the authors of the Dharmasūtras. Instead, this is a justification of the offerings. I suggest that this list is the ritualists' way to assert that the *śrāddha*-rite does indeed offer eternal benefit for the Ancestors. A consideration of Gautama's list, which will show further development of this trope, will support this assertion.

Gautama's list, which expands upon the list that Āpastamba provides us, shows a similar intention.[16] "A gift of sesame seeds, beans, rice, barley, and water gratifies the Ancestors for a month; meat of a fish, deer, Ruru antelope, rabbit, turtle, boar, or sheep for years; cow's milk or rice milk for twelve years; the meat of the Vārdhrīṇasa crane, *kālaśāka*, the meat of a goat, a red goat, or a rhinoceros, mixed with honey eternally" (*GDhS* 15.15).[17] Gautama not only adds several varieties of meat, he increases the benefit of the intermediary group. Whereas Āpastamba makes the lesser duration one year or more than that, Gautama merely indicates the meats on his list will last several years. Gautama makes the import clear: these offerings last one month, hence the householder performs the *śrāddha*-rite every month; otherwise the Ancestors are without food.[18] The other offerings prolong the duration of the benefit of the offering, that is, prolong the benefit of the ritual for the Ancestors beyond the monthly *śrāddha*-rite. Like Āpastamba, Gautama highlights the eternality of the meat offerings by including the monthly offerings in the list. In addition to the structural similarities, Gautama also uses the same word, *anantya*, to indicate that the offerings will serve without end.

The brevity of Āpastamba's list indicates a period before the scholastic tendency to multiply lists that increases with time in the *dharma* tradition, something seen more clearly in Gautama's somewhat later list. But the point of these lists is not to compare the values of different offerings, but rather to indicate which offerings one can make that will generate eternal benefit for one's ancestors. The vagueness of Gautama's "several years" also supports the notion that the emphasis is on the eternal offerings. These two *dharma* authors are reacting to the renouncer tradition's assertion that the heaven won through ritual does not last forever. They react by outlining details of the ritual that ensure an eternal heaven. Ideologically the renouncer's soteriology calls into question the ritualist's soteriology, but more importantly, anything that challenges the notion that the stay in heaven won through the performance of the *śrāddha*-rite is a threat to the Brahmin's role as ritual expert. The ideological challenge leveled by those advocating an ascetically-oriented soteriology had real implications for the livelihood of those Brahmins who supported themselves through ritual performance. In short, the ritualist authors expressed their concerns about the renouncers' challenge to the centrality of ritual and thereby to the livelihood and worldview of and central place in society given to the brahmanical ritual experts.

The enumeration of meats fit for the *śrāddha*-rite and the duration for which they serve the Ancestors in the Dharmasūtras pale in comparison to the list that Manu records (*MDhŚ* 3.266–272). Table 6.1 compares the lists of Manu and Yājñavalkya list with the two lists found in the Dharmasūtras and includes lists from the *Mahābhārata* and the *Viṣṇu Smṛti* to help illustrate the historical trend.[19]

This scheme has the same purpose as it did in the *Gautama Dharmasūtra*, to detail the requirements for the ritual to secure an eternal heaven, though the scholastic tendency to enumerate every possibility has certainly grown stronger. The lists imply at least a tacit admission that the older ritual has its limits, that is, that the ancestral rites as they had been performed did not grant an eternal heaven—as the ascetic opponents of the ritual lifestyle argue. But the *dharma* authors reinterpret the ritual to show that it does indeed produce imperishable food for the Ancestors located in heaven, as long as the proper offerings are made. While normal offerings will last a month—in keeping with tradition—these offerings will last longer, even eternally (*anantya*).[20]

Table 6.1 Duration of benefit for the Ancestors from different offerings

	sesame, rice, barley, beans, water, roots, and fruit	Fish	Common deer	Sheep	Birds	Goat	Spotted Deer	Eṇa Antelope	Ruru antelope	Buffalo	Boar	Hornless Goat	Rabbit	Turtle	Cow	Milk or milk-rice	Rhinoceros	Śatabali fish	Vārdhrāṇasa crane	Sacred basil	Mahāśalka crustacean	Red goat	Honey	Sage's Food
ĀpDhS										1y					1y		∞	∞	∞					
GDhS		1+y		1+y		∞	1+y		1+y		1+y		1+y	1+y			∞	∞	∞	∞		∞		
MDhŚ	1m	2m	3m	4m	5m	6m	7m	8m	9m	10m	10m		11m	11m	1y	1y	∞		12y	∞	∞	∞	∞	∞
ViSmṛ	1m	2m	3m	4m	5m	6m	7m			10m		11m			9m	1y	∞		∞	∞	∞			
MBh	1m	2m		3m	7m	5m	8m	10m	9m	11m	6m		4m		1y		∞		12y	∞		∞	∞	
YS	1m	2m	3m	4m	5m		6m	7m			8m		9m			1y	∞		∞		∞			

Asserting the eternality of heaven by quantifying the durability of the food offered does not occur in the later two Dharmasūtras. It is replaced, I argue, by a more consistent assertion of the older concept that the heaven won through *śrāddha*-rite is eternal. Neither Baudhāyana nor Vasiṣṭha engage the issue of the durability of the offerings made in the *śrāddha*-rite; they assert that the offerings of the *śrāddha*-rite do not decay. Unlike the authors who list the meat offerings, who consistently use the word *anantya*, these two *dharma* authors revive the older language for describing the eternal heaven won through the ritual, and this trend gains ground in the subsequent literature.

The notion of an eternal heaven is quite old, for example, in describing the offerings to the ancestors, *AVŚ* 12.2.32 indicates that the offerings to the ancestors should be undecaying.[21] More commonly, the older ritualists describe the food offered with words derived from the verb *kṣi*, to diminish, waste away, and perish. Derivatives of this root have been used to describe both heaven and the food offered to the Ancestors since at least the Vedas. *Ṛg Veda* 9.113.7, discussed earlier, describes heaven as undecaying (*akṣita*). *Atharva Veda* 18.4.32 describes the food on which the Ancestors subsist with the same word. Āpastamba described the benefit of performing the Four-Monthly Sacrifices as inexhaustible (*akṣayya*) (*ĀpŚS* 8.1.1). However, the word *akṣaya*—and its twin *akṣayya*[22]—enjoys an increasingly central place in subsequent literature and is used in mantras employed in the ancestral rites.

Conversely, the default mantra used in the householder ancestral rites employing the word *akṣaya* is replaced when the eternality of the offering is not implied. In the *ekoddiṣṭa śrāddha*-rite, the usual mantra is replaced. As discussed earlier, the shift from "Inexhaustible" (*akṣayya*) to "May he approach the Ancestors" (*upatiṣṭhatām*) changes the focus of the ritual from the ancestors to the single deceased father. The term *akṣayya* refers to the food offered to the Ancestors, expressing the hope that the offering to the Ancestors will last forever. Since the ritual aims to effect the transfer of the deceased to the status of Ancestor, and not the regular feeding of the Ancestors, the mantra that replaces the standard mantra emphasizes that transition. A similar substitution occurs in the *ābhyudayika śrāddha*-rite (*ŚGS* 4.4.1–15) and this trend continues in the later literature.

Baudhāyana gives more details regarding the procedure than the other Dharmasūtra authors and even includes three mantras to be recited when the Sacrificer touches the food to be presented to the Brahmins. The first is to the father and the other two to each subsequent Ancestor.

"You are the whole of the earth! Agni sees you and the *Ṛg* verses are your greatness for avoiding negligence in giving you. The earth is your vessel; heaven is your cover. I offer you into the mouth of *brahman;* I offer you into the in-breath and the out-breath of learned Brahmins. You are undecaying! May you not decay for the Ancestors over there in the other world" (*BDhS* 2.14.12).[23] Baudhāyana specifically refers to the food offered to the Ancestors as undecaying (*akṣita*) continuing the trend I have just illustrated (See also *HGS* 2.4.11.4).

Vasiṣṭha records a similar opinion about the duration of the oblations made to the Ancestors: "During the eighth part of the day the sun moves slowly; this period is known as 'midday'; and anything given to ancestors at this time becomes inexhaustible (*akṣaya*)" (*VDhS* 11.36, Olivelle 2000, 393).[24] The oblation, if given at the proper time of the day, will give inexhaustible benefit to the Ancestors. Vasiṣṭha, like Baudhāyana, asserts that the *śrāddha*-rite grants an eternal reward.

In the subsequent literature, the word *akṣaya* (or *akṣayya*) commonly describes heaven in a broader context, for example, *BDhS* 2.11.7; *MDhŚ* 3.79, *MBh* 3.219.5. But there develops a preference for using this and related words to describe the benefits of performing a *śrāddha*-rite. The number of occurrences of these derivatives in the subsequent literature testifies to this trend. The term *akṣita* occurs in this capacity in the *Baudhāyana Dharmasūtra* once. (2.14.12); *akṣaya* occurs in the *Baudhāyana Dharmasūtra* once (2.11.7) and *Vasiṣṭha Dharmasūtra* twice (11.22; 11.36), but in the *Mānava Dharmaśāstra* three times (3.122; 3.202; 3.273, 275) and in the *Mahābhārata* numerous times in association with the *śrāddha*-rite (e.g., 1.1.203; 1.56.29). The phrase *pitṝṇāṃ dattam akṣayam*, occurs already in the *Vasiṣṭha Dharmasūtra (VDhS* 11.36), but becomes common, with slight variations, only by the time of the *Mahābhārata*, for example, *MBh* 3.80.106; 3.82.72; 3.85.8; 13.61.92. The *dharma* authors do not abandon the notion that the heaven won through ritual is eternal; in fact, the terms and phrases associated with the *śrāddha*-rite reinforce this idea throughout the later literature.

As he does with other aspects of religious practice, Manu adopts both of these strategies, weaving them into a single soteriology. He preserves both discourses, that is, that the food offering is inexhaustible and that an eternal stay in heaven is won with different meat offerings.

In a section that addresses the proper time for performing the *śrāddha*-rite, Manu too asserts the perpetual nature of certain offerings made at certain times.

> 273 Something mixed with honey offered on the thirteenth day of the fortnight during the rainy season when the moon is in Maghā would be undecaying. 274 Would that a man would be born in our family who would give milk-rice with honey and ghee on the thirteenth day during the eastern shadow of the elephant. 275 Whatever a man endowed with faith gives according to the rules, that becomes eternal and undecaying for the ancestors in the next world. *MDhŚ* 3.273–275[25]

Like Vasiṣṭha, Manu ties the success to the proper moment. The terminology he employs underlines the dual heritage of this view. Manu says that the offerings become eternal (*anantya*), explicitly drawing on vocabulary used in the lists of meat offerings, and inexhaustible (*akṣaya*), using the term employed by the later two Dharmasūtras.

Manu reiterates the eternality of heaven in each aspect of the discussion of the ancestral rites, the offerings made in the ritual and the timing of the ritual. He integrates the two ways of demonstrating the eternality of the heaven won through the *śrāddha*-rite, strengthening the ritualists' arguments.

The Ritualist Soteriology

One final piece of evidence will strengthen my argument that both these strategies—the lists of durations won in heaven by certain meats and the increased concern with expressing the eternality of heaven, specifically the heaven won through the *śrāddha*-rite—are aimed at advancing a ritualists soteriology in defense against the encroaching renunciate soteriology. The one passage in which Baudhāyana uses the term *akṣayya* provides some clues.

In his discussion of the Five Great Sacrifices, Baudhāyana defines the sacrifice to *brahman* (*brahmayajña*) as the recitation of the Vedas and discusses the rewards of performing it at length. Relevant for our discussion is this *sūtra*: "When a man performs the recitation of his Veda with this knowledge, he wins as great a heavenly residence as a man who gives as a gift this world filled with wealth—indeed, he wins a heavenly residence even greater than that, a residence that is unending; and he overcomes repeated death" (*BDhS* 2.11.7, Olivelle 2000, 279).[26] Of the Five Great Sacrifices Baudhāyana only connects the attainment of heaven with the sacrifice to *brahman* and immediate after doing so, he mentions redeath (*punarmṛtyu*). This is the key to better understanding the intended audience of the work more generally.

The term *punarmṛtyu* occurs almost exclusively in the Late Vedic literature and Bodewitz argues that the term, "introduced together with its solution and with emphasis on its solution, reflects the reaction of the ritualists to attempts made by nonritualists to devalue the ritualist claims" (Bodewitz 1996b, 36). Bodewitz shows in his analysis of the term that it was strongly associated with certain rituals, particularly the *brahmayajña* (40–41). This passage indicates that Baudhāyana shared this concern over the devaluation of ritual in general. The overt defense he and other authors of the Dharmasūtras make of the ritual life described earlier (e.g., *ĀpDhS* 2.23.3–12) supports this interpretation. This concern helps us understand the long list of meats and increasingly longer stays in heaven they secure.

The lists are best understood, as are the much older discussions of redeath and the efforts by the authors of the Dharmasūtras to defend the householder life, as a reaction to the ascetically-oriented ideologies, specifically, the nonritualists attack on the notion of an eternal heaven. Āpastamba reacts by outlining the ritual procedures that ensure an eternal heaven. Gautama continues the trend with a greater need to classify and list things. The later Dharmasūtra authors do not argue that *śrāddha*-rite wins an eternal heaven; they accept the fact and describe it thus, increasingly using the term *akṣaya* and its derivatives. Manu, as he does with the different ways of classifying the householder's ritual duties more generally, uses both strategies, synthesizing them into a stronger, cohesive defense of the ritual life. All these authors recognize reincarnation, but refuse to integrate the two soteriologies; they refer to both soteriological ends, but no effort to integrate them occurs. Efforts to synthesize do not occur until much later, in the later *dharma* literature, Epics, and Purāṇas.

The Śrāddha-Rite in the Buddhist Literature

While the Buddhists experts embraced the renunciate soteriology more easily than the Brahmanical ritualists, the householders who patronized Buddhist religious specialists shared many of the assumptions about the efficacy and benefit of performing the ancestral rites, as seen in the *Jāṇussoṇisutta*. The former of these two facets of early Buddhism account for the more rapid assimilation of the *śrāddha*-rite;[27] thus it is already little more than a cultural memory in the Pāli Canon, which was in its current form at least by the first few centuries of the Common Era when these issues were still hotly debated in the early *dharma* tradition of the Brahmins. The centrality of ancestral rites to the ritual life of the householder indicates one reason for the staying power of that cultural memory and the structural influence on the offerings as described in the *Petavatthu*. The Buddhist authors granted their householder devotees some of the benefits of the ancestral rites, but gradually steered the ritual practice toward a different goal, religious gifting, which produced different benefits.

Jāṇussoṇi's dialogue with the Buddha makes it clear that he, like other householders, performs the *śrāddha*-rite and is concerned about its efficacy. His two primary concerns are the receipt of the offerings by the deceased and his receipt of the benefits derived therefrom. The first concern is allayed rather easily, but even after the Buddha shifts the focus from the actual ritual of the *śrāddha*-rite to gifting more generally, Jāṇussoṇi still expresses a concern that the "giver is not without fruit" (*A* v.273).[28] The householder does not engage in ritual merely to remain active or because it is his obligation; he derives benefit from its performance. These benefits are increasingly associated with Buddhist goals, as the scholars who trace the development of the transfer of merit have shown,[29] but the Buddhist religious experts dared not eliminate the benefits drawn from ritual, despite their efforts to move to the discussion to a more abstract level. They draw upon this common practice, integrating it into the Buddhist view of ritual activity, marketing themselves as the most efficacious way to successfully fulfill one's ritual obligations.

The Buddhist authors altered the rituals of ancestor worship only insofar as to locate it within their own social and cosmological world, that is, aligning its interpretation with the Buddhist reinterpretation and practice of sacrifice and other ideological values. More significantly, they shifted the focus of the ritual performance of the ancestral rites. Gifting had become more central to the Buddhist expression of religiosity (Heim 2004), and thus the ancestral rites were construed as a manifestation of gifting, as I showed in my reading of the *Petavatthu* (see also Egge 2002, 29–32). Beyond this redefinition of the immediate mechanism of ancestor worship, there is a tacit acceptance of the older conceptions of the aims of the rituals. The *Jāṇussoṇisutta* shows us that the tradition did not dismiss the concern over the feeding of the dead Ancestors, and the narratives of the *Petavatthu* reinforce the connection made between the obligatory performance of ancestral rites and the cultivation of the proper moral attitude. Further, narratives from both texts avoid underestimating the concern over the benefit sought by the patron who performs the ritual. In short, the Buddhists authors could not abandon the underlying concerns of ancestor worship, that is, sustaining one's ancestors and benefiting in turn from the performance of those rituals. The householders' concern over the benefits they drew from the performance of ritual, ancestor rites in particular, shaped the religious experts' (of both Brahmanical and Buddhist traditions) redefinition of the ritual obligations. The benefits drawn from those performances were surely the same as those expressed in the Brahmanical texts, though the Buddhist authors tended to downplay these "lesser" rewards.

In addition, without altering the practice significantly, the Buddhist authors imbued the ritual with newer values and constructed new notions of what determined the ritual's proper performance. In the *Jāṇussoṇisutta* the discussion of the efficacy of the ritual is turned to the destiny of those who act morally. Similarly, the *Petavatthu* advocates living a moral life, but, more significantly, the authors advocate gifting, specifically to the Saṅgha. The ritual is effective, but only if offered through religious experts worthy of that honor. Both traditions make extensive efforts to define the qualifications of those to whom the practitioner would go to for ritual expertise. It is to the role of the religious expert that I now turn.

7

*Mediation**

ONE FEATURE OF the recentering from the sacrificial model of Vedic religion to newer models of religious practice was the introduction and authorization of a new role for the religious expert, discussed briefly in the discussion of the ancestral rites in the Gṛhyasūtras. One important factor of this new role is the mode of mediation that the religious expert was said to effect between the ritualist and the supernatural entity he sought to propitiate through ritual.

This new model of religious expert also reflected the authors' conception of the proper orientation to the universe he sought to manipulate. That is to say, the qualities described as desirable reflected the authors' conception of a proper mediator. The role of mediator was contested by multiple groups—Buddhist, Brahmin, and Jain among others—and each had a vested interest in defining the role of mediator in such a way as to advocate their own worldviews.[1] In addition to the competition between these groups, competition between Brahmins that advocated ritual performance and ascetically oriented Brahmins has a role here. The learned Brahmin was the counterpart to the ascetic. The latter became a symbol of religious, almost magical, power (Thapar 1982, 294) a power that could be tapped into by presenting them with alms. Theologians constructing the new religious expert needed to describe that expert in a way that made him as worthy of gifts as the ascetic. This also highlights the stakes of these discursive constructions of the religious expert: these authors argue for their very livelihood. They argue about who will serve the householder best as he performs those rituals central to his religious life.

* A previous version of this article "Claiming Modes of Mediation in Ancient Hindu and Buddhist Ancestor Worship" appeared in the *Journal of Ritual Studies* 26(1) 2012 and is reprinted in part here with the permission of the Journal's Editors, Pamela J. Stewart and Andrew J. Strathern.

The initial innovations in the development of this new ritual expert are enacted first in the construction of the new paradigm for ancestor worship found in the Gṛhyasūtras, and the later development of this trend throughout South Asian religion is predicated, in part, upon this model of ancestor worship.

In the solemn model of sacrifice the Vedic priest was the primary human mediator between the patron and the supernatural beings he wished to influence through sacrifice. Through the reconstruction of the ancestral rites in the Gṛhyasūtras, certain Brahmins created a new model of religious expert as mediator, the professional guest. Religious gifting (*dāna*), specifically ritual gifts made to those same religious experts, became central to Indian modes of religiosity. Of particular importance in understanding the construction of this new role is the substitution of the Brahmin—who stands in for the deceased in the *śrāddha*-rite—for the ritual fire. The Buddhist authors also made efforts to appropriate the role of the religious expert as mediator in sacrifice. Masefield touches upon this role in his discussion of sacrifice in the development of the doctrine of the transfer of merit (Dhammapāla 1996). Egge (2002) traces similar motifs in the development of the Buddhist notion of *karma*. In the development of Buddhist doctrine and practice, as these authors, and others, have shown, Buddhists drew upon Vedic conceptions of sacrifice and ritual (e.g., Norman 1991, Frieberger 1998). I argue that the Buddhist efforts with respect to the role of mediation—with the Buddha or the Saṅgha as stand in for the ritual fire—are most apparent in their handling of ancestor worship and inform the later, fuller development of the *dāna* tradition. In both the Brahmanical and Buddhist texts the shift from older models of religious practice revolve, to no little degree, around the creation of this new mediator as first expressed in the discourse on ancestral rites.

Agni and Vedic Mediation

The Vedic sacrifice offers the Sacrificer the opportunity to, among other things, set up stores for his afterlife. This is seen already in one of the funeral hymns of the *Ṛg Veda*: "Join with the Ancestors, with Yama by means of your sacrifices and gifts in the highest heaven" (*ṚV* 10.14.8).[2] The *Śatapatha Brāhmaṇa* says, "He is born into that world he made; therefore, they say 'A man is born into the world he made'" (*ŚBM* 6.2.2.27).[3] Central to the performance of ritual is Agni, thus his connection to the building of heaven is unsurprising. "May you (Agni), along with them, create a body and this heaven, O resplendent one, according to your desire" (*ṚV* 10.15.14).[4] It is through the performance of sacrifice that one makes a place for himself in heaven (see Malamoud 1983, 31).

But the ancient ritualist could not secure heaven by himself; nor could he perform the Vedic sacrifices by himself. The Vedic priests extensive ritual knowledge and ritual purity qualified him to approach the sacred fire, Agni, i.e., and perform the ritual on the householder's behalf.

It is in this context, a sacrificial religious context, that the reconstruction of the domestic rites took place. The various groups competing for the patronage of those interested in attaining heaven—as well as the other benefits of ritual performance—all constructed their ideologies in response to the Vedic world view. Some groups responded by rejecting it outright—as did most of the renunciate traditions that were born from the *śramaṇa* movement—but others—inside and outside the Brahmanical community—reflected on the older tradition, often appropriating sacrificial language, to describe and validate other religious activities.

However, those Brahmins working to create this new role for a religious expert chose not to emulate the Vedic priest in constructing this new role for themselves, they drew upon the metaphors applied to Agni himself to authorize this new role, if not to circumvent the old human intermediary they sought to displace. By focusing on Agni as mediator they were able to transform the ritual interaction between humans and the supernatural. By substituting themselves for Agni, they were, in effect, cutting out the middle man, that is, the Vedic priest.

With efforts centered on substituting human agents for the sacred fire, the religious experts of both traditions understood this new role as that of an intermediary. Instead of logistical expert assisting Agni in establishing a connection between sacrifice and deity or ancestor, Brahmins now occupy a role they themselves constructed on the model of Agni and influenced by the changing conceptions of proper ritual practice. This role served the needs of these Brahmins well in that they established themselves as ritual experts better able to serve the needs of practitioners seeking religious experts to mediate between them and the gods or the Ancestors, making themselves indispensable in the performance of domestic ritual. Buddhists similarly engaged the conversation about the role of the religious expert, offering their services as mediators in the ritual obligations that defined the householder: divine worship, hospitality, and ancestor worship. The efforts in both traditions were predicated on securing for themselves a livelihood as the religious expert best suited to mediate between the practitioner and the object of veneration.

Agni's role as the mediator between the Sacrificer and the gods is well known; he enacts the exchange between the human Sacrificer with his supernatural counterpart, not only transferring the food to the gods and the Ancestors, but bringing the gods to the ritual space and even transferring the deceased to the next world (*ṚV* 10.14). The very first hymn of the *Ṛg Veda* describes Agni's role as mediator.

> 2. Agni must be invoked by the Sages—both those past and present. He will convey the gods here. 3. Through Agni, the sacrifice will attain wealth, a prosperity day after day, which brings glory and many heroes. 4. O Agni, the sacrifice, the ceremony which you encompass on every side—that very one goes to the gods. *ṚV* 1.1.2–4 (Brereton and Jamison, forthcoming)[5]

Agni brings the gods to the ritual space and brings the sacrifice to the gods. Through him one wins the rewards of sacrifice, e.g., prosperity, sons, long life, and heaven.

In one funeral hymn from the *Ṛg Veda* Agni's role as intermediary in both rituals to the gods and those to the Ancestors is stated explicitly.

> 11. The flesh-conveying Agni who will sacrifice to the forefathers, who are strong through truth, he will proclaim the oblations to the gods and the forefathers.
>
> 12. Eagerly we would install you; eagerly we would kindle you. Eagerly convey the eager forefathers here, to eat the oblation. *ṚV* 10.16.11–12 (Brereton and Jamison, forthcoming)

Agni carries the corpses to heaven and he carries the sacrifice to the Ancestors. Agni is the intermediary for both offerings of food to the gods and to the Ancestors. Finally, Agni even brings the Ancestors to the ritual so that they can consume the offerings made in the ritual. His role as divine intermediary is the foundation of the exchange enacted in Vedic sacrifice and it is clear that he is the mediator for both divine and ancestral rites.

The Brahmin and Human Mediation

As the appeal of large-scale sacrifice in the Vedic world began to wane, the religious experts who had a vested interest in the continuation of a priest-managed Vedic ritual found their role in the religious life challenged. The Brahmins who reworked the domestic rites during the composition of the domestic ritual manuals created a new role for a human actor to fill; a man who possessed the proper character could stand in the place of Agni as intermediary.

The later tradition preserves this role for Agni in the divine rites. In his Gṛhyasūtra, Āśvalāyana indicates that Agni is the mouth of the gods. "A Brāhmaṇa (says) 'The gods have Agni as their mouth, the Ancestors have the hand as their mouth'" (*ĀśGS* 4.7.22). The metaphor of the mouth indicates that the gods are fed through the ritual, as we saw in *Śatapatha Brāhmaṇa* 2.4.2. The Ancestors are said to have the hand as their mouth because the offerings made to the Ancestors are offered into the hands of the Brahmins. Thus, as the food for the gods is given to them through the sacrificial fire, the food for the Ancestors is offered into the hands of the Brahmins. Just as Agni mediates between the householder and the gods he seeks to feed through sacrifice, the Brahmin mediates between the householder and his Ancestors, by accepting the food given in the *śrāddha*-rite. The author's—and his audience's—understanding of the metaphor rests on their conception of Agni as the mediator in ritual. This and similar passages highlight the elision of Vedic priests; the authors of the late Vedic and early classical material do not model their new religious role on the older religious experts, but draw directly on the divine model.

In the mythic introduction to the ancestral offerings, Āpastamba says, "In this (ritual) the Ancestors are the deity, but Brahmins stand in for the offertorial fire" (*ĀpDhS* 2.16.3). The Brahmin stands in for Agni and, as Agni does, conveys the oblations to the gods. Beyond the comparison of the Brahmin to the offertorial fire found in the Gṛhyasūtras and the Dharmasūtras, Manu asserts that offerings made to Brahmins are superior to those made in the fire. "It never spills, it never falls, it never perishes at all—an offering made in the mouth of a Brahmin is far superior to oblations made in the fire" (*MDhŚ* 7.84, Olivelle 2005, 158).[6] The hyperbole of this passage indicates two things: Manu's conviction that the Brahmin as mediator is qualified to act as religious expert and the established state of this human mediator in the ritual culture of his time. It is also not coincidence that he is advocating a Brahmin specifically; he has a vested interest in perpetuating the institution of ritual that relies on ritual experts such as himself.

The Brahmins' new role had become an integral part of the domestic ritual by the time of the Gṛhyasūtras, but the role was not open to any Brahmin; it is available only to the Brahmin knowledgeable of the Brahmanical tradition. The authors of the domestic ritual manuals enjoin the feeding of Brahmins in outline of the basic ritual paradigm, but add a qualification; only certain Brahmins qualify to be invited. While the concern about the qualifications is not limited to the context of ancestral rites, I will show that that concern is particularly strong in the context of ancestor worship. Additionally, the preoccupation with the quality of the Brahmin invited to the *śrāddha*-rite increases and receives considerable more attention in the later tradition.

In these texts the Brahmanical theologians construct a mode of religiosity that includes them in a central role, that of professional guest. The role of guest is certainly not new, just as ancestor worship is not new, however, the development seen in the Gṛhyasūtras indicates that the specifics of that role were under development in those texts, therefore we can see in the Gṛhyasūtras and the subsequent *dharma* literature a formalization and authentication of this role. These Brahmins define this new role for the religious expert in sharp contrast to the older Vedic ritual priests, though the two groups were certainly not mutually exclusive.

In defining the new ritual expert the Brahmanical theologians circumscribe the group of qualified mediators in very specific ways. They seek to guard the gateways to ritual performance, to discursively legitimate their own religious expert and exclude others. What is at stake here are competing claims for the role of religious intermediary; experts in each tradition make the case for who is, and isn't, qualified to serve as religious expert for the rituals that householders perform. The Brahmins did not want religious experts from different religious communities to encroach upon a ritual behavior that they considered their domain. In order to secure this role for themselves Brahmins—and Buddhists—defined the qualifications for the new ritual expert in terms of learning, but the learning sought in a guest reflects their own ideological perspective. This first arises in the domestic ritual manuals.

The Gṛhyasūtras express concern over the character and learning of the Brahmins invited to be fed at domestic rituals, but the concern is not widely expressed early on. Only four of the fifty-eight instances where the Gṛhyasūtras indicate that Brahmins should be fed explicitly indicate qualities. The simplest of these appears in the *Hiraṇyakeśin Gṛhyasūtra*. "With that [the remains of the rice-milk offering] he serves a Brahmin possessed of learning" (*HGS* 1.7.23.5).[7] Learning qualifies the Brahmin for receiving food at the ritual. Āpastamba indicates that the proper Brahmin to be invited is virtuous (*śucin*), and verses in the mantras (*mantravat*) (*ĀpGS* 8.21.2). Śāṅkhāyana reiterate this emphasis on learning, calling for Brahmins who are learned in the Vedas (*śrotriya*) (*ŚGS* 2.14.9).

Despite the different terminology the authors of these texts clearly agree that learning is important to the success of the ritual. Not all authors explicitly state that only Brahmins of learning and good moral character should be invited to a ritual, but later authors stress this characteristic, especially in the context of ancestor worship. The overall trend in this period is of an increase in this concern, driven by the increased importance of the qualifications of the recipient in the success of any gift.

Śāṅkhāyana speaks of the qualities of the recipients elsewhere in greater detail.

> 1 At the conclusion of rites (there is) the feeding of Brahmins. 2 Voice, (pleasing) form, age, learning, moral character, moral conduct: These are the qualities (sought). 3 Learning exceeds them all. 4 He should not overlook learning. 5 About the gods, about the self, and about sacrifice: These are the three (knowledges) given in the mantras and Brāhmaṇa; they are called learning. 6 One who performs the rites properly, one who is studying, one who is experienced in learning, one who practices austerities: Hunger will never again gnaw at that one who feeds one of them. *ŚGS* 1.2.1–6[8]

The emphasis on learning—*śrutam*, specifically religious learning—echoes the terms seen above: *vidyāvat*, *mantravat*, and *śrotriya*. Further the terms employed here, and elsewhere, specify a conception of learning that is intimately tied to knowledge of the Vedas. The Brahmins—and the Buddhists in kind—value knowledge and moral character, but they also take this opportunity to validate and position their own worldview. Both traditions agree that knowledge and good character are required to take on the role of intermediary, but they differ on the type of knowledge and the particular aspects of character that are to be valued.

This broad concern about the worthiness of ritual guests takes on special import in the context of ancestral offerings. The passages discussed above from Hiraṇyakeśin and Āpastamba specifically mention the qualification in the context of offerings made at a *śrāddha*-rite. Additionally, Āśvalāyana indicates that Brahmins invited to a *śrāddha*-rite should be "endowed with fame, character, and good behavior, or with one (of these)" (*ĀśGS* 4.7.2).[9] Śāṅkhāyana (4.1.2) describes the ideal invitee as learned in the Vedas (*vedavid*). This concern over the qualities of the Brahmins invited to a *śrāddha*-rite increases dramatically in the subsequent literature, the treatises on *dharma*. Discussions of the properly qualified ritual expert must be understood as a central part of the discursive efforts to define the Brahmanical tradition against the competitors in the religious marketplace. The Dharmasūtra authors work to define the proper *dharma* in contrast to the *dharma* of the Buddhist tradition (Olivelle 2004a) and the efficacy of the ritual experts to be employed in rituals in a key aspect of this work. The extent to which the *dharma* authors care about the proper qualities of the Brahmin plays a part in the promotion of their ritual experts and the exclusion of the ritual experts of other traditions.

While the Brahmanical authors are concerned about the quality of guests invited to any ritual, the concern is most ardently expressed in the ancestral rites. I will argue that the Brahmin ritual expert's role, namely as stand-in for the Ancestors in the *śrāddha*-rite and other ancestral rituals, is the locus for this increased concern.

Each of the Dharmasūtra authors lists specific qualities and rules for making compromises if Brahmins of quality are unavailable. Baudhāyana is unambiguous; the invited Brahmins should be well-behaved (*caraṇavat*) and well versed in the Vedas (*anūcāna*), as well as virtuous (*śuci*) and versed in the mantras (*mantravat*) (2.14.6). Āpastamba lists only one quality to be sought, well-versed in the Vedas (*brahmavid*) (2.17.4). Gautama describes Brahmins who are learned in the Vedas (*śrotriya*), and endowed with eloquence (*vāc*), beauty (*rūpa*), youth (*vayaḥ*), and moral character (*śīla*) (15.6–11). Vasiṣṭha is more specific, indicating certain persons: ascetics (*yati*), virtuous householders (*gṛhasthān sādhūn*), and those learned in the Vedas (11.16). In all the Dharmasūtras we can see the conservative nature of the tradition at work; several of these terms are borrowed from earlier authors (e.g., *mantravat* in *HGS* 2.4.10.2–3 and *ĀpGS* 8.21.2).

Baudhāyana restricts which Brahmins can be invited; he indicates that the invitees should not be related to him by birth, by *gotra*, a different kinship relationship, or by the associations created in performing a sacrifice (2.14.6) (See also *ĀpGS* 8.21.2). Āpastamba indicates that ideally the householder will find such a Brahmin that is not related to him by birth, by *gotra*, or by the associations created in performing a sacrifice, or being in a student-teacher relationship (2.17.4). Vasiṣṭha mention only restrictions on inviting pupils (11.16). Gautama is explicit that these rituals should not be used to strike up a friendship (15.16). An offering to such people, Āpastamba tells us, does not reach the Ancestors and bears no merit for the Sacrificer (2.17.8); in other words it is a complete failure. In explaining the connection between hospitality and the *śrāddha*-rite, Stephanie Jamison has pointed out that the point of the *śrāddha* is "naked hospitality." That is, the true expression of hospitality is feeding guests (*atithi*) who are "functionally strangers." She then adds an insight into the care with which guests are chosen, "This is perhaps also why more attention is paid to the worthiness of the invited guests in this rite than in one dedicated to the gods; they must represent the very type of the proper Aryan" (1996, 183). I will address another reason behind this careful attention shortly.

The remainder of the lists of invitees enumerates negative qualities to be avoided in an invitee (See also *ĀpDhS* 2.17.21). The Brahmins should not be too old (*apariṇatavayasa*) nor engage in improper occupations (*avikarmastha*), nor be a pupil of the Sacrificer, though he may feed his pupils if they are of the best character. The other characteristics to be avoided, with the exception of the naked, share a common trait: they disqualify a Brahmin from ritual participation. Since they are unable to participate in ritual, it follows that they would be prohibited from participating in a *śrāddha*-rite, but other prohibitions indicate more than concern about ritual sanctity. Some proscriptions are aimed specifically at excluding the ritual experts of other traditions.

For example, the meaning of the term naked (*nagna*) in this context has generated many different interpretations, including someone with an unlucky horoscope and one negligent in his duties (Olivelle 2000, 661n11.19). Vasiṣṭha, who describes the punishment for perjury as including shaving of the head (*VDhS* 16.33), may indicate another possibility: criminals. Additionally, a bald person is disqualified from participating in ritual. In the end, the common factor is clear: these people stand outside normal social parameters for participation in ritual, be it someone who has failed to fulfill his ritual obligations or someone more socially sanctioned. Beyond these concerns, however, this term may also refer to the Jain monks who walked about in the nude and are often defined by this practice.[10] Thus this passage would reflect the competition for patrons that the Brahmin authors must surely have felt in a culture with a diversity of religious experts.

This rule may offer another insight into the broader culture of ancestor worship. With reference to *Arthaśāstra* 3.20.16, which recommends a fine for anyone who feeds "contemptible Buddhist or Ājīvika ascetics" at rites for the gods or ancestors,[11] James Egge says: "If this rule was formulated in response to actual practice, we may conclude that some laypeople and Buddhist monastics did regard *śrāddha*-rite rites observed by Brāhmaṇs and Buddhists to be the same rite, and did not see such rites as inherently Brahmanical, and therefore not Buddhist" (2002, 33). Vasiṣṭha's injunction similarly implies that the *śrāddha*-rite was not limited to Brahmins in practice, though lists such as his represent an effort impose such discrimination. The Brahmins did not want non-brahmanical religious experts encroaching upon what they considered their ritual domain. What is at stake here is the livelihood of the religious intermediary; experts in each tradition make the case for their religious expert as the best qualified for the rituals that householders perform.

In all these lists, the central characteristic to be sought in a Brahmin is learning. Vasiṣṭha reinforces this with his next *sūtra*. "Now, if a man who knows the Veda is afflicted with a bodily (defect) that corrupts those among whom he eats, Yama has declared him to be incorruptible; he certainly purifies those among whom he eats" (*VDhS* 11.20).[12] Learning is enough to overcome the detrimental effect of the bodily defects just listed, even those which would disqualify him from ritual performance or defile those who eat with the afflicted. In fact, the learning of a man who knows the mantras will purify those with whom he is seated at the *śrāddha*-rite. Such comparisons reinforce the priority of learning in evaluating the qualities of a Brahmin.

In addition to the question of quality the authors of the domestic manuals address the issue of quantity, though the aim is the same. In his Gṛhyasūtra, Āśvalāyana expresses the sentiment that the greater the number of Brahmins served, the greater the merit accrued thereby (4.7.3). While Gautama and Baudhāyana (*GDhS* 15.7–8; *BDhS* 2.14.6) advocate higher numbers of invitees, Vasiṣṭha takes a more different view, "Even a rich man should not indulge in feeding a large number" (*VDhS* 11.27, Olivelle 2000, 391).[13] Beyond advocating a view of moderation, this admonition against inviting too many, has the same aim as the passages about learning: to praise quality over quantity. He follows his admonition with reasoning.

> 28 A large number is detrimental to five things: offering proper hospitality, doing things at the right place and time, carrying out

> purifications, and finding Brahmins of quality. Therefore he should refrain from feeding a large number. 29 Or else, he may feed a single Brahmin who has mastered the Veda, is endowed with learning and virtue, and is free of any unfavorable bodily marks. *VDhS* 11.28–29 (Olivelle 2000, 393)[14]

Certainly, there is a degree of practicality behind this admonition of excess, but the primary intention is to praise the value of the quality of invitees over the quantity of invitees. While the practical concerns do exist, the primary purpose of inviting many Brahmins would be to receive greater merit, as Āśvalāyana tells us. Vasiṣṭha informs us that feeding a single Brahmin with the proper qualities is a better idea.

The emphasis on the qualities of the recipient appears in the section on gifts as well, with a similar escalation commensurate with the level of learning. "A gift bears an equal reward when it is given to a non-Brahmin, twice as much when given to a Brahmin, a thousand times as much when it is given to a vedic scholar, and an infinite reward when it is given to one who has mastered the entire Veda" (*GDhS* 5.20, Olivelle 2000, 133).[15] The escalation correlates to the increase in the value placed on the type of knowledge possessed by the invitee, not the number; in this way the author further nuances the discussion over the qualities of Brahmins to be invited. The concern over the quality of Brahmins invited to a *śrāddha*-rite intensifies again in the *Law Code of Manu*, further illustrating the increase of that concern over time.

With respect to the number of invitees, Manu agrees with Vasiṣṭha, who outlines the problems one encounters with too many invitees (*MDhŚ* 3.125–126). The context, immediately before the section addressing the qualities of the Brahmin invitees, however, suggests that Manu's intention is the same as Vasiṣṭha's: to praise the quality of Brahmins over the quantity. In similar manner, Manu asserts, "Should he feed just one learned (Brahmin) at a divine or ancestral (rite) instead of many who do not know the Vedas, he obtains abundant fruit" (*MDhŚ* 3.129).[16] Manu's intent, like Vasiṣṭha's, does not preclude the practical proscription against excess, but it does serve to heighten the importance of the qualities of the Brahmins. While the quantity of Brahmins is considered less important that the quality, Manu does not restrain himself in addressing those qualities at length. Whereas no Dharmasūtra author uses more than five *sūtras* to enumerate the positive qualities sought, Manu employs twenty-one verses. The concerns are not different, Manu simply goes into greater detail on much of the same concerns; his primary concern too is the learning of the Brahmins invited to the *śrāddha*-rite.

The lists of Brahmins unfit for invitation are also considerably longer than his predecessors' as well. While Gautama's list—forty-three types of people (*GDhS* 15.16–19)—dwarfs the lists in other Dharmasūtras, Manu lists ninety-six (*MDhŚ* 3.150–168), complete with a partial list of the effects of giving food to such people (*MDhŚ* 3.174–182). The length and details of the list imply that his concern over the proper qualifications of the ritual expert was far greater as well. In addition to listing far more disqualifications, Manu felt the need to detail the negative results derived from inviting such people. The lists make clear Manu's aim: to disqualify all but the best Brahmin for this role; this certainly excluded ritual experts from other traditions. Giving to the children of wrongful unions, that is, mixed caste marriages, negate the benefits of performing the ritual, as does giving to traders. Others in the list bring worse results. Certain unfit invitees negate the effect of those qualified Brahmins next to whom they are seated at the *śrāddha*-rite or other ritual. Manu makes it clear that the rules about who is invited apply equally to rituals oriented toward the gods and those oriented toward the Ancestors (*daive pitrye ca*) (3.129), but the fact that these lists occur in the section dedicated to explaining the ancestral rites indicates the association of these qualifications with ancestor worship.

Manu also addresses those who, rather than negating beneficial effects, cause detriment to the offering to the Ancestors. Food given to the seller of Soma is not food; by the time it reaches the Ancestors it is excrement (3.180). The physician, the temple priest, and the usurer likewise taint the offerings made to them (3.180). The quality of the invitee influences the offerings made to that person. The sin of selling Soma taints the person and any ritual transaction in which they partake. The impurity necessary for a physician carries over into any role he takes in a ritual. This section reinforces not only the importance of the quality of the Brahmins invited, as it is through them that the Ancestors receive the offerings, but more importantly how dangerous it would be to invite a on-Brahmin to a *śrāddha*-rite.

Given this sentiment and the value placed on learning, the hyperbole surrounding the detriment of giving food to someone ignorant of the Veda is not surprising, "The departed man eats as many red-hot spikes, spears, and iron balls as rice-balls that the man ignorant of the Vedas eats at the divine and ancestral offerings" (*MDhŚ* 3.133).[17] As with the Soma seller and the physician, those ignorant of the Veda do not merely fail to mediate between the performer of the *śrāddha*-rite and his Ancestors, he actually taints the transfer, ruining the food that sustains the Ancestors.

The details of different authors' lists diverge, but they all assume that the recipient determines the efficacy of the offering made to the Ancestors; that is, that the mediator is responsible for the successful, or unsuccessful, transfer effected in the ritual. Manu makes this clear in his praise of Brahmins more generally.

> 85 A gift to a non-Brahmin brings an equal reward; to a Brahmin by name, a double reward; to one who is advanced in vedic study, a thousand-fold reward; and to a man who has completely master the Veda, an infinite reward. 86 For, whether the reward a man received after death is large or small is contingent on his spirit of generosity and on the excellence of the recipient. *MDhŚ* 7.85–86[18] (Olivelle 2005, 158)

The comparative of the first verse and the explicit reference to the excellence of the recipient in the second verse demonstrate Manu's conviction that the recipient influences the reward of the offering made to him.[19] These verses belong to the sustained effort to emphasize the importance of the recipient of ritual gifts and to delegitimize any non-Brahmin ritual expert. This direct comparison explicitly undermines any authority that Manu's audience may have granted a non-Brahmin ritual expert, but the specifics of the negative effects—such as the extreme nature of the detrimental effects that one would open their Ancestors to—must have had a tremendous impact on the competition that underlies the generation of these lists.

The importance of these qualifications is underscored by the rule with which Manu concludes his section on fit invitees, "One who knows *dharma* would not investigate (the qualities of) a Brahmin at a divine ritual, but when he completes an ancestral ritual he should investigate diligently" (*MDhŚ* 3.149).[20] The Ancestors depend on the oblations given in the *śrāddha*-rite as food, one cannot be too careful then in assuring that they receive it. Additionally, this points to the importance and centrality of the ancestral rites in the householder tradition; the role of mediator between the householder and ancestors requires significant validation of the qualities of the recipient.

Understanding the Brahmin's role as mediator illuminates the reason for this regulation. The Brahmins fed at the divine rite do not actually mediate between the householder and the gods; Agni does. The Brahmins that are fed are present merely to facilitate, to add a degree of auspiciousness, and to proclaim the endeavor a success (e.g., *HGS* 2.7.17.13). The Brahmins who stand in for the Ancestors, however, are mediating for the Ancestors directly. Whereas one cannot question Agni's authority to act as mediator, the householder is enjoined to query the Brahmin about his qualities to ensure that he is qualified to act as mediator. Jamison's point, discussed earlier, that the regulations about guests at a *śrāddha*-rite aim to made him the "proper Aryan" is relevant here as well. The metaphor connecting the Brahmin guest to Agni invests the Brahmin with the authority to act as mediator. The emphasis on the guest "representing the very type of the proper Aryan" (Jamison 1996, 183) would similarly serve to legitimize this new ritual expert and delegitimizing any expert outside the Brahmanical community.

Manu's enumeration of those Brahmins who purify the line of people among whom they sit when fed at the *śrāddha*-rite show a clear preference for Vedic learning. He praises men who know all the Vedas and expository texts; men who are descendent from Vedic scholars; those who have knowledge of the three Nāciketas fires, the Trisuparṇa verse, the six Vedāṅgas, or the Jyeṣṭha Sāmans; one who knows the meaning of the Vedas or one who teaches it (*MDhŚ* 3.183–186). The emphasis on the proprietary knowledge valued most by Brahmins occurs throughout. The concern over the recipient, and some of the details, match the Dharmasūtra lists of those who purify those whom they sit next to in the line to be fed (See *BDhS* 2.14.2–3 and *ĀpDhS* 2.17.22). As in the Dharmasūtras, the most common attribute that distinguishes one of these men is learning. Specifically, it is Vedic learning that set men apart as purifying.

The success of the rite that feeds the Ancestors depends on the guest's legitimacy, as the above list of mishaps caused by feeding the wrong persons illustrates quite vividly. This also highlights what is at stake in determining who is qualified, the material support offered to the religious expert by a patron. The Brahmin authors encourage a test of qualifications to reinforce that only learned Brahmins are qualified to mediator, that is, to exclude other who may be competing for the patronage of the householder.

This concern over the qualities of the mediator, seen in both traditions, supports my argument that the *śrāddha*-rite became the model for a new mode of religiosity—valuing gifting especially—one that is constructed by the theologians of both traditions. The concern over the quality of the invitees is not unique to the ancestral rites, but it finds its most ardent expression with respect to the offerings made to one's ancestors. The importance of the qualities of the mediator, the recipient of gifts in the subsequent tradition, increases over time.

The *dharma* literature's concern over the qualities of Brahmins invited to a *śrāddha*-rite increases dramatically in the subsequent tradition, i.e., the Epics and Purāṇas. The new importance granted this aspect of the *śrāddha*-rite is significant for understanding the efforts, and the parameters of those efforts, made by both Brahmins and Buddhists to secure the role of mediator. Additionally, the fact that this trend has a strong association with the *śrāddha*-rite early in its development suggests that the conception of ancestor worship was influential on the development of general models of religious patronage.

While the Brahmins and, as I will argue presently, the Buddhists share a conception of the role the religious expert plays and occupy the same discursive space in their efforts to define the most appropriate person to fill this role, they do so in a way that advocates their own ideology. The Brahmins, unsurprisingly, advocate Vedic learning. While sharing the emphasis on learning and moral character found in the Brahmanical literature, Buddhist reflections on the proper religious expert value different kinds of knowledge, that more relevant to the Buddhist worldview. The discourse on the proper religious expert indicates explicit competition for the patronage of the householder. The Brahmins and the Buddhists are marketing themselves as the heir to Agni.

The Buddha and Human Mediation

The success of Buddhism certainly follows from its success in finding a niche to fill in the social milieu of its time. One important role for religious specialists in a ritual culture was the role of mediator, and Masefield argues forcefully that the Buddhists made considerable effort to take on this role.[21] When reading the Pāli Canon for evidence of the authors' concern about mediation, one can detect two distinct tactics, though some passages employ both. First, the Buddhist authors often endeavor to devalue the Brahmin as an effective recipient of religious offerings. Second, the authors work to substitute the Buddha or the Saṅgha for the older mediator, that is, Agni, and establish both as effective recipients. The first is a general trend to undermine the authority of the Buddhists' rivals,[22] the intellectual elites among Brahmins who claim special knowledge and moral superiority and through those the role of mediator. This effort operates on the same level as the Brahmanical effort to define the appropriate invitee, that is, the Buddhists engage the

Brahmins in a character debate. In the second tactic, the authors appropriate Agni's role for the Buddha, as the Brahmins did with the learned Brahmin in the domestic rites to the Ancestors. That substitution involves a strategic use of language and metaphor to transfer the power before associated with the fire to a human agent, specifically the Buddha, or the Saṅgha in his place.

In the light of this strategic effort to appropriate the role of mediator, we can more fully understand the purpose of the many disparaging comments about contemporary Brahmins in the Pāli Canon. The authors commonly compared Brahmins to the Sages of old (*ṛṣi*); the Brahmins never benefit by the comparison.

> [The Buddha:] Now what think you, Ambaṭṭha? What have you heard when Brahmans, old and well stricken in years, teachers of yours of their teachers, were talking together—did those ancient Rishis, whose verses you so chant over and repeat, parade about well groomed, perfumed, trimmed as to their hair and beard, adorned with garlands and gems, clad in white garments, in the full possession and enjoyment of the five pleasures of sense, as you, and your teacher too, do now?
>
> [Ambaṭṭha:] Not that, Gotama.
>
> [The Buddha:] Or did they live, as their food, on boiled rice of the best sorts, from which all the black specks had been sought out and removed, and flavoured with sauces and curries of various kinds, as you, and your teacher too, do now?
>
> [Ambaṭṭha:] Not that, Gotama.
>
> [The Buddha:] Or were they waited upon by women with fringes and furbelows round their loins, as you, and your teacher too, do now? Or did they go about driving chariots, drawn by mares with plaited manes and tails, using long wands and goads the while, as you, and your teacher too, do now? Or did they have themselves guarded in fortified towns, with moats dug out round them and crossbars to let down before the gates, by men with girt with long-swords, as you, and your teacher too, do now?
>
> [Ambaṭṭha:] Not that, Gotama.
>
> [The Buddha:] So then, Ambaṭṭha, neither are you a Rishi, nor your teacher, nor do you live under the conditions under which the Rishis lived. *D* i.104–5 (Rhys Davids 2007, 129–130)

The Buddha's admonition of Ambaṭṭha emphasizes the standard of living of contemporary Brahmins; he purports to hold the Brahmin up to his own standard, then shows that he is lacking.

The comparisons sometimes employed more direct attacks, openly criticizing the Brahmins for lacking the virtues they themselves held most high. Elsewhere Kaccāna addresses a rowdy group of pupils, and their teacher the Brahmin Lohicca.

> Foremost in virtue were the men of old,
> Those Brahmins who remembered ancient rules.
> In them well guarded were the doors of sense.
> They had achieved the mastery of wrath.
> In meditation and the Norm they took delight,
> Those Brahmins who remembered ancient rules.
> But these backsliders with their "Let us recite,"
> Drunk with the pride of birth, walk wrongfully.
> O'ercome by wrath, exceeding violent,
> They come to loss 'mongst weak and strong alike.
> Vain is the penance of the uncontrolled,
> Empty as treasure gotten in a dream. *S* iv.117
> (Woodward 1996b, 74)

Kaccāna harkens back to a better time, when Brahmins were virtuous, then opines about the lack of virtue in contemporary Brahmins. Those Brahmins, the backsliders of today, fail in their attempts to live up to that standard. Kaccāna criticizes both the character of the Brahmins and their preoccupation with the importance given to "Brahmins by birth."[23] The phrase "Let us recite" *(japāmase)* is a sarcastic reference to the recitation of the Veda, which is disparaged as rote memorization. Richard Gombrich (1992) and Oliver Frieberger (2009) have both explored the use of humor in disparaging Brahmins. Frieberger is explicit about the uses to which such comparisons—in his example Brahmins are compared to dogs and found lacking—these texts are "resources that could be used by Buddhist monks and nuns for propaganda purposes, to attract followers, and to reinforce their own religious identity" (61–62). The Buddhist author undermines the Brahmanical authority by devaluing their claims to moral character and religious learning, substituting their own definition of the proper values in the process.

The qualities of the recipient of a charitable act is of supreme importance; those qualities ensure that the act is effective and beneficial to the donor. Thus the aim of this systematic discrediting of the contemporary Brahmins is clear: the Buddhist authors tried to establish the Saṅgha as the preferable choice as a recipient of meritorious giving. In addition to calling the Brahmins' character into question, they establish the Buddha and the Saṅgha as equal to the task of the older mediator, Agni, or the contemporary ones, Brahmins.

The Buddhist author "employs vocabulary and concepts borrowed from the Vedic tradition to attribute meaning to the act of giving" to the Saṅgha (Egge 2002, 19). In doing so they equate the giving of alms to the Saṅgha with sacrifice and the rewards of the former are implied to be equal to or better than the latter. Like the Brahmins, the Buddhist authors looked to the ritual fire as an exemplar intermediary. The Buddha is identified with the sacrificial fire in the *Theragāthā*, "I sacrifice to the fire worthy of the donation/gift (*dakkhiṇeyya*); I venerate the Tathāgata" (*Thag* 343cd).[24] This relies on the ideology of gifting; the donation/gift (*dakkhiṇā*) derives from the sacrificial gift (*dakṣiṇā*) of the Vedic ritual model (White 1986), which was the model for the later practice of giving. Additionally, this parallels the Brahmanical substitution of the Brahmin for the fire seen above in the *śrāddha*-rite ritual of the *Āpastamba Dharmasūtra* (*ĀpDhS* 2.16.3).

Beyond this substitution, which employs the tropes and metaphors of ritual to facilitate the transition, the later tradition evidences the simple assertion that the Buddha or the Saṅgha are the proper recipients of gifts, particularly of gifts to the deceased. In the "Ghost Story of the Biscuit Doll" in the *Petavatthu* (*Pv* 1.4), gifts, specifically the offerings of the *śrāddha*-rite in this context, established in the Saṅgha will benefit the intended recipient, "But this donation, firmly established in the Saṅgha, will immediately serve to benefit them for a long time" (*Pv* 1.4.13). More significant is the second story reviewed, "The Ghosts Outside the Walls" (*Pv* 1.5), in which the Buddha informs the King that offerings made to him, if dedicated to his ancestors, would reach them. The Buddha explicitly states his role as mediator between the living and the dead, between a householder and a supernatural being.

The nexus of this theological understanding of the efficaciousness of giving gifts rests on the qualities of the recipient, the Buddha being the most qualified of all recipients, as is shown throughout the Pāli Canon (Amore 1971). That notion often finds expression in the metaphor of a field.

Intersections: The Field of Merit

As in Brahmanical thought, the idea that the benefit yielded from a gift rests on the merit of the recipient finds repeated expression in the Buddhist materials (Dhammapāla 1989, xxvii–xxviii). In the *Petavatthu* we find this sentiment expressed in the mouth of Aṅkura, who is suffering due to his lack of gifts. "As a seed planted on a sterile field, even many (seeds), neither becomes abundant fruit nor please the planter, Just like a plentiful gift, bestowed upon one of bad moral character, neither becomes abundant fruit nor pleases the giver" (*Pv* 2.9.68–70).[25] This metaphor is shared by Brahmin and Buddhist authors alike; Manu expresses it this way,[26] "142 Just as when the sower sows seeds in barren soil he obtains no fruit, when the giver gives an oblation to one who doesn't know the *Ṛg Veda* he obtains no fruit. 143 When he gives the sacrificial gift given to a learned man according to the rules he makes the giver and the receiver share in the fruit here in this world and in the hereafter" (*MDhŚ* 3.142–143).[27] That both a Buddhist and a Brahmin author employ this metaphor is not surprising in itself, but it does strengthen the sense that both authors occupy a single discursive space; they are engaged in the same exercise of ideology construction, sometimes using the same language (See Masefield in Dhammapāla 1989 and Egge 2002, 15–39). They agree that the recipient of religious gifts should be qualified and go to great lengths to show that the religious expert of their tradition is best qualified.

Another example of this overlap in argumentative style and substance occurs in the formula that describes the Buddha as the unsurpassed field of merit,[28] clearly derived from the above metaphor. In the *Suttanipāta* the Buddha is called "the unsurpassed field of merit, the sacrificial recipient for all the world," and "what is given to the Blessed One yields great fruit" (*Sn* 486).[29] The analogy of the field and seed is combined with the sacrificial imagery; the threads are woven together—as Manu did with the two soteriological threads that he inherited—resulting in a formula that emphasizes the effectiveness of the Buddha, and by extension the Saṅgha, as mediator. By combining the metaphor of the seed with the sacrificial terminology the Buddhist author taps into two themes that resonate strongly in this culture; the effect associates the Buddha—and the Saṅgha—with the efficacious modes of mediation.

The formula occurs in many places throughout the Pāli Canon, in a consistent fashion, for example, "The Assembly of Disciples of the Lord is worthy of sacrifice, worthy of hospitality, worthy of offerings, worthy of veneration, an unsurpassed merit-field for the world" (*A* 1.208).[30] This formula is constructed to demonstrate the Saṅgha's qualification for all manner of religious gift, all the possible ways that a religious expert could mediate for the householder. The appellation worthy of sacrifice (*āhuṇeyyo*) indicates that the Saṅgha is worthy of accepting the offering made in sacrifice. The term for worthy of hospitality (*pahūṇeyyo*) indicates that the Saṅgha, not only Brahmins, are also worthy of hospitality and, more significantly, are capable of bestowing the merit derives from offerings hospitality. The third term worthy of donations/gifts (*dakkhiṇeyyo*) indicates that the Saṅgha qualifies for the sacrificial gift of the Vedic tradition and those gifts modeled on the older sacrificial gift, as discussed previously. The last descriptor worthy of veneration (*añjalinaraṇīyo*) refers to the veneration due a teacher. The sum of these appellations indicates that the Saṅgha is justified to serve as religious expert for any form of religious ritual one might choose to perform.

The term *āhuṇeyyo* derived from the same verb, *hu*, as is the Sanskrit term *āhavanīya*, the name of the eastern fire of the Vedic ritual; this explicitly associates this aspect of the field of merit formula with the Buddhist efforts to substitute the Saṅgha for Agni as mediator. Here the deployment of sacrificial terminology is most clear; the verb *ā-hu*, seen in such passages as *ŚBM* 11.2.2.6, quoted above, is central to the language used to describe sacrifice. The Buddhist authors cleverly constructed this formula to advertise their equality with, if not superiority to, Brahmins as effective recipients of all sorts of religious offerings: One stop for all your merit-making needs.

It is impossible to say with any degree of accuracy the relative dating of the texts from which I have drawn data, that is, we cannot say definitively whether Buddhist authors are contemporaneous with the composition of the Gṛhyasūtras, or are much later and reflecting on a developed domestic ritual tradition. It is clear, however, that elements of the discursive construction of the religious expert qualified to act as mediator between the householder and the gods and the Ancestors appear in both traditions. The degree of overlap in the approach, language, and concerns of both traditions' texts strongly suggests that the Brahmin and Buddhist authors both constructed the notion of a human mediator from similar preconceptions. Further both actively sought to construct the category in a way that favored their conception of the role of religious expert, that is, they were doing the same thing, with the same tools, namely, trying to woo the householder as patron.

The influence of the model of mediation that develops in the Gṛhyasūtra's descriptions of the *śrāddha*-rite—a model reinforced and given new prominence in the *dharma* literature—had a significant influence on the development of the role available to the religiously educated. Brahmin authors participated in the early construction of the new role for religious experts to play as they reflected on the common practice of ancestor worship and the Vedic models of ritual propitiation of, among others, the Ancestors. Buddhist authors joined the conversation about the proper religious life for a householder and shaped for themselves a central role in the ritual duties that the householder sought to fulfill. In both traditions the development of new modes of religious behavior included the practice of religious giving. The *śrāddha*-rite had a significant influence on the conception of mediation that characterized the transition from the Vedic model of sacrifice and the later model of religious practice, one factor of which was an emphasis on religious giving (*dāna*).

In the Buddhist tradition, the emphasis on ancestral rites per se erodes quite early in the tradition. Already in the *Petavatthu* the notion of filial piety is still strongly felt in some places, but less so in other stories. The notions of *karma* and reincarnation and the *dāna* tradition subsume the cultural memory of the ancestral offerings in the Buddhist texts. Yet, in the Hindu tradition the performance of the *śrāddha*-rite persists despite a strong *dāna* tradition and the growing acceptance of reincarnation. The defense mounted by the *dharma* authors strengthened the soteriology that aims at an eternal heaven and advocates the propitiation of the Ancestors through ritual, ensuring its survival to the present day.

Conclusion

THE RITUAL TEXTS of the Brahmanical tradition include a strong tradition of ancestor worship, but the inheritance is not simply passed down from generation to generation. The authors of each subsequent genre contribute to the collective reflection on the practice of ancestral offerings and discuss the practice of ancestral rites more frequently. As the Vedic religion developed into Classical Hinduism, the rituals of ancestor worship became more central to the understanding of the proper religious life and the development of a new religious expert that was central to this redefinition was instrumental in the development of Classical Hinduism.

The inclusion of the funerary hymns near the end of the *R̥g Veda*, a text primarily employed in the Soma ritual, shows the earliest example of this broadening interest. The two ancestral rites described in the Brāhmaṇas and the Śrautasūtras, the *pitr̥yajña* and the *piṇḍapitr̥yajña*, demonstrate the inclusion of ancestral rites in the literary conversation about solemn ritual and the infusion of domestic ritual elements into the solemn ritual cycle. The *piṇḍapitr̥yajña* orients the Sacrificer and his desires toward the Ancestors. It represents the integration of elements of the domestic propitiation of the Ancestors and the most common structural elements of the Vedic model of sacrifice. The *pitr̥yajña* more closely follows the paradigmatic ritual procedure described throughout the Brahmanical material yet retains its concern with appeasing the Ancestors. While the former integrates ancestor worship loosely into the solemn model of sacrifice, the latter more comprehensively synthesizes the impulse to honor the dead into the solemn modes of worship. Neither integration is abrupt or smooth; a review of the ritual terminology and its use in the Saṃhitās and Brāhmaṇas indicates a slow, uneven process of synthesis.

The authors of the domestic ritual manuals, the Gr̥hyasūtras, draw upon the dual traditions of ritual practice—the solemn ritual tradition formalized in the Brāhmaṇas and the Śrautasūtras and untextualized domestic tradition of ancestor worship—in the textualization and codification of the domestic ritual obligations. The authors invoke the Vedic models as paradigmatic structures for ritual practice, which is evidence of the infusion of solemn ritual elements into the domestic ritual, but the authors begin to undermine the monopoly of the Vedic priest. They grant the Sacrificer the responsibility of the primary ritual actor, minimizing the role of Vedic priests. Simultaneously, the Brahmin authors created a new role, that of professional guest, who was central to the efficacy of the rites. Despite the fact that the householder was able to perform the rites largely on his own, the role that Brahmins constructed for themselves played a key role in the conception of domestic ritual obligations. Nearly every rite in the domestic ritual manuals involves feeding a Brahmin. Working within the long-established literary tradition, the authors were able to authorize their new role as a culmination of the older tradition, integral to the success of the proper religious life. These Brahmins created a cycle of ritual dependency and thereby established a livelihood for themselves, constructing a new role that would put them at the center of the religious life.

The process was not uniform, however. The process of integrating the domestic ritual practices into the educated discourse is visible in a review of the terminology used in the Gṛhyasūtras, including the label *śrāddha*, and in the gradual shift from employing Vedic rituals as prototypes to the establishment of the *śrāddha*-rite as the paradigmatic form of ancestor worship. The broader change from Vedic models of religious practice to those of Classical Hinduism is evident in the Gṛhyasūtras, especially in the context of ancestor worship.

Two threads in the Brahmanical discourse on ancestor worship contributed to both the shift in modes of religiosity and the increasingly central place that the *śrāddha*-rite took in the conception of the householder's ritual life: mediation and soteriology. While the Brahmin theologians constructed this new religious expert, which was often expressed in terms of mediation between the householder and the supernatural entities he wishes to propitiate through ritual, they grappled with two soteriologies. The Brahmanical authors increasingly associated the performance of the *śrāddha*-rite with the full spectrum of the benefits won through the Vedic rites, namely, prosperity, sons, long life, and heaven. In this way they advocated the heaven-oriented soteriology that is crucial to their role as ritual experts. In addition, these ritualist Brahmins actively resist synthesizing the notion of reincarnation, an ideology that undermined the centrality of ritual to the proper religious life. They championed the attainment of heaven, which required ritual participation, and through the construction of a new conception of ancestor worship authorized and integrated the new religious expert into the Brahmanical ideology. This ritually oriented religiosity came to shape the discourse on *dharma* for centuries.

In the Buddhist theological camp, a similar integration of the practice of ancestor veneration took place. They Buddhist authors drew upon the common conception of the householder's obligation to their ancestors under the influence of the Brahmanical formulations of the primary associations of ancestral offerings, that is, food, clothing, and housing. Gradually the authors of the Buddhists texts oriented the practice toward religious giving more broadly, though the cultural memory of the *śrāddha*-rite was still visible in the *Petavatthu*. Like the Brahmanical theologians, the Buddhist authors worked to redefine the role of the religious expert. In the period of the composition of the Gṛhyasūtras the Brahmins made efforts to advocate a role of professional guest instead of priest. Subsequently the Brahmins, in the *dharma* literature, and the Buddhists, in the Pāli Canon, worked to define the proper qualifications for the religious expert who was to take on the role of profession guest, the role of mediator.

While the Brahmanical and Buddhist texts point to the *śrāddha*-rite as one of several key factors central to the shift from Vedic to Classical Indian modes of religiosity, the developments in each tradition head in dramatically different directions in the early centuries of the first millennium C.E. The Brahmanical tradition begins to wrestle with the synthesis of the two soteriologies, the heaven-oriented soteriology of the ritualists and the liberation-oriented soteriology, which developed in the renunciation tradition, but won wide-spread acceptance across the subcontinent. In both the epics and the Purāṇas we first find efforts, though uneven and inconsistent, to integrate the notion of heaven won through ritual into the process of transmigration (Brockington 1998, 246–248 and Hill 2001, 42). The Buddhist literature, for example, the *Jāṇussoṇi Sutta*, shows that the Buddhists integrated the destination of the dead, *petivisaya*, with the possible realms of rebirth. That is, they had already, at least by the beginning of the Common Era, assimilated the heaven won through ritual into the transmigration process.

The centrality of ancestor worship to Classical and Contemporary Hindu practice is well known, though the early history is far more complicated than scholars have previously recognized. The specific developments within the Brahmanical literature with respect to the *śrāddha*-rite had a profound impact on the transition from Vedic to Classical modes of religious practice and helped fertilize the ground in which the seeds of the continuation of the Brahmanical hegemony were sewn. The householder was the primary religious consumer in ancient India and his main religious obligations—divine worship, ancestor worship, and hospitality—required a religious expert. While the Vedic literature enshrines internal conversations about a ritual cycle open to few, the *dharma* literature evidences an increasing concern with the *proper* definition of *dharma*. The Brahmins make a sustained effort to define the proper religious life and those efforts indicate a keen concern for securing their role as religious expert. The Buddhists marketed themselves as the primary competitor in a religious marketplace that was driven by consumer demands and shaped by theological discourse. Patrick Olivelle's (2004a) reimagining of the genesis of the *dharma* tradition within Brahmanical circles and Johannes Bronkhorst's (2007) efforts to describe the diverse cultural landscape in the second half of the first millennium for the Common Era show us that the Buddhists were not merely reacting to a hegemonic Brahmanical culture—there were, in fact, several different groups of Brahmins working to define the Brahmanical worldview. Instead, theologians in both traditions sought to define the religious life in their own terms in a religious milieu characterized by a complex ideological discourse involving several heterogeneous groups.

One way that they sought to define the proper life involved constructing for themselves the role of mediator, who would serve the needs of the householder seeking to fulfill his ritual obligations to guests with hospitality, to the gods with divine rites, and to his ancestors with the ancestral rites. The literature on ancestor worship highlights these efforts well and indicates at least one reason why those discussions were particularly relevant to ancestor worship. It is in these discussions that we see the most careful attention to the specific qualifications for the proper mediator, the effective mediator, and criticisms of the mediator who puts the householder's ritual obligations in danger. The competition for the patronage of the householder is strongest in the discussions of which religious expert will convey the householder's offerings to their ancestors. The repeated process of synthesis within the traditions of ancestor worship had a tremendous impact on the development of both Buddhism and Classical Hinduism.

Appendix

For readers interested in reading the fuller accounts mentioned in this text I emend this list, by no means exhaustive, of texts in which the rituals are described. I include references for editions and translations of the texts at the first citation of the text (unless otherwise noted, translations are in English).

pitṛyajña:

- *ṚV* 10.16 (Edition: Müller 1890. Translation: Brereton and Jamison, forthcoming; German: Geldner 1951; Griffith 1992 *outdated*. Selected translations: Doniger 1981.); *AVŚ* 12.2 (Edition: Roth 1924. Translation: Griffith 1963 *outdated*); *TS* 1.8.5 (Edition: Weber 1973. Translation: Keith 1967.); *MS* 1.10.3 (Edition: Schroeder 1970–1972); *ŚBM* 2.6.1.1–43 (Edition: Caland 1983. Translation: Eggling 1882–1900); *ŚBK* 1.6.1 (Edition: Caland 1983. Beyond a handful of clarifying notes, differences from the Mādhyaṃdina recension are almost exclusively limited to word choice or order.) *KB* 5.8–9 (Edition: Sarma 1968. Translation: Keith 1920.); *TB* 1.4.10; 1.6.8–10 (Edition: Mitra 1981; Kumar 1998. Selected translations: Dumont 1948; 1951; 1954; 1957; 1959; 1960; 1961; 1962; 1963a; 1963b; 1964; 1965; 1969.); *TĀ* 2.10 (Edition: Mitra 1982.); *ĀpŚS* 8.13.1–8.16.6 (Edition and translation: Thite 2004. Translation: German, Caland 1921.); *KŚS* 5.8.5–5.9.13 (Edition and translation: Thite 2006. Translation: Ranade 1978.); *ŚŚS* 3.16 (Edition: Hillebrandt 1981.); *BŚS* 5.11–17 (Edition and translation: Kāśīkar 2003.); *BhŚS* 8.16–23 (Edition and translation: Kāśīkar 1964.); *AśŚS* 2.19 (Edition: Vidyāratna 1874; Jha 2001.); *LŚS* 5.2; *MŚS* 1.7.6 (Edition: Kāśīkar 1985. Translation: Gelder 1963.)

piṇḍapitṛyajña:

- *ŚBM* 2.4.2.7–24; *ŚBK* 1.3.3 (Differences from the Mādhyaṃdina recension are almost exclusively limited to word choice or order.); *TB* 1.3.10–11; 2.6.3; *JB* 4.4.19–21; *ĀpŚS* 1.7–1.10; *KŚS* 4.1; *BŚS* 3.10–11; *BhŚS* 1.7–10; *ŚŚS* 4.3–5; *AśŚS* 2.6–7; *MŚS* 1.1.2

piṇḍadāna:

- *AB* 3.37.19 (Edition and translation: Haug 2003.); *KB* 16.2.15; 16.8.22; *ĀpŚS* 13.12.9–12; *ĀśŚS* 5.17.5–6; *BŚS* 8.17; *BhŚS* 14.12.1–3; *KŚS* 10.5.11–12; *LŚS* 2.10.4; *MŚS* 2.5.1.35–36; *ŚŚS* 8.2.13; *VaitS* 22.22–23

anvaṣṭakya:

- *ĀpGS* 8.22.9–12; *ŚGS* 3.13.7; *ĀśGS* 2.5.1–9; *GGS* 4.2–4.4.1; 2.5.15; *PGS* 3.3.10–12; *HGS* 2.5.15 (Edition: Āpastamba: Pandey 1971. Āśvalāyana: Gokhale 1978. Gobhila: Bhattacarya 1982. Hiraṇyakeśin: Kirste 1889. Pāraskara: Malaviya 1991. Śāṅkhāyana: Rai 1995. Translation: Oldenberg 1967.); *BGS* 2.11 (Edition: Sama Sastrin 1982.); *BhGS* 2.15 (Edition: Salomons 1981.); *KhGS* 3.5 (Text and translation: Oldenberg 1967.); *JGS* 2.3 (Edition and translation: Caland 1922)

śrāddha:

- *ĀpGS* 8.21–22; *ŚGS* 4.1–4; 5.9; *ĀśGS* 2.5.10–15; 4.7; *GGS* 4.4.2–26; *HGS* 2.4.10–13; *PGS* 3.10.1, 27, 46–55; *BGS* 2.11; 3.12; *BhGS* 2.11–14; 3.16–17; *JGS* 1.6; 2.1; 2.5; *ĀpDhS* 2.16.1–2.20.2; *GDhS* 15.1–30; *BDhS* 2.14.1–15.12; *VDhS* 11.16–44 (Edition and Translation: Olivelle 2000.); *MDhŚ* 3.122–286 (Edition and translation: Olivelle 2004b.); *YS* 198–270 (Edition and translation: Joshi 2005.); *Viṣṇusmṛti* 20.32–36; 21; 73–85 (Edition and translation: Olivelle 2009.)

Notes

INTRODUCTION

1. *Brahmin,* first and foremost, refers to the highest class in the *varṇa* system. I use it here most often to refer to those educated Brahmins who composed the texts I have read to understand their world.
2. The term *dharma* has been variously translated as duty, Law, religion, etc.; it refers to the proper behavior as determined by various aspects of one's social identity, for example, gender, age, class. For a thorough understanding of the term see *Journal of Indian Philosophy* 32(5–6), a volume dedicated to the history of the term.
3. *bhojanābhyañjanād dānād yad anyat kurute tiliaḥ | śvaviṣṭhāyāṃ kṛmir bhūtvā pitṛbhiḥ saha majjatīti ||* Unless otherwise noted, all translations are my own.
4. Bronkhorst addresses the tension between these ideologies in a broader context (2007). Hill discusses the relationship between these two soteriologies in the Epic as "a process of coalescence and adjustment, with varying signs of tension" (2001, 42). One example of this tension appears in the *Viṣṇu Smṛti*: "Whether he is a god, in hell, an animal, or a human being, the ancestral offerings made by his relatives will reach him" (*devatve yātanāsthāne tiryagyonau tathaiva ca | mānuṣye ca tathāpnoti śrāddhaṃ dattaṃ svabāndhavaiḥ ||*) (*ViSmṛ* 20.35, Olivelle 2009, 79). See also *BrP* 1.28.88–91 and *GP* 2.10.20; for examples from the Epics, see Saindon 1999. The synthesis takes on a different tenor in the *Gayā Mahātmyā*, which repeatedly indicates that liberation (*mukti*) can be won through performance of the *śrāddha*-rite (e.g., *GM* 1.11–12). The tension between the two soteriologies is never completely resolved, but, as Parry (1994) remarks, this does not bother Hindus, "The lack of consistency between these eschatological theories does not seem to bother my informants, who make little attempt to reconcile them—probably in part because they tend to invoke the

theory of rebirth to explain the present, and the theory of heaven, hell and salvation to visualize the future" (209).

5. For a diagram of the ritual space, see Jamison 1991, 19. For the expanded ritual space used in the Soma Sacrifice, as well as pictures of the implements employed, see Caland and Henry 1906–07, 1:Plates I–IV.
6. There is considerable scholarly debate over the identity of the plant originally used in this rite; the classic text on the identity of the soma plant is Wasson 1968.
7. The tradition explains the sacrificial victim's willingness to participate in order to preclude violence from the sacrifice; see, for example, *ŚBM* 3.7.3.1–13.
8. It is common in the Epics and Purāṇas to speak of an activity as generating benefit equal to a Horse Sacrifice, e.g., *GM* 1.26, which indicates that the benefit derived from the *aśvamedha* arises with each step taken by a man on his way to the pilgrimage site (*pade pade 'śvamedhasya yatphalaṃ gacchato gayāṃ* | *tatphalaṃ ca bhavannṝṇāṃ samagraṃ nātra saṃśayaḥ* ||).
9. See Staal et al. (1983) and Gardner (1976) for the 1975 performance of the Agnicayana.
10. Indra's weapon is often said to be a thunderbolt, but descriptions and effects of its use vary (see Macdonell 1995, 55).
11. For descriptions and citations for the various gods, see Macdonell 1995 and Oldenberg 1894. For an example of mythic exegesis from the Vedic texts, see Jamison 1991.
12. There were diverse worldviews within the Brahmanical tradition; see Olivelle1993, 35f; 2006b, 2011; Heesterman 1982; Bronkhorst 2007, 77f. For the perspective of the non-Brahmanical groups within the *śramaṇa* groups, see Jaini 1970; Dutt 1970; Long 2009, 29–56; Chakravarti 2009; Varma 1960. For the Buddhist perspective on contestation between Brahmins and Buddhists, see Black 2009 and Frieberger 2009; 2011. Thapar (1982) compares the householder-renouncer dichotomy in the Brahmanical and Buddhist traditions.
13. For a summary of the three most common theories for the origins of the *śramaṇa* movement, see Long 2009, 45–55.
14. This is a gross simplification of the complicated nature of the practices and aims of, as well as the relationship between, the laity and monastics. For more detail, see Samuels 1999 and Schopen 1997a, 1997b.
15. In addition, *M* ii.186 and *A* iii.45 describe the householder's ritual obligations in broad terms.
16. I am aware of the dangers posed by relying only upon or privileging textual sources over others—which is well-articulated by Schopen (1997c)—but the nature of ritual in the period under discussion leaves almost no material remains, thus the reliance on textual sources is unavoidable.
17. For more detail on the nature of *sūtra* literature, see Gonda 1977b, 1980, Oldenberg 1967, and Olivelle 2000.

18. Gonda (1977b) gives a detailed review of the scholarly views on the dating of all the *sūtra* texts (465–488). For the Gṛhyasūtras, see pp. 478–479.
19. This period "between the empires" of the Mauryans and the Guptas is the subject of an anthology bearing that name (Olivelle 2006a). In the preface, the editor says this period "saw unparalleled developments within the Indian subcontinent, developments that defined the classical Indian culture and society" (v).
20. The dating of Dhammapāla is very complex. In fact, Cousins posits three different authors for the works generally ascribed to Dhammapāla, one in the sixth century, one probably in the seventh century C.E., and the last circa 960 C.E. (Cousins 1972, 163 and passim).
21. The word *piṇḍa* means lump, ball, or clod; it can be made of anything, but it has a particular association with the rice-balls offered in the ancestral rites. The rice offerings made into *piṇḍas* are commonly mixed with other materials, for example, barley (*yava*, e.g., *ŚGS* 4.4.9–10) and meat (*māṃsa*, e.g., *GGS* 4.2.13). In the classical period the term also comes to mean food more generally.
22. In reaction to Keith's suggestion that priestly assimilation of popular rites explains the inclusion of domestic ritual in the Vedic corpus, Smith suggests it is "just as possible to posit an 'Aryan' or 'priestly' origin for domestic ritualism as not…" (1986, 80).
23. In his study of saints in Latin Christianity, Peter Brown shows that the "popular" is not monolithic and unchanging and a model that relies on the elite-popular dichotomy "has the disadvantage that it assumes that 'popular religion' can be understood only from the view point of the elite" (1981, 19).
24. For example, *ṚV* 1.1, in which Agni is called domestic chaplain (*puróhita*), priest (*ṛtvíj*), and *hótṛ*, (*agním īḷe puróhitaṃ yajñásya devám ṛtvíjam | hótāraṃ ratnaghā́tamam* |).

CHAPTER 1

1. The term also occurs only once in the *Atharva Veda* (12.2.7) in a borrowing of *ṚV* 10.16.10.
2. In addition to one's own power (*eigenkraft*), Mayrhofer also says that it refers to the invigorating drink (*labetrank*) offered in ritual, which is later accompanied by the ritual call *svadhā* (*KEWA*, 3:559). Similarly, Oldenberg translates the term *Geisterspeise*, though he considers it related to the broader meaning, which he glosses *Selbstbestimmung* (1894, 531n2). I will argue that these senses are later developments.
3. *gárbham ā́ dadhuḥ*
4. *purū́ rétāṃsi pitṛ́bhiś ca siñcataḥ*
5. For a discussion of the many classes of *pitṛs*, see *HoD* 4:340–351.
6. In the later tradition destination of the deceased is called the world of the Ancestors (*pitṛloká*), e.g., *ŚBM* 12.7.3.7; *PB* 5.4.11; *TB* 1.3.10.10, but in the Ṛg

Veda it is referred to as heaven (e.g., *paramé vyòman*, *ṚV* 10.14.8; *mádhye diváḥ*, 10.15.14). The authors of the *Kauṣītati Brāhmaṇa* seem to be keenly aware of the difference between the heavenly realm of the Ancestors and the heaven in which the gods dwell; they mention Ancestors moving from the *pitṛloká* to the *devaloká* by means of ritual offerings (*KB* 5.9.18–19; 16.5.25–26; 16.8.28). Despite the occurrence of the compound *pitṛloká* in the Śaunaka recension of the *Atharva Veda* (14.2.52), it does not carry the sense of the heavenly home of the Ancestors; elsewhere the poets refer to that place without using the compound (*AVŚ* 3.29.4; 6.117.3; 12.2.9; 12.2.45; 18.1.55; 18.2.25; and 18.3.73) (See also Bodewitz 1999). Bodewitz's (1994) excellent study makes clear the different destinies of the dead in the *Ṛg Veda*, I am here interested only in the destination of those conceived of as *pitṛ́s*, which, according to Bodewitz, belong to the latest layers of the *ṚV* and are therefrom borrowed by the authors of the *AVŚ*.

7. *kravyā́d agníṃ prá hiṇomi dūráṃ yamárājño gachatu ripravāháḥ | iháivā́yám ítaro jātávedā devébhyo havyáṃ vahatu prajānán* || 9 *yó agníḥ kravyā́t pravivéśa vo gṛhám imáṃ páśyann ítaraṃ jātávedasam | táṃ harāmi pitṛyajñā́ya deváṃ sá gharmám invāt paramé sadhásthe* || 10 *yó agníḥ kravyavā́hanaḥ pitṛ́n yákṣad ṛtāvṛ́dhaḥ | préd u havyā́ni vocati devébhyaś ca pitṛ́bhya ā́* || 11 *uśántas tvā ní dhīmahy uśántaḥ sámidhīmahi | uśánn uśatá ā́ vaha pitṛ́n havíṣe áttave* || 12
8. In his thorough and convincing analysis of this term and its varying interpretations, Findly connects Jātavedas to several aspects of Agni's relation to the Sacrificer, including the continuity of the family. He argues that it means "in whose possession are the creatures" (1981, 353) and suggests that "Jātavedas responds to the need for assurance of the familial continuity as it is based in an effective ritual," and this refers both to the acquisition of wealth through ritual and the care and transformation of the deceased to the status of ancestor (373).
9. Poleman suggests that *ṚV* 10.15.1–8 most closely resembles the later rite of *sapiṇḍīkaraṇa śrāddha*-rite, but the hymn under discussion better matches the aim of the transformation wrought in the later, domestic ancestral rite.
10. *ásūta pṛ́śnir mahaté ráṇāya tveṣáṃ ayā́sāṃ marútāṃ ánīkam | té sapsarā́so 'janayantā́bhvam ā́d ít svadhā́m iṣirā́ṃ páryapaśayan* ||
11. *tváṃ māyā́bhir ápa māyíno 'dhamaḥ svadhā́bhir yé ádhi śúptāv ájuhvata | tváṃ pípror nṛmaṇaḥ prā́rujaḥ púraḥ prá ṛjíśvānaṃ dasyuhátyeṣv āvitha* ||
12. *yád indrāgnī údítā sū́ryasya mádhye diváḥ svadháyā mādáyethe | átaḥ pári vṛṣaṇāvā́ hí yātám áthā sómasya pibataṃ sutásya* ||
13. *dáivyā hótārā prathamā́ ny ṛ̀ñje saptá pṛkṣā́saḥ svadháyā madanti | ṛtáṃ śáṃsanta ṛtám ít tá āhur ánu vratáṃ vratapā́ dī́dhyānāḥ* ||
14. *sá nídadhāti | yé rūpā́ṇi pratimuñcámānā ásurāḥ sántaḥ svadháyā cáranti parāpúro nipúro yé bháranty agníṣ ṭā́ṃ lokā́t prā́ṇudāty asmā́d íty agnír hí rákṣasām apahantā tásmād eváṃ nídadhāti* |
15. ...*tā́n abravīd yajñó vó 'nnam amṛtatváṃ vá ū́rgvaḥ sū́ryo vo jyótir íti* | 1...*tā́n abravīn māsí māsi vó 'śanaṃ svadhā́ vo manojavó vaś candrámā vo jyótir íti* | 2...*tā́n abravīt sāyám prātarvó 'śanam prajā́ vo mṛtyúr vo 'gnír vo jytótir íty* | 3

16. The passages in the funeral context that use the term *svadhā́* are 10.14.3; 10.14.7; 10.15.3; 10.15.12–14; 10.16.5; 10.17.8. I discuss only a few of these.
17. *mā́talī kavyáir yamó áṅgirobhir bŕ̥haspátir ŕ̥kvabhir vāvr̥dhānáḥ | yā́ṃś ca devā́ vāvr̥dhúr yé ca devā́n svā́hānyé svadháyānyé madanti ||*
18. *devébhyo havyáṃ vahatu*
19. *pitr̥yajñā́ya*
20. *préd u havyā́ni vocati devébhyaś ca pitŕ̥bhya ā́*
21. *svadhākāró hí pitr̥̄ṇā́ṃ…*
22. *ā́ham pitŕ̥̄n suvidátrān avitsi nápātaṃ ca vikrámaṇaṃ ca víṣṇoḥ | barhiṣádo yé svadháyā sutásya bhájanta pitvás tá ihā́gamiṣṭhāḥ ||*
23. Sāyaṇa understands *svadhā́* to refer to the food offered along with the Soma (*svadhayā puroḍāśadyannena*) (Müller 1890, 37).
24. *préhi préhi pathíbhiḥ pūrvyébhir yátrā naḥ pū́rve pitáraḥ pareyúḥ | ubhā́ rā́jānā svadháyā mádantā yamáṃ paśyāsi váruṇaṃ ca devám ||*
25. *áva sr̥ja púnar agne pitŕ̥bhyo yás ta ā́hutaś cárati svadhā́bhiḥ | ā́yur vásāna úpa vetu śéṣaḥ sáṃ gachatān tanvā́ jātavedaḥ ||*
26. For a detailed comparison of exactly which verses are borrowed from which hymns of the *R̥g Veda*, Whitney's synoptic statements at the beginning of each of the hymn in Book 18 are invaluable (Joshi 2000, 132–221).
27. Other examples of verses that occur in a funerary context but are used in the more general meaning of independent power are *AVŚ* 18.1.43; 18.3.8, 42; 18.4.39.
28. *apūpā́pihitān kumbhā́n yā́ṃs te deva ádhārayan | té te santu svadhā́vanto mádhumanto ghr̥taścútaḥ ||yás te dhānā́ anukirā́mi tilámiśrāḥ svadhā́vatīḥ | tā́s te santu vibhvī́ḥ prabhvī́s tā́s te yamó rā́jā́nu manyatām ||*
29. Though some do this very thing, e.g., Joshi 2000, 217.
30. *svadhākāréṇa pitŕ̥bhyo yajñéna devatābhyaḥ | dā́nena rājanyò vaśā́yā mātúr héḍaṃ ná gacchati ||*
31. *abhí tvórṇomi pr̥thivyā́ mātúr vástreṇa bhadráyā | jīvéṣu bhádraṃ tán máyi svadhā́ pitŕ̥ṣu sā́ tváyi ||*
32. *tā́ṃ kr̥táṃ lokáṃ abhí jāyate tásmād āhuḥ kr̥tá lokam púruṣo 'bhí jāyate íti |*
33. *asaṃbādhé pr̥thivyā́ uráu loké dhīyasva | svadhā́ yā́ś cakr̥ṣé jī́van tás te santu madhuścútaḥ ||*
34. In fact, the notion that ancestral rites secure a place in heaven for both the performer and the ancestor is common in the Purāṇas and, though less commonly, occurs in the *Mahābhārata*, but I have not seen this elsewhere in the earlier literature.
35. *vyā́karomi havíṣāham etáu táu bráhmaṇā vy aháṃ kalpayāmi | svadhā́ṃ pitŕ̥bhyo ajárāṃ kr̥ṇómi dīrghéṇā́yuṣā sám imā́nt sr̥jāmi ||*
36. *sódakrāmat sā́ pitŕ̥̄n ā́gacchat tā́ṃ pitára úpāhvayanta svádha éhī́ti | tásya yamó rā́jā vatsá ā́sīd rajatapātráṃ pā́tram | tā́m ántako mārtyavó 'dhok tā́ṃ svadhā́m evā́dhok | tā́ṃ svadhā́m pitára úpa jīvanty upajīvanī́yo bhavati yá eváṃ véda |*
37. *sáṃ gachasva pitŕ̥bhiḥ sáṃ yaméneṣṭāpūrténa paramé vyòman | hitvā́ yávadyáṃ púnar ástam éhi sáṃ gachasva tanúvā suvárcāḥ ||*

38. *té nò avantu pitáro háveṣu* | *R̥V* 10.15.1d This may have prompted Caland to suggest that the rituals of ancestor worship began as rites to these Ancestors, not the direct descendants of the Sacrificer (1893, 153).
39. *ūpahūtāḥ pitáraḥ... barhiṣyéṣu nidhíṣu priyéṣu*
40. *attā́ havī́ṃṣi práyatāni barhíṣy*
41. *áthā rayíṃ sárvavīraṃ dadhātana*
42. *tébhiḥ svarā́ḷ ásunītim etā́ṃ yathāvaśáṃ tanvā́ṃ kalpayasva*

CHAPTER 2

1. The references to ancestor worship in the Upaniṣads add nothing the historical development of the ritual. The remaining occurrences demonstrate merely an awareness of the ancestral rites, and they frequently occur in a narrative as a list that demonstrates a character's knowledge of ritual, or completeness of proper behavior remainder, e.g., *KaU* 3.17; *BU* 3.8.9; *CU* 2.22.2; 7.1.2, 4; 7.2.1; 7.7.1; *PU* 2.8; and *TU* 1.11.2.
2. Offerings to the Ancestors—called Giving Rice-Balls (*piṇḍadāna*)—also occur during the third pressing of Soma in the Agniṣṭoma (*KB* 16.2.15; 16.8.22; *ĀpŚS* 13.12.9–12; *ĀśŚS* 5.17.5–6; *BŚS* 8.12; *KŚS* 10.5.11–12; *LŚS* 2.10.4; *MŚS* 2.5.1.35–36; *ŚŚS* 8.2.13; *VaitS* 22.22–23), but these brief additions to the Soma ritual are abbreviated versions of the larger *piṇḍapitr̥yajña* (see Caland and Henry 1907, 350–352).
3. More often than not the Śrautasūtras include details not mentioned in the Brāhmaṇa of the same *śākhā*; contradictory instructions are rare. I include some variations in the notes.
4. This is a summary of the account given in *ĀpŚS* 1.1–3. Dumont (1957, 217–218) offers a similarly brief summary, and Kane has a much more detailed summary (*HoD* 2(2):1010–1085).
5. *triḥ phalīkaroti* | *KŚS* 2.4.22
6. For a far more detailed description of this rite, see *HoD* 2(2):1085–1090.
7. *sakr̥tphalīkaroti* | *KŚS* 4.1.8; see also *ŚBM* 2.4.2.13
8. Āpastamba (1.8.3–4) includes an oblation to Yama but recognizes that not all schools call for this. Unlike the Brāhmaṇas, Āpastamba instructs the Adhvaryu to switch his sacred thread for these two divinely oriented oblations. The only other mention of this in a discussion of the *piṇḍapitr̥yajña* appears in *ĀśŚS* 2.6.13, where an option is given with regard to the offering to Agni Kavyavāhana: the offering may be made, having switched the sacred thread and using *agni kavyavāhanāya svāhā* instead of the customary *agni kavyavāhanāya svadhā namaḥ*. *BŚS* 3.10 mentions this option as well, in the same context.
9. *ŚBM* 2.4.2.14; *ĀpŚS* 1.8.8; *KŚS* 4.1.9.
10. *...asāv avanenikṣva...* *KŚS* 4.1.10; *ŚGM* 2.4.2.16
11. *etat te tatāsau*. *ĀpŚS* 1.9.1

12. The *Śatapatha Brāhmaṇa* also explains that men, the gods, and the Ancestors eat together, but without seeing each other, whereas in the past they did so visibly: "And verily both the gods and men, and the Ancestors drink together, and this is their symposium; of old they drank together visibly, but now they do so unseen" (... *té ha smaitá ubháye devamanuṣyā́ḥ pitáraḥ sámpibante saìṣā́ sampā té ha sma dṛ́ṣyámānā evá purā sámpibanta utaìtaryádṛṣyamānāḥ*) (*ŚBM* 3.6.2.26, Eggeling 1882–1900, 155).
13. *ĀpŚS* 1.9.14–10.1; *BhŚS* 1.9.7–8. *KŚS* 4.1.17 mentions only the wool.
14. *Taittirīya Brāhmaṇa* differs in this, using the term *daśā,* as opposed to the *Śatapatha Brāhmaṇa,* which uses the term *nīvi.* Sāyaṇa glosses *nīvim udvṛhya* at *ŚBM* 2.4.2.24 with the phrase, "Having drawn out, i.e., having unfastened the fringe of his undergarment" (*paridhānīyasya vāsaso daśā tām udvṛhya visramsya*). The differences appear to follow the *śākhās,* though the association with clothing, which I will discuss later in the chapter, is the same.
15. At this point in the ritual Āśvalāyana describes a sequence of mantras used to praise the Ancestors, offering them reverence and invoking several emotions/aspects: strength (*ūrjā*), vigor (*śuṣmā*), terror (*ghora*), life (*jīva*), and sap (*rasa*) (*ĀśŚS* 2.7.7). This is an altered form of the same sequence that appears in *TB* 1.3.10.8.
16. Another innovation found first in the Śrautasūtras gives the Sacrificer an option of feeding the second rice-ball—which is dedicated to his grandfather—to his wife, in order to produce a son (*ĀpŚS* 1.10.10–11; *KŚS* 4.1.22; *ĀśŚS* 2.7.12–13).
17. *ĀpŚS* 1.10.16. *BhŚS* 1.10.5 also gives the option of throwing them in the fire. *ĀpŚS* 1.10.12 gives the Sacrificer the option of eating one of the rice-balls.
18. Āpastamba and Kātyāyana both suggest a diseased person will benefit from eating the remaining rice-balls (*ĀpŚS* 1.9.13 and *KŚS* 2.7.17).
19. Most authorities (*ĀpŚS, MŚS,* and *BhŚS*) indicate either of these two months, but Kātyāyana specifies Kārttika (*KŚS* 5.6.1). For the debate on how integral the rite is to the seasonal ritual, see Bhide 1979, 94.
20. The contrast between the waning and waxing moon in relation to the Ancestors is dealt with explicitly in reference to the *ābhyudayika śrāddha* in Chapter 4.
21. Sources disagree on whether it occurs in Bhādrapada or Aśvin, but it generally falls in October (Shastri 1963, 137–141).
22. For a more detailed description of this rite, see *HoD* 2(2):1101–1103.
23. Kātyāyana indicates this should happen to the east of the fire (*KŚS* 5.8.14).
24. In the *Śatapatha Brāhmaṇa* the remainder of the oblation is smelled by the Hotṛ, the Brahman, and the Āgnīdhra, in turn, but this remainder is not eaten (*ŚBM* 2.6.1.33).
25. *ĀpŚS* 8.16.8 also adds the instruction to wipe the portion of the material used to make the rice-balls that sticks to one's hands on the last corner; this is for the Ancestors beyond the great-grandfather.

26. The *Taittirīya Brāhmaṇa* (1.6.9.8) specifies that they are to move to the north and that they are to ask for forgiveness. *Śatapatha Brāhmaṇa* (*ŚBM* 2.6.1.38–39) specifies that they are to switch their sacred cords to the left shoulder and recite verses that praise Indra and Manas.
27. The priest circumambulates the altar three times as he sprinkles water to wash the Ancestors. The Kaṇva recension of the *Śatapatha Brāhmaṇa* explicitly connects the three circumambulations with the three Ancestors and adds that the point of this action is to signal the Sacrificer's return to his world (*sá yā́s trayā́n pitṝ́n anvaváiti tébhya evaìtát púnar apodetīmā́m abhí svā́ṃ lokám*) (*ŚBK* 1.6.1.28).
28. The *Taittirīya Brāhmaṇa* ends here, but *Śatapatha Brāhmaṇa* instructs the ritualists to switch their sacred threads again and concludes with a few closing offerings (*ŚBM* 2.6.1.43ff.).
29. *dakṣiṇāto varṣīyasīṃ prākpravaṇāṃ prāgukpravaṇāṃ vā* || *ĀpŚS* 2.2.9
30. *dakṣiṇāprāgagrair bhardakśiṇam agniṃ paristīrya*...|| *ĀpŚS* 1.7.5
31. *sakṛ́d ù hy èva párāñcaḥ pitáras*
32. E.g., *ŚBM* 2.6.1.24 *KŚS* 5.9.9–12; ĀpŚS 8.15.10–13; BhŚS 8.19.21–24; *BŚS* 2.15.4–5; *MŚS* 1.7.6.32–36. *ĀpŚS* 8.15.12 indicates that the *Ṛg-vedic* and *Vājasaneyi* traditions prohibit the *svadhā*-call, but this does not accord with those traditions, though *ŚBM* 2.6.1.25 mentions another authority that calls for the normal call and response.
33. *TB* 1.3.10.3 indicates there should be three offerings (*tisrá ā́hutīr juhoti*), the third of which, according to Sāyaṇa, is made to Yama. Yama's connection with the deceased, on the other hand, is obvious; he is the god of the dead. His inclusion in these rites may have cemented the association of these three with the Ancestors and further supported their inclusion in the Ancestor-oriented rite.
34. The *piṇḍapitṛyajña* is described in at least three of the Brāhmaṇas (*JB* 4.4.19–21, *ŚBM* 2.4.2, *TB* 1.3.10; 2.6.3) and the *pitṛyajña* can be found in three as well (*ŚBM* 2.6.1, *TB* 1.4.10; 1.6.8–10, *KB* 5.6).
35. *etat te tata*
36. *āñjanādi piṇḍapitṛyajñavad ā paṇktyāḥ*
37. This uncommon term appears at *ṚV* 10.15.11; *AVŚ* 18.3.44; *TS* 2.6.12.2 (which is identical to the previous); *ŚBM* 2.6.1.22; and *KB* 5.8.17. Outside a funerary context, the three types of Ancestors are invoked in the Sautrāmaṇī ritual to Indra (*ŚBM* 5.5.4.28).
38. *tad ye sómenejānāḥ | té pitáraḥ sómavantó 'tha yé datténa pakvéna lokaṃ yájanti té pitáro barhiṣadó 'tha ye 'tha táto nānyatarác cana yā́n agnír eva dáhantsv adáyati té pitáro 'gniṣvāttā́ etá u yé pitáraḥ ||*
39. *agniṣvāttā angina khāditā etatnāmakāḥ pitaraḥ*
40. One last bit of data that Caland offers obfuscates the terminological lines. "In der Vājasaneyisaṃhitā sind die ritualsprüche zu beiden opfern vorhanden; hier stehen sie neben einander; daher kann es nicht auffallen, dass hier der

pitṛyajña im gegensatz zum piṇḍapitṛyajña 'mahāpiṇḍpitṛyajña' genannt wird" (Caland 1893, 153). While *The Vājasaneyi Saṃhitā* does contain the mantras used in both the *pitṛyajña* and the *piṇḍapitṛyajña*, I was unable to find anywhere in the text the term *mahāpiṇḍapitṛyajña* or even the term *mahāpitṛyajña*. [Kane (1941, 1101), Eggeling (1882, 420n1), and Shastri (1963, 103) all attest this term for the *pitṛyajña*, all without a citation. I have found only three instances of this term—BŚS 5.11; *HŚS* 5.4; *VŚS* 9.4—though it is significant that it only occurs in a minority of the Śrautasūtras and never in any earlier text to my knowledge.] The presumption that Caland refers to the commentaries fails to bear fruit. Sāyaṇa does use the term *mahāpitṛyajña*, but not the other term. Uvaṭācārya refers only to the *pitryo 'adhyāya* not to the ritual itself and Mahīdhara, who does refer to the ritual, uses the term *pitṛmedha*—a term most frequently used to refer to the cremation and funeral (Paṇaśīkara 1992, 768–769). Even if this term is to be found, it would support the supposition that the *piṇḍapitṛyajña* is the basic, and the newer one is called the *mahā-* in order to praise it over the older model. The prefix *mahā-* is quite frequently a laudatory adjective; examples abound: *mahāyajña*, *mahāyāna*, etc.

41. For the multivalence of Vedic ritual see Thite 1975, 54 and en passim.

CHAPTER 3

1. For example, Oldenberg argues that the Gṛhyasūtras that treat the *pākayajñas* then turn to marriage are generally older (1967 2:xxxix). He shows that *KhGS* is dependent upon *GGS*, as is *HGS* upon *ĀpGS* (1:xxxvii). I have left out of my discussion Gṛhyasūtras that are generally agreed to be much younger, e.g., Vaikānasa and Agniveśya.
2. Authorities disagree on whether there are three or four *aṣṭakās* and in which months they occur (See Gonda 1980, 450–451).
3. For the later, more fully developed ancestral rites, see Knipe 1977 and *HoD* 4:334–551.
4. Oldenberg (1967, xxxi) indicates that the Śrautasūtra of the Atharva Veda tradition presupposes the Gṛhyasūtra of that tradition.
5. See *MŚS* 1.1.2.5
6. Nārāyaṇa, commenting on the *Āśvalāyana Gṛhyasūtra*, indicates that other Brahmins are also invited to represent the Vaiśvadevas.
7. . . .*'sāv etat te tilodakaṃ ye cā 'tra tvā 'nu yāṁś ca* | *GGS* 4.2.35
8. *agnau kariṣyāmīti āmantraṇaṃ hoṣyataḥ* | 38 *kurv ity ukte kaṁse carū samavadāya mekṣaṇeno 'paghātaṃ juhuyāt svāhā somāya pitṛmata iti pūrvāṃ svāhā 'gnaye kavyavāhanāya ity uttarām* | *GGS* 4.2.38–39
9. Khādira does not mention this in his Gṛhyasūtra. This is probably because Khādira is, in general, an abridgement of Gobhila (Oldenberg 1967, 1:371).
10. *atha pitṝn āvāhayaty eta pitaraḥ somyāsa iti* | *GGS* 4.3.4

11. …'sāv avanenikṣva ye cā 'tra tvā 'nu yāṁś ca tvam anu tasmai te svadhā…| *GGS* 4.3.6
12. …'sāv eṣa te piṇḍo ye cā 'tra tvā 'nu yāṁś ca tvam anu tasmai te svadhā…| *GGS* 4.3.8
13. If he does not know their names he offers with mantras to the Ancestors dwelling in the earth, the air, and heaven, respectively (*GGS* 4.3.10).
14. *apaparyāvṛtya puro 'cchavāsād bhiparyāvartamāno japed mīmadanta pitaro yathābhagam āvṛṣāyiṣate 'ti* | *GGS* 4.3.12
15. Gobhila also describes the householder asking for forgiveness with a series of mantras that offers reverence to the Ancestors and invokes several emotions/aspects: life (*jīva*), vigor (*śuṣmā*), terror (*ghora*), sap (*rasa*), independence (*svadhā*), and rage (*manyu*). Like that appearing in the *Āśvalāyana Śrautasūtra* (*ĀśŚS* 2.7.7) this is a version of those mantras that appear in *TB* 1.3.10.8. The borrowing across theological schools is one indication of the weakening of those boundaries that is occurring during the composition of the *Gṛhyasūtras*.
16. *gṛhan avekṣate gṛhān naḥ pitaro date 'ti* | 22 *piṇḍāṇ avekṣate sado vaḥ pitaro deṣme 'ti* | *GGS* 4.3.22–23
17. …'sāv etat te vāso ye cā 'tra tvā 'nu yāṁś ca tvam anu tasmai te svadhā…| *GGS* 4.3.24
18. *śvo 'nvaṣṭakāsu sarvāsāṃ pārṣvasakthisavyābhyāṃ parivṛte piṇḍapitṛyajṇavat* |
19. Pāraskara refers to them with the word *strī*, "(the ancestor's) wives." It is unclear if *pitṛ* was meant, in the older language, as a gender neutral term inclusive of the female ancestors, but it is first in the Gṛhyasūtras that their inclusion is explicit. Śāṅkhāyana refers to the householder's female ancestors as wives, *tatpatni* (*ŚGS* 4.1.11), in one place and *matṛ* in another (4.4.3), yet another indication of the fluid nature of these rites during this period. Later authors call the female ancestors *matṛs*, literally "mother" in imitation of *pitṛ*, "father," and this tradition increases in frequency in the subsequent literature, as evidenced in the *MBh* and several Purāṇas.
20. Oldenberg's (1967) cross references throughout his translation are invaluable in comparing the domestic and solemn rituals.
21. E.g., *ŚBM* 2.4.2.17; *TB* 1.3.10.5; *ĀpŚS* 1.7.4; *BhŚS* 1.7.8; *GGS* 4.2.20.
22. E.g., *ĀpŚS* 1.7.5; *KŚS* 4.1.2; *GGS* 4.2.20.
23. E.g., *ŚBM* 2.6.1.11; *ĀpŚS* 1.7.11; *BhŚS* 1.7.6; *GGS* 4.2.11.
24. E.g., *ŚBM* 2.4.2.24; *KŚS* 4.1.15; *ĀpŚS* 1.10.3; *GGS*4.3.22–23
25. E.g., circumambulating the altar before making an offering *ŚBM* 2.6.1.34; pouring out water to the left *ĀpŚS*1.8.11; *KŚS* 4.1.9; taking up the portions to be cut in his left hand *ŚBM* 2.6.1.35; *KŚS* 5.9.14; taking up the grass with his left hand *GGS* 4.3.2; placing the fire-brand with his left hand *GGS* 4.3.3; *KhGS* 3.5.13; meat for the rite is taken from the left thigh of the sacrificial animal *GGS* 4.1.5.
26. E.g., *ŚBM* 2.4.2.14; *ĀpŚS* 1.8.8; *KŚS* 4.1.8; *GGS* 4.3.3
27. E.g., *ĀpŚS* 1.10.11; *KŚS* 4.1.22; *MŚS* 1.1.2.31; *BhŚS* 1.10.8; *GGS* 4.3.27

28. E.g., *ŚBM* 2.4.2.21; *ĀpŚS* 1.9.9; *GGS* 4.3.12.
29. For example, *VS* 2.30 is used in *ŚBM* 2.4.2.14, *ĀpŚS* 1.8.7, *KŚS* 4.1.9, *ŚŚS* 4.4.2 and *GGS* 4.3.3, and a much distorted version appears in *MŚS* 1.1.2.8.
30. *pitṝn vā eṣa vikrīṇīte yas tilān vikrīṇīte* | ... *BDhS* 2.2.27
31. *ĀpŚS* 1.8.13; *KŚS* 4.1.8; *BhŚS* 1.7.8
32. *prādeśāyāmāś caturaṅgulapṛthivīs tathāvakhātāḥ* || *GGS* 4.2.17
33. *apūpamāṃsaśākair yathāsaṃkyam*
34. *mahāvyāhṛtayaś catasro ye tāṭṛṣur iti catasronudrutya vapāṃ juhuyād* |
35. *tasminn evāgnau śrapayaty edoanacaruṃ ca māṃsacaruṃ ca pṛthaṅ mekṣaṇābhyām prasvayam udāyvan* |
36. See Jamison 1996, 176–184, Bhattacarya 1971, Köhler 1973, Pendse 1977, and Rao 1974.
37. *karmāpavarge brāhmaṇabhojanam*
38. Smith demonstrates that *pākayajña* refers to domestic rituals and expresses the hierarchical relation between the solemn and domestic rituals, it does not mean, as some have supposed, cooked sacrifice (1986, 80). The comparison is between the small sacrifice (*pākayajña*) of the domestic tradition and the big sacrifice (*mahāyajña*) of the solemn domestic tradition (84).
39. *trayaḥ pākayajñāḥ hutā agnau hūyamānā anagnau prahutā brāhmaṇa-bhojane brahmaṇi hutāḥ*
40. See also *PGS* 1.4.1. and Baudhāyana, who lists seven *pākayajñas* (*BGS* 1.1.1).
41. *huto agnihotrahomenāhuto balikarmaṇā* | *prahutāḥ pitṛkarmaṇā prāśito brāhmaṇe hutaḥ* |
42. *annadhanadāne tv atrāniyate*
43. *agnau kariṣyāmīty āmantraṇaṃ hoṣyataḥ* | 38 *kurv ity ukte kaṁse carū samavadāya mekṣaṇeno 'paghātaṃ juhuyāt...*
44. *brāhmaṇān annena pariviṣya puṇyāhaṃ svastyayanam ṛddhim iti vācayitvātheitāṃ rātriṃ vasanti* |

CHAPTER 4

1. Brahmins are invited to attend the Ninth-Day Ancestral Offerings, and Oldenberg thinks that those Brahmins are thought to stand in for the Ancestors (1967, 2:105n33; 1:106n2), and this is likely the case. I discuss it in the context of the *śrāddha*, because the *śrāddha* texts speak to this point much more explicitly and the new ritual expert in the domestic rites and the specific burden this expert takes on in the ancestral rites merit separate discussion.
2. For a detailed description of this process and the ritual whereby it is effected, see Knipe 1977.
3. The *Caraka Saṃhitā* (8.40) lists materials used in the *nāndīmukha śrāddha*, which are gathered in the ninth month of pregnancy to prepare for the birth (Selby 2005, 269).

4. Śāṅkhāyana also describes the *sapiṇḍīkaraṇa* in the fifth *adhyāya* of the Pariśiṣṭa to the Gr̥hyasūtra (*ŚGS* 5.9).

5. Parry's treatment of the culture and industry of death in the sacred city of Banaras is an excellent source for understanding the relationship between the living and the dead in contemporary India. His treatment—including pictures—of the modern practice of the *śrāddha*-rites in that city is invaluable for those interested in the living tradition of *śrāddha* (1994, 191–222 and Plates 11–12).

6. For descriptions of this rite, see Lamb 2000, 169–176; Inden & Nichols 1977, 63–64; Das 1982, 122; Nicholas 1988, 375–376; Parry 1982, 84–85; 1994, 204–206.

7. Generally, this kind of statement refers to the *ābhyudayika śrāddha*, and it is possible that this is the origin of the *ābhyudayika*.

8. In addition, Śāṅkhāyana allows the householder to offer rice-balls to his mother, brother, or wife who has predeceased him (*ŚGS* 5.9.6).

9. *athāta ābhydayika* | 1 *āpūryamāṇapakṣe puṇyāhe* | 2 *mātr̥yāgam kr̥tvā* | 3 *yugmān vedavida upaveśya* | 4 *pūrvāhhr̥ṇe* | 5 *pradakṣiṇam upacārah* | 6 *ptr̥mantravarham japaḥ* | 7 *r̥javo darbhāḥ* | 8 *yavais tilārthaḥ* | 9 *dadhibadarākṣatamiśrāḥ piṇḍāḥ* | 10 *nāndīmukhān pitr̥̄n āvāhayiṣya ity āvāhane* | 11 *nāndīmukhāḥ pitaraḥ prīyantām ity akṣayyasthāne* | 12 *nāndīmukhān pitr̥̄n vācayiṣya iti vācane* | 13 *sampannam iti tr̥ptpaśnaḥ* | 14 *samānam anyad aviruddham iti* ||

10. The later conception of the Nāndīmukha Ancestors as the Ancestors who have been promoted beyond the first three ancestors into a class of more remote, satisfied, and therefore, benevolent supernatural beings may have been an aspect of this term as early as the Gr̥hyasūtras, but there is very little evidence to suggest this.

11. In a modern parallel, Knipe suggests that including the deceased in auspicious events may indicate the hope that offerings made may "for the time being 'satisfy' the deceased, forestalling malevolence that might spoil the party" (1989, 125). While his discussion reflects on relationship between the living and the untimely dead, the *ābhyudayika śrāddha* may indicate a similar concern about the ritual establishment of control over and appeasement of the dead.

12. *brāhmaṇāñ śrutaśīlavr̥ttasampannān ekena vā kale jñāpitān snātān kr̥tapacchaucān ācāntān udanmukhān pitr̥vad upaceśyaikaikam ekaikasya dvau dvau trīṃs trīn vā*

13. *brāhmaṇān vedavido ayugmāṃs tryavarārdhān pitr̥vad upaveśya*

14. *ayugmāny udapātrām tilari avakīryā* | 3 *asāv etat ta ity anudiśya brāhmaṇānāṃ pāniṣu ninayet* | 4 *ata ūrdhvam alaṃkr̥tān* | 5 *āmantrya agnau kr̥tvā 'nnam ca* | 6 *asāv etat ta ity anudiśya bhojayed* | 7

15. *apaḥ pradāya* | 7 *darbhān dviguṇabhugnān āsanam pradāya* | 8 *apaḥ pradāya* | 9

16. *athāgnau juhoti yathoktam purastāt* | 20 *abhyanujñāyām pāniṣv eva vā* | 21

17. *agnimukhā vai devāḥ pāṇilmukhāḥ pitara it ha brāhmaṇam*

18. *athānnam abhimiśrati* | *pr̥thivī te pātraṃ dyaur apidhānaṃ brahmaṇas tvā mukhe juhomi brāhmaṇānāṃ tvā prāṇāpānayor juhomi* | *akṣitam asi mā pitr̥̄ṇāṃ kṣeṣṭhā amutrāmuṣmiṃl loke* | *pr̥thivī samā tasyāgnir upadraṣṭā dattasyāpramādāya* | ...

19. *tatra pitara devatā brāhmaṇās tv āhavanīyārthe*
20. *śvonvaṣṭakyaṃ piṇḍapitṛyajñāvṛtā*
21. *piṇḍapitṛyajñakalpena*
22. *agnaukaraṇādi piṇḍpitṛyajñena kalp vyākhyātaḥ*
23. The word *śrāddha* occurs only once in a text older than the Gṛhyasūtras, *KaU* 3.17, but Olivelle asserts that this and the preceding verses are later additions to the text (Olivelle 1996, 379).
24. The *Khādira Gṛhyasūtra* describes the Ninth-Day Ancestral Offerings, but does not describe the *śrāddha*-rite.
25. Śāṅkhāyana uses the term, but not in the section describing the rite (see below).
26. *māsi māsi pitṛbhyo dadyād*
27. *athāta ekoddiṣṭam*
28. *atha sapiṇḍīkaraṇa*
29. *athāta ābhyudayika*
30. *amāvāsyāyāṃ tat śrāddham*
31. *pretāya piṇḍaṃ dattvā 'avanejanadānapratyavanejaneṣu nāmagrāham* | 27 *mṛnmaye tāṃ rātrīṃ kṣīradake vihāyasi nidadhyuḥ pretātra snāhīti* | 28
32. *ekādaśyām ayugmān brāhmaṇān bhojayitvā māṃsavat* | 48 *pretāyaoddiśya gām apy eke ghnanti* | 49 *piṇḍakaraṇe prathamāḥ pitṝṇāṃ pretaḥ syāt putravāṃś cet* | 50 *nivareta caturthaḥ* | 51 *saṃvatsaram pṛthag eke* | 52 *nyśyas tu na caturthaḥ piṇḍo bhavatīti śruteḥ* | 53 *ahar ahar annam asmai brāhmaṇāyodakumbhaṃ ca dadyāt* | 54 *piṇḍam apy eke nipṛṇanti* | 55
33. *māsi māsi ca evam pitṛbhyo ayukṣu pratiṣṭhāpayet* | 10 *navāvarān bhojayet* | 11 *ayujo vā* | 12 *yugmān vṛddhir pūteṣu* | 13 *ayugmān itareṣu* | 14 *pradakṣiṇam upacāro yavais tilārthaḥ* | 15
34. Nārāyaṇa suggests several ways to understand *ĀśGS* 4.7.5, including understanding it to refer to the *sapiṇḍīkaraṇa*, but this does not convince.
35. Similarly, Śāṅkhāyana records two separate accounts of the *sapiṇḍīkaraṇa* (*ŚGS* 4.3 and 5.9). The two accounts complement each other: both describe one part of the ritual integration of the deceased father into the company of the Ancestors. The complementary nature of the accounts and Oldenberg's view that the latter passage is younger (1967, Part I, 11) suggest that, like Āśvalāyana, Śāṅkhāyana has captured two moments in the development of the rite.
36. Interesting in relationship to the complexity of labeling and categorizing the *śrāddha*-rite is the fact that neither author mentions any type of *śrāddha*-rite beyond the monthly performance.
37. Hiraṇyakeśin does the same (*HGS* 2.4.10–13 and 2.4.14–15).
38. *anvaṣṭakāyām evaike piṇḍanidhānam upadiśanti* | 9 *athaitad aparaṃ dadhna avāñjalinā juhoti yayā 'pūpam* | 10 *ata eva yathārthaṃ māsāṃ śiṣṭvā śvobhute 'nvaṣṭakam* | 11 *tasyā māsiśrāddhena kalpo vyākhyātaḥ* | 12

CHAPTER 5

1. *puna ca paraṃ gahapati ariyasāvako uṭṭhānaviriyādhigatehi bhogehi bāhābalaparicitehi sedāvakkhittehi dhammikehi dhammaladdhehi pañca balīkattā hoti: ñātibaliṃ, atithibaliṃ, pibbapetabaliṃ, rājabaliṃ, devatābaliṃ. ayaṃ catuttho bhogānaṃ ādiyo.*
2. Other references to the *pañcabali* include: *M* ii.186, *A* iv.244–245, *A* iii.43–44, *D* iii.189.
3. *"api nu naṃ brāhmaṇā bhojeyyuṃ saddhe vā thālipāke vā yaññe vā pāhune vā?"ti*
4. *abhisaṅkhataṃ nirārambhaṃ yaññaṃ kālena kappiyaṃ, tādisaṃ upasaṃyanti saññatā brahmacārayo. vivattachaddā ye loke vītivattā kulaṃ gatiṃ, yañña metaṃ pasaṃsanti buddhā puññassa kovidā. yañña vā yadi vā sadde hutaṃ katvā yathārahaṃ, pasannacitto yajati sukhette brahmacārisu. suhutaṃ suyiṭṭhaṃ suppattaṃ dakkhiṇeyesu yaṃ kataṃ, yañño ca vipulo hoti pasīdanti ca devatā. evaṃ yajitvā medhāvī saddho muttena cetasā, abyāpajjhaṃ sukhaṃ lokaṃ paṇḍito upapajjatīti.*
5. *mayamassu bho gotama brāhmaṇā nāma dānāni dema saddhāni karoma: idaṃ dānaṃ petānaṃ ñātisālohitānaṃ upakappatu, idaṃ dānaṃ petā ñātisālohitā paribhuñjantu 'ti. kacci taṃ bho gotama dānaṃ petānaṃ ñātisālohitānaṃ upakappati? kacci te petāñāṭisālohitā taṃ dānaṃ paribhuñjanti ti?*
6. *so kāyassa bhedā paraṃ maraṇā petti visayaṃ upapajjati. yo pettivesayikānaṃ sattānaṃ āhāro, tena so tattha yāpeti. tena so tattha tiṭṭhati. yaṃ vā panassa anuppavecchanti mittā amaccā vā ñāti vā, sālohitā vā tena so tattha yāpeti. tena so tattha tiṭṭhati. idaṃ kho brāhmaṇa ṭhānaṃ, yattha ṭhitassa taṃ dānaṃ upakappatī ti.*
7. *sace pana bho gotama so peto ñātisālohito taṃ ṭhānaṃ anuppano hoti, ko taṃ dānaṃ paribhuñjatīti? aññepissa brāhmaṇa petā ñāti sālohitā tāṃ ṭhānaṃ anupapattā honti. te taṃ dānāṃ paribhuñjantī ti. sace pana bho gotama so ceva peto ñāti sāholito taṃ ṭhānaṃ anupapanno hoti, aññepissa petā ñātisālohitā taṃ ṭhānaṃ anupapannā hontī. ko taṃ dānaṃ paribhuñjatī ti? aṭṭhānaṃ kho etaṃ brāhmaṇa, anavakāso yaṃ taṃ ṭhānaṃ vicittaṃ assa iminā dīghena addhunā yadidaṃ petehi ñāti sālohitehi. api can brāhmaṇa dāyakopi anipphali hoti.*
8. *acchariyaṃ bho gotama, abbhūtaṃ bho gotama, yāvañc idaṃ bho gotama alameva dānāni dātuṃ, alaṃ saddhāni kātuṃ, yatrahi nāma dāyako pi anipphalo hoti.*
9. *evam etaṃ brāhmaṇa, evaṃ etaṃ brāhmaṇa, dāyakopi hi brāhmaṇa anipphalo hoti.*
10. White (1986) has explored this as well and, though I disagree with some of the details of his argument, my argument is largely compatible with his.
11. *ViSmṛ* 20.30–31 expresses a similar sentiment.
12. *yaṃ kiñ cārammaṇaṃ katvā dajjā dānaṃ amaccharī | pubbapete ca ārabbha atha vā vathudevatā ||* 10 *cattāro ca mahārāje lokapale yasassino | kuveraṃ dhataraṭṭhañ ca virūpakkhaṃ virūḷhakaṃ | te ceva pūjitā honti dāyakā ca anipphalā ||* 11 *na hi ruṇṇaṃ vā soko vā yā caccā paridevanā | na taṃpetassa atthāya evaṃ tiṭṭhanti*

ṇātayo || 12 ayac ca kho dakkhiṇā dinnā saṅgham hi suppatiṭṭitā | dīgharattaṃ hitāyassa ṭhānaso upakappatīti || 13

13. *dānāni dema*
14. *saddhāni karoma*
15. *dāyakā ca anipphalā*
16. Horner points out that the introductory material is commentary, but then suggests that that does not necessarily mean it is much later. She fails to make a more definitive statement about the relationship of the prose introduction to the verses (Horner and Gehman 1974, iiix).
17. His name likely means something like 'one who gives food to the unprotected.'
18. *mama dhīta matā*
19. *tava dhītudhānaṃ dassāṃi*
20. *anumodanaṃ karonto*
21. *tirokuṭṭesu tiṭṭhanti snadhisiṅghāṭakeṣu ca | dvārabāhāsu tiṭṭhanti āgantvāna sakaṃ gharaṃ* || 14 *pahūte annapānamhi khajjabhojje upaṭṭhite | na tesaṃ koci sarati sattānaṃ kammapaccayā* || 15 *evaṃ dadatni ñātīnaṃ ye honti anukampakā | suciṃ paṇītaṃ kālena kappiyaṃ pānbhojanaṃ* || 16 *idaṃ vo ñātīnaṃ hotu sukhitā hontu ñātayo | te ca tattha samāgantvā ñātipetā samāgatā | pahūte annapānamhi sakkaccaṃ anumodare* || 17 *ciraṃ jīvantu no ñāṭīyesaṃ hetu labhāmase | amhākacca kata puja dāyakā ca anipphalā* || 18 *na hi tattha kasi atthi horakkhettha na vijjati | vaṇikkā tādisī natthi hiraccena kayākayaṃ | ito dannena yāpenti petā kālagatā tahiṃ* || 19 unnamed *udakaṃ vuṭṭhaṃ yathā ninnaṃ pavattati | evam eva ito dinnaṃ petānaṃ upakappati* || 20 *yathā vārivahā pūrā paripūrenti sāgaraṃ | evam eva ito dinnaṃ petānaṃ upakappati* || 21 *adāsi me akāsi me ñātimittā sakhā ca me | petānaṃ dakkhiṇaṃ dajjā pubbe katamanussaraṃ* || 22 *ne hi ruṇṇaṃ vā soko vā yā caccā paridevanā | na taṃ petānamatthāya evaṃ tiṭṭhanti ñātayo* || 23 *ayac ca kho dakkhiṇā dinnā saṅghamhi supppatiṭṭitā | dīgharattaṃ hitāyassa ṭhānaso upakappatīti* || 24 *so ñātidhammo ca ayaṃ nidassito petāna puja ca katā ulāra | balacca bhikkūnam anuppadinnaṃ tumehi puccaṃ pahutaṃ annappakanti* || 25
22. *idaṃ vo ñātīnaṃ hotu sukhitā hontu ñātayo*
23. *asāv eṣa te piṇḍo ye cātra tvānu yāṃś ca tvam anu tasmai te svadheti*
24. *mam putto mahābhinikkhamanaṃ nikkhamitvā buddho jāto, mayham buddho, mayhaṃ dhammo, mayhaṃ saṅgho*
25. Gayāsīsa refers to a particular site at Gayā, a popular Hindu place of pilgrimage since early in the Common Era. The Buddhist tradition frequently associates these three ascetics with the village of Gayā. Gayā has a strong association with the *śrāddha*-rite in Brahmanical literature as early as the first century C.E., (see Sayers 2010 and Jacques 1962, 1979, 1980).
26. *te tāni paribhuñjitvā pīṇitindriyā ahesuṃ.* I follow Masefield in reading *pīṇitindriyā* instead of *pi nindiyā* or *piṇindriyā*; he follows the *PED* suggestion that this is a wrong reading, *sv nindiya* (Dhammapāla 1989, 34n25).
27. *nāndīmukhāḥ pitara prīyantāṃ*

28. *pratnavadbhiḥ prattaḥ svadhayā pitṝn imāṃl lokān prīṇayā hi naḥ svadhā nama.* See also *ĀśGS* 1.1.4 with respect to satisfying the gods with an oblation, *ĀśGS* 4.8.29 with respect to satisfying snakes in a propitiatory offering, and *TB* 1.6.8.3, in the context is the *pitṛyajña* in the Sākamedha. The verb is also common in the *Śatapatha Brāhmaṇa*, where it is more commonly associated with satisfying the gods in sacrifice; in these examples, there is similarly a correspondence to achieving heaven as well. The word is similarly employed in the *Mahābhārata*.
29. *yadeva tarpayaty adbhiḥ pitṝn snātvā dvijottamaḥ | tenaiva sarvam āpnoti pitṛyajñakriyāphalam ||*
30. *gṛhā́n naḥ pitaró dattéti gṛhā́ṇāṃ ha pitára īśatá éṣo etásyāśī́ḥ kármaṇo*
31. *gṛhā́n naḥ pitaro datta...*

CHAPTER 6

1. *māsi māsi kāryam*
2. *dadyād ahar ahaḥ śrāddham annādyenodakena vā | payomūlaphalair vāpi pitṛbhyaḥ prītim āharan ||* 82 *ekam apy assayed vipraṃ pitrarthe pāñcayajñike | na caivātrāśayet kiṃ cid vaiśvadevaṃ prati dvijam ||* 83
3. *pitṛyajñaṃ tu nirvartya vipraś candrakṣaye 'gnimān | piṇḍānvāhāryakaṃ śrāddhaṃ kuryān māsānaumāsikam ||* 122 *pitṝṇāṃ māsikaṃ śrāddham anvāhāryaṃ vidur budhāḥ | tadāmiṣeṇa kartavyaṃ praśastena prayatnataḥ ||* 123
4. Critiques of the sacrificial model of religiosity can be found throughout the Upaniṣads, e.g., *KaU* 1.1–4. Vedic texts also ridicule of those Brahmins who accepted gifts in the ritual as greedy (e.g. *AB* 7.29 and *CU* 1.13.4–5, quoted in Siegel 1987, 199).
5. *yátra jyótr ájasraṃ yásmiṃ loké svàr hitám | tásmin mā́ṃ dhehi pavamāna amṛ́te loké ákṣita índrāyendo pári srava ||*
6. *prajā́ḥ sṛṣṭvā́nho 'vayájya vṛtā́ṃ hatvā́ devā́ amṛtatvā́ṃ evā́kāmayanta svargó vái lokó 'mṛtatvā́ṃ saṃvatsarā́ḥ svargó lokó yád dvā́daśā́hutayo 'mṛtatvā́m evá téna spṛṇoty...*
7. *pitryam āyuṣyaṃ svargyaṃ yaśasyaṃ puṣṭikarma ca |*
8. *bhojanābhyañjanād dānād yad anyat kurute tiliaḥ | śvaviṣṭhāyāṃ kṛmir bhūtvā pitṛbhiḥ saha majjatīti ||*
9. *yat tu śmaśānam ucyate nānākarmaṇām eṣo 'nte puruṣasāṃskāro vidhīyate |* 11 *tataḥ param anantyaṃ phalaṃ svargaśabdaṃ śrūyate |* 12
10. *tasyāśramavikalpam eke bruvate | GDhS* 3.1
11. There is some variety in the terminology used for the different orders of life. Āpastamba uses the terms *ācāryakula, gārhasthya, vānaprasthya, and mauna (ĀpDhS 2.21.1)*. Gautama uses *brahmacārin, gṛhastha, vaikānasa, and bhikṣu.* Baudhāyana (*BDhS* 2.11.12) and Vasiṣṭha (*VDhS* 7.1) both use *brahmacārin, gṛhastha, vānaprastha,* and *parivrājaka*. For a detailed study of the development of the *āśrama* institution see Olivelle 1993.

12. *ekāśramyaṃ tv ācāryāḥ prayakṣavidhānād gārhasthyasya gārhasthyasya* |
13. See Bronkhorst for more examples of the criticism of asceticism within the Vedic tradition (2007, 84).
14. In this context the word *tīrtha* can also mean 'at a place of pilgrimage.'
15. *tatra dravyāṇi tilamāṣā vrīhiyavā āpo mūlaphalāni* | 23 *snehavati tv evānne tīvratarā pitṝṇāṃ prītir drāghīyāṃsaṃ ca kālam* | 24 *tathā dharmāhṛtena dravyeṇa tīrthe pratipannena* | 25 *saṃvatsaraṃ gavyena prītiḥ* | 26 *bhūyāṃsam ato māhiṣeṇa* | 27 *etena grāmyāraṇyānāṃ paśūnāṃ māṃsaṃ medyaṃ vyākhyātam* | 28 *khaṅgopastaraṇe khaḍgamāṃsenānantyaṃ kālam* | 1 *tathā śatabaler matysasya māṃsena* | 2 *vāṛdhyāṇasasya ca* | 3
16. Olivelle indicates that the Gautama passage is missing from five of the thirteen manuscripts he compiled and he doubts its authenticity (Olivelle 2000, 555n15.15). Though it is not commented upon by either Maskarin or Haradatta, I include it here because it appears to indicate a manner of thinking about the issue that is more in keeping with the older authors than that of Manu, as I hope will become more clear presently.
17. *tilamāṣavrīhiyavodakadānair māsaṃ pitaraḥ prīṇanti* | *matsyahariṇaruruśaśak ūrmavarāhameṣamāṃsaiḥ saṃvatsarāṇi* | *gavyapayaḥpāyasair dvādaśa varṣāṇi* | *vārdhrīṇasena māṃsena kālaśākacchāgalohakhaḍgamāṃsair madhumiśraiś cānantyam* | 15
18. Interestingly, failures in proper behavior with regard to preparation for the *śrāddha* are also expressed in terms of food, for example, "The Ancestors of a man who engages in sexual intercourse having given or eaten a *śrāddha*-rite eat (his) semen for that month" (*śrāddhaṃ dattvā ca bhuktvā ca maithunaṃ yo 'dhigacchati* | *bhavanti pitaras tasya tanmāsaṃ retaso bhujaḥ* ||) (*VDhS* 11.37).
19. *Baudhāyana Gṛhyasūtra* includes a similar list, but its context and corrupted nature suggest it is a later addition: *atha yadi gāṃ na labhate meṣamajaṃ vā ''labhate* | 51 *āraṇyena vā māṃsena yathopapannena* | 52 *khaṅgamṛgamahiṣam eṣavarāhapṛṣataśaśarohitaśārṅgatittirikapotakapiñjalavārdhrāṇasānām akṣayyaṃ tilamadhusaṃsṛṣṭam* | 53 *tathā matsyasya śatavalaiḥ kṣirodanena vā sūpodanena vā* | 54 *yad vā bhavaty āmair vā mūlaphalaiḥ pradānamātram* | 55 *hiraṇyena vā pradānamātram* | 56 *api vā gogrāsamātram āharet* | 57 *api vā 'anūcānebhya udakumbhān āharet* | 58 *api vā śrāddhamantrān adhīyīta* | 59 *api vā 'raṇye 'gninā kakṣamupoṣedeṣām ekāṣṭaketi* | *BGS* 2.11.51–60
20. The offerings are sesame, rice, barley, beans, water, roots, and fruit (*tilamāṣā vrīhiyavā āpo mūlaphalāni*); fish (*matsya*); common deer (*hariṇa*); sheep (*aurabhra, āvika*); birds (*śākuna*); goat (*chāga, ajaka*); spotted deer (*pārṣata*); eṇa *antelope* (*eṇa*); ruru antelope (*ruru*); buffalo (*māhiṣa*); boar (*varāha*); hornless goat (*tūpara*); rabbit (*śaśa*); turtle (*kūrma*); cow (*gavyaṃ māṃsam*); milk or milk-rice (*gavyaṃ payas pāyasam, gavyasamāyuktaṃ pāyasam*); rhinoceros (*khaḍga*); Śatabali fish (*śatabaler matsyasya māṃsena*); Vārdhrāṇasa crane (*vārdhāṇasa, vārdhrīṇasa*); sacred basil (*kālaśāka*); Mahāśalka crustacean (*mahāśalka*); red

goat (*loha, lohitacchāgalo*); honey (*madhu*); and sage's food (*munyanna*). Manu and subsequent authors tend not to favor fish eating (Olivelle 2002a, 19), but the *Mānava Dharmaśāstra* (5.16) specifies those that are acceptable for the *śrāddha*-rite. For more on changing trends in the acceptance of fish as an edible or inedible food, see Olivelle 2002a, 19f. For a discussion of the rhinoceros' inclusion on this list, see Jamison 1998. See Sax (1997) for a later example of the rhinoceros in Indian myth. For more on sage's food (*munyanna*), see Olivelle 2005, 267 n3.257; 1991, 34.

21. *svadhā́ṃ pitṛ́bhyo ajárāṃ kṛṇómi*
22. Both terms derive from the verb *kṣi*, to perish; *akṣaya* is an adjectival formation and *akṣayya* is a gerundive formation and both take an a-privative, negating the root meaning. Therefore they mean not perishing, not to be destroyed, or not coming to an end.
23. *pṛthivī samantasya te 'agnir upadraṣṭaracaste mahima dattasyāpramādāya pṛthivī te pātraṃ dyaur apihānaṃ brahmaṇas tvā mukhe juhomi brāhmaṇānāṃ tvā vidyāvatāṃ prāṇāpānayor juhomi akṣitam asi mā pitṝṇāṃ kṣeṣṭhā amutrāmuṣmiṃl loke iti* | ...
24. *divasasyāṣṭame bhāge mandībhavati bhāskaraḥ* | *sa kālaḥ kutapo jñeyaḥ pitṝṇāṃ dattam akṣayam* ||
25. *yat kiṃ cin madhunā miśraṃ pradadyāt tu trayodaśīm* | *tad apy akṣayam eva syād varṣāsu ca maghāsu ca* || 273 *api naḥ sa kule bhūyād yo no dadyāt trayodaśīm* | *pāyasaṃ madhusarpirbhyāṃ prāk chāye kuñjarasya ca* || 274 *yad yad dadāti vidhivat samyak śraddhāsamanvitaḥ* | *tat tat pitṝṇāṃ bhavati paratrānantyam akṣayam* || 275
26. ...*yāvantaṃ ha vā imāṃ vittasya pūrṇāṃ dadat svargaṃ lokaṃ jayati tāvantaṃ lokaṃ jayati bhūyāṃsaṃ cākṣayyaṃ cāpa punarmṛtyuṃ jayati ya evaṃ vidvān svādhyāyam adhīte* |...
27. This is in sharp contrast to Jainism, the third major player in the *śramaṇa* movement. While Jains adopted and incorporated many of the sacred ceremonies of the Brahmanical tradition, several Jain texts demonstrate an outright rejection of the rites associated with death, especially the *śrāddha*-rite (Jaini 1979, 302–304). While Jaini discusses the incorporation of the *śrāddha*-rite as a "blatant heresy" in the face of Jaina doctrines pertaining to *karma* (303), at least one source seem to indicate a more practical concern in addition to the theological one—that is, a concern about the competitive religious marketplace discussed above—as well as the vitriolic nature of the competition similar to those to be discussed in the next chapter, e.g., in the *Syādvādamañjarī*, Malliṣena asks, "Who can agree that what is eaten by the brahmans accrues to them [the ancestors]? For only in the brahmans do we see fattened bellies, and transference of these to the departed souls cannot be espied" (quoted in Jaini 1979, 303). In addition, Jeffery Long says "Whenever I have asked Jains about the differences between Jains and Hindus, the topics of *anyeṣṭi* and *śrāddha* inevitably come up" (personal communication). See also Granoff 1992.

28. ... *dāyakopi hi brāhmaṇa anipphalo hoti.*
29. For more on the transfer of merit, see Amore 1971, Bechert 1992; Gombrich 1971a; Hara 1967–68; Holt 1981; Kajiyama 1989; Keyes 1983; Malalasekera 1967; McDermott 1974; Schopen 1997a; White 1986; and Woodward, 1914.

CHAPTER 7

1. Bruce Lincoln's thoughts on myth also apply to texts that describe culture with a prescriptive bent, "myth has tremendous importance and is often the site of contestation between groups and individuals whose differing versions of social ideals and reality are inscribed within the rival versions of the myths they recount" (1991, 123).
2. *sáṃ gacchasva pitṝbhiḥ sáṃ yaméneṣṭāpūrténa paramé vyòman |*
3. *táṃ kṛtáṃ lokáṃ abhí jāyate tásmād āhuḥ kṛtá lokam púruṣo 'bhí jāyate íti |*
4. *tébhiḥ svarā̐l ásunītim etā́ṃ yathāvaśáṃ tanvàṃ kalpayasva |*
5. *agníḥ pūrvebhir ŕ̥ṣibhir īḍyó nūtanair utá | sá devā́ṃ éhá vakṣati ||* 2 *agnínā rayím aśnavat póṣam evá divé dive | yaśásaṃ vīrávattamam ||* 3 *ágne yáṃ yajñám adhvaráṃ viśvátaḥ paribhūr ási | sá íd devéṣu gacchati ||* 4
6. *na skandate na vyathate na vinaśyati kar hi cit | variṣṭam agnihotrebhyo brāhmaṇasya mukhe hutam ||*
7. *tena brāhmaṇaṃ vidyāvantaṃ pariveveṣṭi |*
8. *karmāpavarge brāhmaṇabhojanaṃ |* 1 *vāgrūpavayaḥśrutaśīlavṛttāni guṇāḥ |* 2 *śrutaṃ tu sarvān atyeti |* 3 *na śrutam atīyāt |* 4 *adhidaivam athādyātmam adhiyajñam iti trayam | mantreṣu brāhmaṇe caiva śrutam ity abhidhīyate ||* 5 *kriyāvantam adhīyānaṃ śrutavṛddhaṃ tapasvinam | bhojayet taṃ sakṛd yas tu na taṃ bhūyaḥ kṣud aśnute ||* 6
9. *śrutaśīlavṛttasampannān ekena vā*
10. In fact, just such competition appears in the Jain story of Harikeśa told in the *Uttarādhyayana Sūtra*, in which a Jain monk asks for alms at a sacrifice and is beaten for asking (Jacobi 1895, 50ff).
11. *śākyājīvikādīn vṛṣalapravajitān devapitṛkāryeṣu bhojayataḥ śatyo daṇḍaḥ*
12. *atha cen mantravidyuktaḥ śārīraiḥ paṅktidūṣaṇaiḥ | aduṣyaṃ taṃ yamaḥ prāha paṅktipāvana eva saḥ ||*
13. *bhojayet susamṛddho 'pi na prasajjeta vistare ||*
14. *satkriyāṃ deśākālau ca śaucaṃ brāhmaṇasaṃpadam | pañcaitān vistaro hanti tasmāt tāṃ parivarjayet ||* 28 *api vā bhojayed ekaṃ brāhmaṇaṃ vedapāragam | śrutaśīlopasaṃpannaṃ sarvālakṣaṇavarjitam ||* 29
15. *samadviguṇasāhasrānantāni phalāny abrāhmaṇabrāhmaṇaśrotriyavedapāragebhyaḥ |*
16. *ekaikam api vidvāṃsaṃ daive pitrye ca bhojayet | puṣkalaṃ phalam āpnoti nāmantrajñān bahūn api ||*
17. *yāvato grasate piṇḍān havyakavyeṣv amantravit | tāvato grasate pretya dīptāñ chūlarṣṭyayogaḍān ||*

18. *samamabrāhmaṇe dānaṃ dviguṇaṃ brāhmaṇabruve | sahasraguṇaṃ prādhīte anantaṃ vedapārage || 85 pātrasya hi viśeṣeṇa śraddadhānatayaiva ca | alpaṃ vā bahu vā pretya dānasyāvāpyate phalam* || 86
19. In addition, Manu introduces the notion that the spirit of generosity *(śraddhā)*, which influences the offerings made (See also Heim 2004, 33).
20. *na brāhmaṇaṃ parīkṣeta daive karmaṇy prayatnataḥ | pitrye karmaṇi tu prāpte parīkṣeta prayatnataḥ* ||
21. Dhammapāla 1989. See also Egge 2002, Amore 1971, Michaels and Pierce 1997, and Holt 1981. For a later perspective on the role of mediation in Buddhism, see Holt 2007, in which he suggests that monks of contemporary Sri Lanka "do not in any way offer to broker relations between the living and the dead in a priestly guise," instead this role is taken up in the "informal sector" by priestly practitioners in independently operated shrine (330–331).
22. Though the authors critique all their rivals, I will focus here on critiques of Brahmins. Frieberger categorizes the different ways that Buddhists dealt with non-Buddhists (2011).
23. Consider also the *Ambaṭṭhasutta* of the *Digha Nikāya* (*D* i.87).
24. *juhāmi dakkhiṇeyyaggiṃ namassāmi tathāgataṃ*
25. *ujjaṅgale yathā khette bījaṃ bahukampi ropitaṃ, na vipulaṃ phalaṃ hoti napi toseti kassakaṃ. tatheva dānaṃ bahukaṃ dussīlesu patiṭṭhitaṃ, na vipulaṃ phalaṃ hoti napi toseti dāyakaṃ.*
26. This metaphor occurs a number of times in the subsequent literature, e.g., *MBh* 13.90.37. A similar use of the field metaphor appears in a Jain story of Harikeśa, in the *Uttarādhyayana Sūtra* (Jacobi 1895, 50ff).
27. *yatheriṇa bījam uptvā na vaptā labhate phalam | tathānṛce havir dattvā na data labhate phalam* || 142 *dātṝn pratigrahītṝṃś ca kurute phalabhāginaḥ | viduṣe dakṣiṇāṃ dattvā vidhivat pretya ceha ca* || 143
28. Egge also discusses this metaphor (2002, 19–20).
29. *puññakkhettam anuttaraṃ/āyāgo sabbalokassa bhoto dinna mahaphalan*
30. *bhagavato sāvaksaṅgho āhuneyyo pāhuṇeyyo dakkhiṇeyyo añjalikaraṇīyo anuttaram puññakkhettaṃ lokassā 'ti*

Glossary of Sanskrit Terms

ābhyudayika śrāddha prosperity *śrāddha*. ancestral rite to celebrate an auspicious occasion

Adhvaryu priest of the *Yajur Veda*, responsible for ritual action

Agni Fire. 1. mundane fire, 2. deified Fire, central deity of Vedic sacrifice

Agni Kravyād Flesh-eating Agni. Agni in his persona that consumes the corpse in the cremation

Agni Kravyavāhana Flesh-conveying Agni. Agni in his persona that conveys the corpse to heaven

Agni Sviṣṭakṛt Agni Who Makes the Sacrifice Correct. Agni in his persona that receives an oblation to end the chief offerings in the New and Full Moon Sacrifices

ahuta lit. "not offered" into the ritual fire. class of domestic offering

akṣaya (akṣayya) inexhaustible. describes offerings

anantya without end, eternal. describes offerings

anvaṣṭakya (anvaṣṭakā) lit. "following the *aṣṭakā*," Ninth-Day Ancestral Offerings. ancestral offering on the ninth day of the new moon

Arthaśāstra *Code of Statecraft*. text outlining the ruling of a kingdom

aṣṭakā Eighth-Day Offerings. 1. the eighth day after the new moon, on which ancestral rites are performed, 2. the rites themselves

asura demon. enemies of the gods (*deva*) in the Brāhmaṇas

Atharva Veda collection of hymns dedicated to magical and healing rites

ātman Self. the eternal aspect of humans, identical to *brahman*

bandhu equivalence. identities at the heart of the Vedic ritual homologization of the human, sacrificial, and cosmic worlds

barhis grass strewn in Vedic ritual to create seat for the gods

bhakti devotion. religious practice centered on devotion to a deity

Brahman priest of the *Atharva Veda*, responsible for overseeing the sacrifice

bráhman 1. sacred formula, 2. underlying substrate of reality, identical to *ātman*

Brāhmaṇa prose commentarial text, primarily exegesis of Vedic ritual

brahmayajña sacrifice to *brahman*. one of the Five Great Sacrifices

Brahmin priestly class, highest of the four classes (*varṇa*)

Cāturmāsya Four-Monthly (Sacrifices). seasonal sacrifices

dakkhiṇā donation/gift. offerings made to the Buddha and the Saṅgha
dakṣiṇā sacrificial gift. compensation given to Vedic priests
dāna gifting, almsgiving. practice of giving a gift, which is said to generate religious merit
darbha grass used in Vedic ritual
darśapūrṇamāsa New and Full Moon (Sacrifices)
deva god
dhamma [Pāli for *dharma*] 1. the teachings of the Buddha 2. proper moral behavior
dharma duty Law, religion. proper behavior as determined by various aspects of one's social identity
Dharmaśāstra Law Code. texts prescriptively codifying *dharma*
Dharmasūtra texts describing *dharma*
ekoddiṣṭa śrāddha *śrāddha* directed to one (person). ancestral rite to sustain deceased during first year after death
gārhapatya householder's (fire). one of three sacred fires used in Vedic ritual
gṛhya domestic ritual, rites requiring only one fire
Gṛhyasūtra texts codifying domestic ritual
Hotṛ priest of the *Ṛg Veda*, responsible for recitation of hymns
huta offered into the ritual fire. class of domestic offering
Jātavedas Agni in Whose Possession Are the Creatures. epithet for Agni connected to familial continuity and ritual success
kapāla pieces of pottery. on which oblations are made in the Vedic ritual
karma action. in the later tradition actions that influence rebirth
kuśa grass used in Vedic ritual
Mahābhārata epic poem
mantra a sacred verse or formula
matṛ mother. 1. mother 2. in the later tradition, the female Ancestors
māyā magical power
mokṣa (mukti) release. liberation from the cycle of rebirth
pākayajña Small Sacrifices. a general term for domestic rituals
Pāli the literary language of Early Buddhist scripture
pañcabali Five Offerings. Buddhist term denoting a set of five ritual obligations
pañcamahāyajña Five Great Sacrifices. a set of five ritual obligations outlined in the *dharma* literature
pārvaṇa śrāddha new moon *śrāddha*. monthly ancestral rite performed on the day of the new moon
peta [Pāli *preta*] departed. generally understood to be a ghost
piṇḍa rice-ball. offering of rice made to the Ancestors
piṇḍapitṛyajña Rice-Ball Sacrifice to the Ancestors. Vedic ancestral ritual, that includes offering of rice-balls
pitṛ father. 1. father, 2. Ancestor
pitṛloka world of the Ancestors. heavenly world in which the ancestors live after death

pitṛyajña Sacrifice to the Ancestors. Vedic ancestral ritual
prācīnāvītin wearing one's sacrificial cord over the right shoulder and under the left arm, this is used for divine ritual
pradakṣiṇa clockwise, with one's right hand toward. the auspicious direction of circumambulation
prahuta offered up. class of domestic offering
prasavya with one's left hand toward, counterclockwise. the direction of circumambulation employed in ancestral rites
prāśita eaten. class of domestic offering
preta departed. name for the deceased before translation to ancestorhood
punarmṛtyu re-death. concept used in the Late Vedic arguments about ritual
Purāṇa encyclopedic compendia of religious materials
ṛc verse. sacred verses collected in the *Ṛg Veda*
rākṣasa demon
Ṛg Veda text composed of hymns used in the liturgy of Vedic sacrifice
saddha [Pāli *śrāddha*] domestic ancestral offering
Sākamedha third of the Four-Monthly Sacrifices, it is offered in the autumn
śākhā lit. branch, theological school, the intellectual traditions that composed and preserved Vedic texts
Sāma Veda text composed of chants sung in the Vedic sacrifice
sāman song or tune verses are set to in the sacrifice, collected in the *Sāma Veda*
samaṇa [Pāli *śramaṇa*] an ascetic, monk, religious mendicant
Sāyaṇa Brahmanical commentator from the 14th century C.E.
saṃhitā collection. text compiling liturgical verses and formula
saṃsāra lit. "wandering through." the world, the process of passing through various states of transmigration
saṃskāra lit. "perfecting," sacred ceremonies. series of twelve ceremonies, generally life-cycle rituals
Saṅgha lit. "assembly." the Buddhist monastic community
sapiṇḍīkaraṇa śrāddha *śrāddha* that creates the bond of kinship, the ancestral rite to promote the deceased to the ranks of the Ancestors
smṛti remembered. text recording tradition, opposed to *śruti*
soma 1. sacred drink offering in the Soma Sacrifice, 2. the deity who personifies the drink
śrāddha domestic ancestral offering
śraddhā trust, confidence. confidence in the efficacy of the ritual and in power of hospitality
śramaṇa 1. an ascetic or religious mendicant 2. the movement of asceticism in ancient India
śrauta solemn ritual
Śrautasūtra texts outlining the performance of solemn rites
śruti lit. "heard." text recording revelation, opposed to *smṛti*

sūtra lit. "thread." 1. short aphoristic statement, 2. text composed of those statements
sutta [Pāli *sūtra*], narrative text in the Buddhist scripture
svāhā verbal formula used in mantras accompanying divine offerings
svadhā 1. one's own power, independence, the 2. verbal formula used in mantras accompanying ancestral offerings, 3. later, synecdoche for the entire ancestral rite, 4. the oblation made to the Ancestors in that ritual
svar heaven
svarga heaven
Udgatṛ priest of the *Sāma Veda*, responsible for chanting the *sāmans*
Upaniṣad Vedic philosophical texts
vaṣaṭ call made at the end of sacrificial verse, indicates to the Adhvaryu to made the oblation
Vedāṅga lit. "limbs of the Veda." texts recording the knowledge supplementary to the performance of sacrifice
vedi altar. a shallow, hourglass shape space dug out of the ground
vṛddhi śrāddha *śrāddha* of increase. alternate name for the *ābhyudayika śrāddha*
vyoman heaven
Yajur Veda text containing sacred formulas used in Vedic ritual
yajña sacrifice
yajamāna lit. "sacrificing on his own behalf," Sacrificer. the patron of the sacrifice
yajñopavītin wearing one's sacrificial cord over the left shoulder and under the right arm; this is used for ancestral ritual
Yama the god of the dead

Bibliography

Amore, R. C. 1971. *The Concept and Practice of Doing Merit in Early Theravāda Buddhism*. Dissertation: University of Michigan, Ann Arbor.

Apte, Vinayak Mahadev. 1940. *Ṛgvedic Mantras in their Ritual Settings in the Gṛhyasūtras (with Special Reference to the Āśvalāyana Gṛhyasūtra)*. London: Probsthain.

Arya, Ravi Prakash and K. L. Joshi, eds. 1997. *Ṛgveda Saṃhitā: Sanskrit Text, English Translation and Notes*. 4 Vols. Translated by H. H. Wilson. Delhi: Parimal Publications.

Aung, Shwe Zan and Mrs. Rhys Davids, trans. 1960. *Points of Controversy or Subjects of Discourse being a Translation of the Kathā-vatthu from the Abhidhamma-Piṭaka*. London: Pali Text Society.

Bailey, Greg. 1998. "Problems of the Interpretation of the Data Pertaining to Religious Interaction in Ancient India: The Conversion Stories in the Sutta Nipāta." In *Religious Traditions in South India: Interaction and Change*. Edited by Geoffrey A. Oddie, 9–28. Surrey: Curzon.

Bailey, Greg and Ian Mabbett. 2003. *The Sociology of Early Buddhism*. Cambridge: Cambridge University Press.

Bechert, Heinz. 1992. "Buddha-field and Transfer of Merit in a Theravāda Source." *IIJ* 35(2–3): 95–108.

Ben-Herut, Gil. 2009. "Sharing Language: On the Problem of Meaning in Classical Buddhist and Brahmanical Traditions." *RoSA* 3(1): 125–146.

Bhattacarya, Chintamani, ed. 1982. *Gobhilagṛhyasūtram with Bhaṭṭanārāyana's Commentary*. New Delhi: Munshiram Manoharlal Publishers.

Bhattacarya, Gouriswar. 1971. "Studies in the Concept of Śraddhā in Post-Vedic Hinduism." Ph.D. Dissertation, University of Basle.

Bhide, V. V. 1979. *The Cāturmāsya Sacrifices: With Special Reference to the Hiraṇyakeśi Śrautasūtra*. Pune: University of Pune.

Black, Brian. 2009. "Rival and Benefactors: Encounters between Buddhists and Brahmins in the Nikāyas." *RoSA* 3(1): 25–43.

Bloomfield, Maurice. 1890. "The Kāuçika Sūtra of the Atharva Veda." *JAOS* 14: i–424.

Bodewitz, H. W. 1973. *Jaiminīya Brāhmaṇa I, 1–65 Translation and Commentary with a Study Agnihotra and Prāṇāgnihotra*. Leiden: E. J. Brill.

———. 1990. *The Jyotiṣṭoma Ritual Jaiminīya Brāhmaṇa I, 66–364*. Leiden: E. J. Brill.

———. 1994. "Life after Death in the Ṛgvedasaṃhitā." *Wiener Zeitschrift für die Kunde Südasiens und Archiv für indische Philosophie* 38: 23–41.

———. 1996a. "The pancagnividya and the Pitryana/Devayana." In *Studies in Indology: Professor Mukunda Madhava Sharma Felicitation Volume*. Edited by A. A. Goswami and D. Chutia, 51–57. Delhi: Sri Satguru Publications.

———. 1996b. "Redeath and its Relation to Rebirth and Release." *Studien zur Indologie und Iranistik* 20: 27–46.

———. 1998. "The Hindu Doctrine of Transmigration: its Origin and Background." *Indologica Taurinensia* (Professor Gregory M. Bongard-Levin Felicitation Volume) 23–24: 583–605.

Brereton, Joel and Stephanie W. Jamison, trans. Forthcoming. *The Rig Veda*. New York: Oxford University Press.

Brockington, John L. 1998. *The Sanskrit Epics*. Leiden: E. J. Brill.

Bronkhorst, Johannes. 2007. *Greater Magadha: Studies in the Culture of Early India*. Leiden: E. J. Brill.

———. 2009. *Buddhist Teaching in India*. Boston: Wisdom Publications.

Brown, Peter. 1981. *The Cult of the Saints: Its Rise and Function in Latin Christianity*. Chicago: The University of Chicago Press.

Buddhaghosa. 1994. *Saṃyuttanikāye Sāratthappakāsinī*. 3 Vols. Igatpuri: Vipassan Research Institute.

Buitenen, J. A. B. van, ed. and trans. 1973. *Mahābhārata 1. The Book of the Beginning*. Chicago: The University of Chicago Press.

———, ed. and trans. 1975. *Mahābhārata 2. The Book of the Assembly Hall 3. The Book of the Forest*. Chicago: The University of Chicago Press.

———, ed. and trans. 1978. *Mahābhārata 4. The Book of Virāṭa 5. The Book of Effort*. Chicago: The University of Chicago Press.

Burlingame, Eugene Watson, trans. 1999. *Buddhist Legends, Translated from the Original Pali Text of the Dhammapada Commentary Part I*. New Delhi: Munshiram Manoharlal Publishers. First published 1921.

Caland, W. 1893. *Altindischer Ahnencult: Das Çrāddha nach den verschiedenen Schulen mit Benutzung handschirftlicher Quellen*. Leiden: E. J. Brill.

———. 1896. *Die Altindischen todten- und Bestattungsgebräche mit Benutzung handschriftlicher Quellen*. Amsterdam: Johannes Müller.

———, trans. 1921. *Das Śrautasūtra des Āpastamba*. Göttingen: Vandenhoeck & Ruprecht.

———, ed. and trans. 1922. *The Jaiminigṛhyasūtra Belonging to the Sāmaveda with Extracts from the Commentary*. Lahore: Sanskrit Punjab Book Depot.

———. 1930. "On the Relative Chronology of Some Ritualistic Sūtras." *Acta Orientalia* 9(1): 69–76.

———, trans. 1931. *Pañcaviṃśa-Brāhmaṇa: The Brāhmaṇa of Twenty Five Chapters*. Calcutta: Asiatic Society of Bengal.

———, ed. 1983. *The Śatapatha Brāhmaṇa in the Kāṇvīya Recension*. Revised by Dr. Raghu Vira. Delhi: Motilal Banarsidass. First published 1926.

Caland W. and Victor Henry. 1906–07. *L'Agniṣṭoma: Descripton Complète de la forme normale du sacrifice de soma dans le culte védique*. 2 Vols. Paris: Ernest Leroux.

Caland, W and Raghu Vira, eds. 1971. *Vārāha-Śrauta-Sūtra being the Main Ritualistic Sūtra of the Maitrāyaṇī Śākhā*. Delhi: Meharchand Lacchmandas.

Chakravarti, Uma. 2009. "Of Binaries and Beyond: The Dialectics of Buddhist-Brahmanical Relations in India." *RoSA* 3(1): 7–23.

Chemburkar, Jaya. 1987. "Pitṛyajña: A Study." In *Sacrifice in India: Concept and Evolution*. Edited by S. S. Dange, 99–106. Aligarh: Viveka Publications.

Cousins, Lance S. 1972. "Dhammapāla and the Ṭika Literature." *Religion* 2: 159–165.

Dandekar, R. N., ed. 1962–1973. *Śrautakośa: Encyclopedia of Vedic Sacrificial Ritual Comprising the Two Complementary Sections, namely, the Sanskrit Section and the English Section*. Vol. II, the English Section. 2 Parts. Poona: Vaidika Saṃśodhana Maṇḍala.

Das, Veena. 1982. *Structure and Cognition: Aspects of Hindu Caste and Ritual*. Delhi: Oxford University Press.

DeCaroli, Robert. 2004. *Haunting the Buddha: Indian Popular Religions and the Formation of Buddhism*. Oxford: Oxford University Press.

Dhammapāla. 1980. *Elucidation of the Intrinsic Meaning So Named the Commentary on the Peta-Stories (Paramatthadīpanī nāma Petavatthu-aṭṭhakathā)*. Translated by U Ba Kyaw, edited and annotated by Peter Masefield. *Sacred Books of the Buddhists Vol. XXXIV*. London: Pali Text Society.

———. 1989. *Elucidation of the Intrinsic Meaning So Named the Commentary on the Vimāna Stories (Paramatthadīpanī nāma Vimānavatthu-aṭṭhakathā)*. Translated by Peter Masefield assisted by N. A. Jayawickrama. *Sacred Books of the Buddhists Vol. XXXV*. London: Pali Text Society.

———. 1994. *The Udāna Commentary (Paramatthadīpanī nāma Udānaṭṭhakathā)*. Vol. I. *Sacred Books of the Buddhists Vol. XLIII*. Translated by Peter Masefield. London: Pali Text Society.

———. 1995. *The Udāna Commentary (Paramatthadīpanī nāma Udānaṭṭhakathā)*. Vol. II. *Sacred Books of the Buddhists Vol. XLV*. Translated by Peter Masefield. London: Pali Text Society.

———. 1998. *Khuddakanikāye Paramatthadīpanī Petavatthu-Aṭṭhakathā*. Dhammagiri, India: Vipassana Research Institute.

Doniger, Wendy, trans. 1981. *The Rig Veda*. London: Penguin Books.

Donner, O. 1870. *Piṇḍapitṛyajña: Das Manenopfer mit klössen bei den Indern*. Berlin: S. Calvary and Co.

Dumont, Paul-Emile. 1948. "The Horse-Sacrifice in the Taittirīya-Brāhmaṇa: The Eighth and Ninth Prapāṭhaka of the Third Kāṇḍa of the Taittirīya-Brāhmaṇa with Translation." *PAPS* 92(6): 447–503.

———. 1951. "The Special Kinds of Agnicayana (Or Special Methods of Building the Fire-Altar) According to the Kaṭhas in Taittirīya Brāhmaṇa: The Tenth, Eleventh, and Twelfth Prapāṭhaka of the Third Kāṇḍa of the Taittirīya-Brāhmaṇa with Translation." *PAPS* 95(6): 628–675.

———. 1954. "The Iṣṭis to the Nakṣatras (Or Oblations to the Lunar Mansions) in the Taittirīya-Brāhmaṇa: The First Prapāṭhaka of the Third Kāṇḍa of the Taittirīya-Brāhmaṇa with Translation." *PAPS* 98(3): 204–223.

———. 1957. "The Full-Moon and New-Moon Sacrifices in the Taittirīya-Brāhmaṇa (First Part)." *PAPS* 101(2): 216–243.

———. 1959. "The Full-Moon and New-Moon Sacrifices in the Taittirīya-Brāhmaṇa (Second Part): The Third Prapāṭhaka of the Third Kāṇḍa of the Taittirīya-Brāhmaṇa with Translation." *PAPS* 103(4): 584–608.

———. 1960. "The Full-Moon and New-Moon Sacrifices in the Taittirīya-Brāhmaṇa (Third Part): The Part of the Hotar in the Full-Moon and New-Moon Sacrifices—The Fifth Prapāṭhaka of the Third Kāṇḍa of the Taittirīya-Brāhmaṇa with Translation." *PAPS* 104(1): 1–10.

———. 1961. "The Full-Moon and New-Moon Sacrifices in the Taittirīya-Brāhmaṇa (Fourth Part): The Anuvākas 1–6 and 11 of Seventh Prapāṭhaka of the Third Kāṇḍa of the Taittirīya-Brāhmaṇa with Translation." *PAPS* 105(1): 11–36.

———. 1962. "The Animal Sacrifice in the Taittirīya-Brāhmaṇa the Part of the Hotar and the Part of the Maitrāvaruṇa in the Animal Sacrifice: The Sixth Prapāṭhaka of the Third Kāṇḍa of the Taittirīya-Brāhmaṇa with Translation." *PAPS* 106(3): 246–263.

———. 1963a. "Taittirīya-Brāhmaṇa 3.7.7–10 and 3.7.12–14: Seven Anuvākas of the Seventh Prapāṭhaka of the Third Kāṇḍa of the Taittirīya-Brāhmaṇa with Translation." *PAPS* 107(5): 446–460.

———. 1963b. "The Human Sacrifice in the Taittirīya-Brāhmaṇa: The Fourth Prapāṭhaka of the Third Kāṇḍa of the Taittirīya-Brāhmaṇa with Translation." *PAPS* 107(2): 177–182.

———. 1964. "The Agnihotra (Or Fire-God Oblation) in the Taittirīya-Brāhmaṇa: The First Prapāṭhaka of the Second Kāṇḍa of the Taittirīya-Brāhmaṇa with Translation." *PAPS* 108(4): 337–353.

———. 1965. "The Kaulikī-Sautrāmaṇī in the Taittirīya-Brāhmaṇa: The Sixth Prapāṭhaka of the Second Kāṇḍa of the Taittirīya-Brāhmaṇa with Translation." *PAPS* 109(6): 309–341.

———. 1969. "The Kāmya Animal Sacrifice in the Taittirīya-Brāhmaṇa: The Eighth Prapāṭhaka of the Third Kāṇḍa of the Taittirīya-Brāhmaṇa with Translation." *PAPS* 113(1): 34–66.

Dutt, M. N., trans. 1977. *Mahabharata*. 7 Vols. Delhi: Parimal Publications.

Dutt, Nalinaksa. 1970. "Brahmanism and Buddhism." *Bulletin of Tibetology* 7: 7–11.

Egge, James R. 2002. *Religious Giving and the Invention of Karma in Theravāda Buddhism*. Richmond, Surrey: Curzon.

Eggeling, Julius, trans. 1882–1900. *The Śatapatha-Brāhmaṇa According to the Text of the Mādhyandina School.* 6 Vols. *Sacred Books of the East Vol. XII, XXVI, XLI, XLIII, XLIV.* Oxford: Clarendon Press.

Einoo, Shingo. 1988. *Die câturmâsya oder die altindischen Tertialopfer dargestellt nach den Vorschriften der Brâhmaṇas und der Śrauta Sûtras.* Tokyo: Institute for the Study of Languages and Cultures of Asia and Africa.

Falk, Harry. 1988. "Vedische Opfer im Pali-Kanon." *Bulletin d'Études Indiennes* 6: 225–254.

Findly, Ellison Banks. 1981. "Jātavedas in the Ṛgveda: The God of Generations." *Zeitschrift der Deutschen Morgenländischen Gesellschaft* 131(2): 349–373.

Frieberger, Oliver. 2009. "Negative Campaigning: Polemics against Brahmins in a Buddhist sutta." *RoSA* 3(1): 61–76.

———. 2011. "How the Buddha Dealt with Non-Buddhists." In *Religion and Identity in South Asia and Beyond (Essays in Honor of Patrick Olivelle).* Edited by Steven Lindquist, 185–195. New York: Anthem Press.

Gardner, Robert Grosvenor and Frits Staal. 1976. *Altar of Fire.* Berkeley: University of California Extension Media Center.

Gauda, Veniramasarma, ed. 2001. *Pāraskara-Gṛhyasūtram with the Sanskrit Commentary 'Vivṛti' of Śrī Veṇīrāma Śarmā Gauḍa & Appendices 'Mūlasānti', Yamalajanaśānti, and Pṛṣṭodivi.* Varanasi: Chaukhambha Publishers.

Gelder, Jeannette M. van, trans. 1963. *Mānava Śrauta Sūtra. Śata-Piṭaka Series Indo-Asian Literatures* Vol. 27. New Delhi: International Academy of Indian Culture.

Geldner, Karl Friedrich, trans. 1951. *Der Rig-Veda aus dem Sanskrit ins Deutsche Übersetzt und mit einem laufenden Kommentar versehen.* 4 Vols. Cambridge, MA: Harvard University Press.

Ghosh, Shyam. 2002. *Hindu Concept of Life and Death.* New Delhi: Munshiram Manoharlal.

Gokhale, Ganesasastri, ed. 1978. *Āśvalāyanagṛhyasūtram.* Puna: Ānandāśrama.

Goldman, Robert P., ed. 1984–1996. *The Rāmāyaṇa of Valmiki: An Epic of Ancient India.* 4 Vols. Translated by Various Scholars. Princeton: Princeton University Press.

Gombrich, Richard. 1971a. *Precept and Practice: Traditional Buddhism in the Rural Highlands of Ceylon.* Oxford: Clarendon Press.

———. 1971b. "'Merit Transference' in Sinhalese Buddhism: A Case Study of the Interaction between Doctrine and Practice." *History of Religions* 11(2): 203–219.

———. 1992. "The Buddha's Book of Genesis." *IIJ* 35: 159–178.

Gonda, Jan. 1966. *Loka: World and Heaven in the Veda.* Amsterdam: N.V. Noord-Hollandsche Uitgevers Maatschappij.

———. 1969. *Eye and Gaze in the Veda.* Amsterdam: North Holland Publishing Co.

———. 1975. *Vedic Literature (Saṃhitās and Brāhmaṇas)* Wiesbaden: Otto Harrassowitz.

———. 1977a. *Medieval Religious Literature in Sanskrit. History of Indian Literature.* Vol. II. Wiesbaden: Otto Harrassowitz.

———. 1977b. *Ritual Sūtras. History of Indian Literature* Vol. 1. Wiesbaden: Otto Harrasowitz.

———. 1980. *Vedic Ritual: The Non-solemn Rites.* Leiden: E. J. Brill.

———. 1987. *Rice and Barley Offerings in the Veda.* Leiden: E. J. Brill.

Granoff, Phyllis. 1992. "Worship as Commemoration: Pilgrimage, Death and Dying in Medieval Jainism." *Bulletin d'Études Indiennes* 10: 181–202.

Griffith, Ralph T. H., trans. 1963. *The Hymns of the Atharva Veda.* Varanasi: Chowkhamba Sanskrit Series Office. First published 1895–1896.

———, trans. 1992. *Hinduism: The Rig Veda.* New York: Quality Paperback Book Club.

Hara, Minoru. 1967–68. "Transfer of Merit." *Adyar Library Bulletin* 31–32: 382–411.

———. 1994. "Transfer of Merit in Hindu Literature and Religion." *Memoirs of the Research Department of the Toyo Bunko.* 52: 103–135.

Hare, E. M., trans. 2001. *The Book of the Gradual Sayings (Aṅguttara-Nikāya) or More-numbered Suttas.* 2 Vols. London: Pali Text Society. First published 1934.

Haug, Martin, ed. and trans. 1922. *The Aitareya Brahmanam of the Rigveda.* Allahabad: Sudhindra Nath Vasu.

———, ed. and trans. 2003. *Śrī Aitareya Brāhmaṇam.* 2 Vols. Re-edited by S. Jain. Delhi: New Bharatiya Book Corporation.

Hazra, R. C. 1940. *Purāṇic Records on Hindu Rites and Customs.* Calcutta: The University of Dacca.

Heesterman, J. C. 1982. "Householder and Wanderer." In *Way of Life: King, Householder, Renouncer Essays in Honour of Louis Dumont.* Edited by T. N. Madan, 251–271. New Delhi: Vikas Publishing House.

Heim, Maria. 2004. *Theories of the Gift in South Asia.* New York: Routledge.

Hill, Peter. 2001. *Fate, Predestination and Human Action in the Mahābhārata: A Study in the History of Ideas.* New Delhi: Munshiram Manoharlal Publishers.

Hillebrandt, Alfred, ed. 1981. *Śāṅkhāyana Śrauta Sūtra together with the Commentary of Varadattasuta Ānartīya and Govinda.* Vol. I. New Delhi: Maharchand Lachhmandas Publications.

Hinüber, Oskar von. 1996. *A Handbook of Pāli Literature.* Berlin: Walter de Gruyter.

Holt, John Clifford. 1981. "Assisting the Dead by Venerating the Living. Merit Transfer in Early Buddhist Tradition." *Numen* 28: 1–28.

———. 2004. *The Buddhist Viṣṇu: Religious Transformations, Politics, and Culture.* New York: Columbia University Press.

Horner, I. B., trans. 1962. *The Book of the Discipline (Vinaya-Pitaka).* Vol. IV. London: Luzac & Co. First published 1951.

———, trans. 2000. *The Collection of the Middle Length Sayings (Majjhima-Nikāya).* Vol. I. London: Pali Text Society. First published 1954.

Horner, I. B. and H. S. Gehman, trans. 1974. *The Minor Anthologies of the Pali Canon Part IV: Vimānavathu: Stories of the Mansions and Petavatthu: Stories of the Departed.* London: Pali Text Society. First published 1942.

Inden, Ronald B. and Ralph Nicholas. 1977. *Kinship in Bengali Culture*. Chicago: University of Chicago Press.

Jacobi, Hermann. 1895. *Jaina Sutras, Part II. Sacred Books of the East Vol. 45*. Oxford: Clarendon Press.

Jacques, C. 1962. *Gayā Māhātmya*. Pondichery: Institut Francais d'Indologie.

———. that makes sense.he bibliographyails to the bibliographyuction.hic entrynd its Origins 1979. "Gayā Māhātmya—Introductions etc." Giorgio Bonazzoli, trans. *Purāṇam* 21(2): 1–32.

———. 1980. "Gayā Māhātmya—Introductions etc. (Cont.)." Giorgio Bonazzoli, trans. *Purāṇam* 22(1): 33–70.

Jaini, P. S. 1970. "Sramanas: Their Conflict with Brahmanical Society." In *Chapters of Indian Civilization*. Edited by Joseph W. Elder, 39–81. Dubuque, IA: Kendall Hunt.

———. 1979. *The Jaina Path of Purification*. Delhi: Motilal Banarsidass.

Jamison, Stephanie W. 1991. *The Ravenous Hyenas and the Wounded Sun*. Ithaca, NY: Cornell University Press.

———. 1996. *Sacrificed Wife Sacrificer's Wife: Women, Ritual, and Hospitality in Ancient India*. New York: Oxford University Press.

———. 1998. "Rhinoceros Toes, Manu V.17–18, and the Development of the Dharma System." *JAOS* 118(2): 249–256.

Jamison Stephanie W. and Michael Witzel. 2003. "Vedic Hinduism." In *The Study of Hinduism*. Edited by Arvind Sharma, 65–113. Columbia: University of South Carolina Press.

Jayawickrama, N. A., ed. 1977. *Vimānavatthu and Petavatthu. Pali Text Society Text Series No. 168*. London: Pali Text Society.

Jha, Damodar, ed. 2001. *The Āśvalāyana-Śrauta-Sūtram with the Commentary of Siddhāntin*. Hoshiarpur: Punjab University.

Jolly, Julius, trans. 1965. *The Minor Law Books Part I: Nārada. Brihaspati. Sacred Books of the East Vol. XXXIII*. Delhi: Motilal Banarsidass. First published 1889.

Joshi, K. L., ed. 2000. *Atharva-Veda Saṃhitā (Sanskrit Text, English Translation, Notes and Index of Verses According to the Translation of W. D. Whitney and Bhāṣya of Sāyaṇācārya*. 3 Vols. Delhi: Parimal Publications.

———. ed. 2005. *Yājñavalkyasmṛti (Sanskrit Text, English Translation, Notes, Introduction and Index of Verses)*. Translated by Manmatha Nath Dutt. Delhi: Parimal Publications.

Kajiyama, Y. 1989. "Transfer and Transformations of Merits in Relation to Emptiness." *Studies in Buddhist Philosophy (Selected Papers)*. Edited by Katsumi Mimaki, 1–20. Kyoto: Rinsen Book Co.

Kane, P. V. 1930–1962. *History of Dharmaśāstra*. 5 Vols. Poona: Bhandarkar Oriental Research Institute.

Kangle, R. P. 1988. *The Kauṭilīya Arthaśāstra*. 3 Vols. Bombay: University of Bombay.

Kāśīkar, C. G., ed. 1964. *The Śrauta, Paitṛmedhika and Pariśeṣa Sūtras of Bharadvāja.* 2 Vols. Poona: Vaidika Saṃśodhana Maṇḍala.

———. 1968. "A Survey of the Śrautasūtras." *Journal of the University of Bombay* 35(2): i–188.

———, ed. 1970–1994. *Śrautakośa: Encyclopedia of Vedic Sacrificial Ritual Comprising the Two Complementary Sections, namely, the Sanskrit Section and the English Section.* Vol. I, the Sanskrit Section. 2 Parts. Poona: Vaidika Saṃśodhana Maṇḍala.

———, ed. 1985. *The Mānava Śrautasūtra belonging to the Maitrāyaṇī Saṃhitā.* New Delhi: Sri Satguru Publications. First published in 1961.

———, ed. 2003. *The Baudhāyana Śrautasūtra.* New Delhi: Indira Gandhi National Centre for the Arts.

Keith, Arthur Berriedale, trans. 1920. *Rigveda Brahmanas: The Aitareya and Kauṣītaki Brāhmaṇas of the Rigveda.* Cambridge, MA: Harvard University Press.

———. 1925. *The Religion and Philosophy of the Veda and Upaniṣads.* 2 Vols. Cambridge, MA: Harvard University Press.

———, trans. 1967. *The Veda of the Black Yajus School entitled Taittiriya Sanhita. 2 Vols. Harvard Oriental Series Vol. 18–19.* Cambridge, MA: Harvard University Press. First published in 1914.

Keyes, Charles F. 1983. "Merit-Transference in the Kammic Theory of Popular Theravāda Buddhism." In *Karma: An Anthropological Inquiry.* Edited by Charles F. Keyes and E. Valentine Daniel, 261–286. Berkeley: University of California Press.

Kirste, Johann, ed. 1889. *Hiraṇyakeśigṛhyasūtra the Gṛhyasūtra of Hiraṇyakeśin: with Extracts from the Commentary of Matridatta.* Vienna: Hölder.

Knipe, David. 1977. "Sapindikarana: The Hindu Rite of Entry into Heaven." In *Religious Encounters with Death: Insights from the History and Anthropology of Religions.* Edited by Frank E. Reynolds and Earle H. Waugh, 111–124. University Park: Pennsylvania State University Press.

———. 1989. "Night of the Growing Dead: A Cult of Vīrabhadra in Coastal Andhra." In *Criminal Gods and Demon Devotees: Essays on the Guardians of Popular Hinduism.* Edited by Alf Hiltebeitel, 123–156. Albany: State University of New York Press.

Köhler, Hans-Werbin. 1973. *Śrad-dhā—In der Vedischen und Altbuddhistichen Literatur.* Wiesbaden: Franz Steiner Verlag.

Kumar, Pushpendra, ed. 1998. *Kṛṣṇayajurvedīyam Taittirīyabrāhmaṇam: Śrīmatsāyaṇ ācāryaviracitabhāṣyasametam.* 3 Vols. Delhi: Nag Publishers.

Lamb, Sarah. 2000. *White Saris and Sweet Mangoes: Aging, Gender, and Body in North India.* Berkeley: University of California Press.

Langer, Rita. 2007. *Buddhist Rituals of Death and Rebirth: Contemporary Sri Lankan Practice and its Origins.* London: Routledge.

Law, Bimala Churn. 1936. *The Buddhist Conception of Spirits.* London: Luzac and Co.

———, trans. 1969. *The Debates Commentary (Kathāvatthuppakaraṇa-Aṭṭhakathā)*. London: Pali Text Society.

———. 2005. *Heaven and Hell in Buddhist Perspective*. Delhi: Winsome Books.

Lincoln, Bruce. 1991. "The Two Paths." in *Death, War, and Sacrifice: Studies in Ideology and Practice* (Chicago: The University of Chicago Press), 119–127.

Long, Jeffery D. 2009. *Jainism: An Introduction*. London: I. B. Tauris.

Macdonell, A. A. 1995. *Vedic Mythology*. Delhi: Motilal Banarsidass Publishers. First published in 1898.

Malalasekera, G. P. 1967. "'Transference of Merit' in Ceylonese Buddhism." *Philosophy East and West*. 17(1): 85–90.

Malamoud, Charles. 1983. "The Theology of Debt in Brahmanism." In *Debts and Debtors*. Edited by Charles Malamoud, 21–40. New Delhi: Vikas Publishing House.

Malaviya, Sudhakara, ed. 1991. *Gṛhya-Sūtra of Pāraskara with Two Commentaries of Harihar and Gadadhar*. Varanasi: Chaukhambha Publishers.

Mani, Vettam. 1975. *Purāṇic Encyclopedia: A Comprehensive Dictionary with Special Reference to the Epic and Purāṇic Literature*. Delhi: Motilal Banarsidass. First published in 1964.

Mayrhofer, Manfred. 1956. *Kurzgefaßtes etymologisches Wörterbuch des Altindischen*. 4 Vols. Heidelberg: Carl Winter.

McAnany, Patricia A. 1995. *Living with the Ancestors: Kinship and Kingship in Ancient Maya Society*. Austin: University of Texas Press.

McDermott, James P. 1974. "Sādhīna Jātaka: A Case against the Transfer of Merit." *JAOS* 94(3): 385–387.

———. 1977. "Kamma in the Milindapañha." *JAOS* 97(4): 460–468.

———. 1999. "Karma and Rebirth in Early Buddhism." In *Karma and Rebirth in Classical Indian Traditions*. Edited by Wendy Doniger O'Flaherty, 165–192. Berkeley: University of California Press.

Michaels, Axel and Philip Pierce. 1997. "Gift and Return Gift, Greeting and Return Greeting in India: On a Consequential Footnote by Marcel Mauss." *Numen* 44: 242–269.

Mines, Diane Paull. 1990. "Hindu Periods of Death 'Impurity.'" In *India through Hindu Categories*, edited by McKim Marriott, 103–130. New Delhi: Sage.

Mishra Sharma, Kulamani, ed. 1981. *Pāraskara Gṛhyasūtram with Margadarshini*. Puri, Orissa: Harihar Jha.

Mishra, Yugal Kishor, ed. 2004. *The Śatapatha-Brāhmaṇa (According to the Mādhyandina Recension with the Vedārthaprakāśa Bhāṣya of Sāyaṇācārya Supplemented by the Commentary of Harisvāmin)*. Varanasi: Sampurnanand Sanskrit University.

Mitra, Rajendralal, ed. 1981. *The Taittiriya Brahmana of the Black Yajur Veda*. 4 Vols. Osnabrück: Bilbio Verlag. First published in 1885.

———, ed. 1982. *The Taittirīya Āraṇyaka of the Black Yajurveda*. Osnabrück: Biblio Verlag. First published in 1864.

Müller, F. Max, ed. 1890. *Rig-Veda-Samhitâ: The Sacred Hymns of the Brâhmans together with the Commentary of Sâyanâkârya*. 4 Vols. London: Oxford University Press.

Ñānamoli, Bhikku, trans. 1960. *The Minor Readings (Khuddakapāṭha): The First Book of the Minor Collection (Khuddakanikāya)*. London: Pali Text Society.

Nicholas, Ralph W. 1982. "Śrāddha, Impurity, and Relations between the Living and the Dead." In *Way of Life: King, Householder, Renouncer*, edited by T. N. Madan, 368–379. New Delhi: Vikas Publishing.

Norman, K. R. 1983. *Pāli Literature Including the Canonical Literature in Prakrit and Sanskrit of all the Hīnayāna Schools of Buddhism*. Wiesbaden: Otto Harrassowitz.

———. 1992. *The Group of Discourses (Sutta Nipāta)*. Vol. II. London: Pali Text Society.

Oberlies, Thomas. 1998. *Die Religion Des Ṛgveda: Erster Teil—Das Religiöse System des Ṛgveda*. Vienna: Sammlung De Nobili.

———. 1999. *Die Religion Des Ṛgveda: Zweiter Teil—Kompositionsanalyse der Soma-Hymnen des Ṛgveda*. Vienna: Sammlung De Nobili.

Obeyesekere, Gananath. 2002. *Imagining Karma: Ethical Transformation in Amerindian, Buddhist, and Greek Rebirth*. Berkeley: University of California Press.

Ohnuma, Reiko. 1998. "The Gift of the Body and the Gift of Dharma." *History of Religions* 37(4): 323–359.

Oldenberg, Hermann. 1894. *Die Religion des Veda*. Berlin: Verlag von Wilhelm Hertz.

———, trans. 1967. *The Gṛhya-Sūtras: Rules of Vedic Domestic Ceremonies*. Delhi: Motilal Banarsidass. First published in 1886–1892.

Olivelle, Patrick. 1991. "From Feast to Fast: Food and the Indian Ascetic." In *Rules and Remedies in Classical Indian Law*. Panels of the VIIth World Sanskrit Conference, Vol. 9. Edited by Julia Leslie, 17–36. Leiden: E. J. Brill.

———. 1993. *The Āśrama System: The History and Hermeneutics of a Religious Institution*. New York: Oxford University Press.

———, trans. 1996. *Upaniṣads*. New York: Oxford University Press.

———, ed. and trans. 2000. *Dharmasūtras: The Law Codes of Āpastamba, Gautama, Baudhāyana, and Vasiṣṭha*. Delhi: Motilal Banarsidass.

———. 2002a. "Food for Thought: Dietary Regulations and Social Organization in Ancient India." 2001 Gonda Lecture. Amsterdam: Royal Netherlands Academy of Arts and Sciences.

———. 2002b. "Abhakṣya and abhojya: An Exploration in Dietary Language." *JAOS* 122(2): 345–354.

———. 2004a. "The Semantic History of dharma the Middle and Late Vedic Periods." *Journal of Indian Philosophy* 32(5–6): 491–511.

———, trans. 2004b. *The Law Code of Manu: A New Translation Based on the Critical Edition*. Oxford: Oxford University Press.

———, ed. and trans. 2005. *Manu's Code of Law: A Critical Edition and Translation of the Mānava-Dharmaśāstra*. Oxford: Oxford University Press.

———, ed. 2006a. *Between the Empires: Society in India 300 BCE to 400 BCE*. Oxford: Oxford University Press.

———. 2006b. "The Ascetic and the Domestic in Brahmanical Religiosity." In *Asceticism and Its Critics: Historical Accounts and Comparative Perspectives*. Edited by Oliver Frieberger, 25–42. Oxford: Oxford University Press.

———, ed. and trans. 2009. *The Law Code of Viṣṇu: A Critical Edition and Annotated Translation of the Vaiṣṇava Dharmaśāstra*. Harvard Oriental Series, No. 73. Cambridge, MA: Harvard University Press.

———. 2011. "Introduction to Renunciation in the Hindu Traditions." In *Ascetics and Brahmins: Studies in Ideologies and Institutions*, 11–26. London: Anthem Press.

Pandey, Umesh Chandra, ed. 1971. *Āpastamba-Gṛhya-Sūtra with the 'Anākulā' Commentary of Śrī Hardatta Miśra, the 'Tātparyadarśana' Commentary of Śrī Sudarśanācārya and Notes in Sanskrit by Mahāmahopādhyāya A. Chinnasvamāī*. Varanasi: Chowkhambha Sanskrit Series Office.

Paṇiśīkara, Vāsudeva Lakṣmaṇa Śāstrī, ed. 1992. *Śrīmad-Vājasaneyi-Mādhyandina Śuklayajurveda-Saṃhitā (Text and Padapāṭha) with the Mantra-Bhāṣya of Śrīmad-Uvaṭācārya & the Vedadīpa of Śrīman Mahīdhara (With Appendices & Mantra-Koṣa)*. Varanasi: Chowkhamba Vidyabhawan.

Parry, Jonathan P. 1982. "Sacrificial Death and the Necrophagus Ascetic." In *Death and the Regeneration of Life*, edited by Maurice Bloch and Jonathan Parry. Cambridge: Cambridge University Press, 74–100.

———. 1994. *Death in Banaras*. Cambridge: Cambridge University Press.

Pendse, G. S. 1977. *The Vedic Concept of Śraddhā*. Pune: M. V. Barve.

Poleman, Horace J. 1934. "The Ritualistic Continuity of Ṛgveda X.14–18." *JAOS* 54(3): 276–281.

Prasad, R. C. 1997. *The Śrāddha: Hindu Book of the Dead*. Delhi: Motilal Banarsidass.

Pratap, Surendra, ed. 1990. *Yajurvedasaṃhitā*. Translated by Ralph T. H. Griffith. Delhi: Nag Publishers.

Premasiri, P. D. 1991. "Significance of the Ritual Concerning Offerings to Ancestors in Theravāda Buddhism." In *Buddhist Thought and Ritual*. Edited by David J. Kalupahana, 151–158. New York: Paragon Press.

Rai, Ganga Sagar, ed. and trans. 1995. *Śāṃkhāyana Gṛhyasūtra with Nārāyaṇa Bhāṣya, Sāṃkhāyana Gṛhyasaṃgraha of Vāsudeva; Hindi Translation of Sūtras, Introduction and Appendices*. Varanasi: Ratnā Publications.

Ranade, H. G., trans. 1978. *Kātyāyana Śrauta Sūtra (Rules for the Vedic Sacrifice)*. Pune: Ranade.

Rao, K. L. Seshagiri. 1974. *The Concept of Śraddhā in the Brāhmaṇas, Upaniṣads and the Gītā*. Delhi: Motilal Banarsidass.

Rhys Davids, Caroline A. F., trans. 1986c. *Psalms of the Brethren. Sacred Writings of the Buddhists Vol. III*. New Delhi: Cosmo Publications. First published in 1913.

———. 1986a. *Psalms of the Sisters. Sacred Writings of the Buddhists Vol. I.* New Delhi: Cosmo Publications. First published in 1913.

———, trans. 1986b. *Psalms of the Brethren. Sacred Writings of the Buddhists Vol. II.* New Delhi: Cosmo Publications. First published in 1913.

———, trans. 1999. *The Book of Kindred Sayings (Saṃyutta-Nikāya) or Grouped Suttas. Vol. I.* London: Pali Text Society. First published in 1917.

Rhys Davids, Thomas William, and C. A. F. Rhys Davids, trans. 2007. *Dialogues of the Buddha.* 2 Vols. Delhi: Motilal Banarsidass Publishers. First published in 1910–1921.

Rocher, Ludo. 1980. "Karma and Rebirth in the Dharmaśāstras." In *Karma and Rebirth in Classical Indian Traditions.* Edited by Wendy Doniger O'Flaherty, 61–89. Berkeley: University of California Press.

———. 1986. *The Purāṇas.* Wiesbaden: Otto Harrasowitz.

Roth, Rudolph von and William Dwight Whitney. 1924. *Atharva Veda Sanhita.* Corrected by Max Lindenau. Berlin: F. Dümmler. First published in 1856.

Roy, Pratap Chandra, trans. 1962. *The Mahabharata of Krishna-Dwaipayana Vyasa.* Vols. 1–12. Calcutta: Oriental Publishing Co.

Saindon, Marcelle. 1999. "The Pertinence of the Śrāddha rituals in the Context of Transmigration and Liberation according to the Pitṛkalpa of the Harivaṃśa." *Purāṇam* 41(1): 5–17.

Salomons, Hanriette J. W., ed. 1981. *Bharadvājagṛhyasūtram: The Domestic Ritual, According to the School of Bharadvāja.* New Delhi: Meharchand Lachmandas Publications. First published in 1913.

Sama Sastrin, Ruda-patna, ed. 1982. *The Bodhāyana Gṛhyasūtra.* New Delhi: Panini.

Samuels, Jeffrey. 1999. "Views of Householders and Lay Disciples in the Sutta Piṭaka: A Reconsideration of the Lay/Monastic Opposition." *Religion* 29: 231–241.

Sand, Erik Reenberg. 1986. "The śrāddha (ancestor worship) According to Some Important Purāṇas: Some Facets." In *South Asian Religion and Society.* Edited by Asko Parpola and Bent Smidt Hansen. London: Curzon Press.

Sarma, E. R. S. 1968. *Kauṣītaki-Brāhmaṇa.* Three Volumes. Wiesbaden: Stiener.

Sax, William S. 1997. "Fathers, Sons, and Rhinoceroses: Masculinity and Violence in the Pandav Lila." *JAOS* 117(2): 278–293.

Sayers, Matthew R. 2010. "Gayā-Bodhgayā: The Origins of a Pilgrimage Complex." *RoSA* 4(1): 9–25.

———. 2012. "Claiming Modes of Mediation in Ancient Hindu and Buddhist Ancestor Worship." *Journal of Ritual Studies* 26(1): 5–18.

Schopen, Gregory. 1997c. "Archaeology and Protestant Presuppositions in the Study of Indian Buddhism." In *Bones, Stones, and Buddhist Monks: Collected Papers on the Archaeology, Epigraphy, and Texts of Monastic Buddhism in India* (Honolulu: The University of Hawai'i Press), 1–22.

———. 1997a. "Two Problems in the History of Indian Buddhism: The Layman/Monk Distinction and the Doctrines of the Transfer of Merit." In *Bones, Stones, and Buddhist Monks: Collected Papers on the Archaeology, Epigraphy, and Texts of Monastic Buddhism in India* (Honolulu: The University of Hawai'i Press), 23–55.

———. 1997b. "On Monks, Nuns, and 'Vulgar' Practices: The Introduction of the Image Cult into Indian Buddhism." In *Bones, Stones, and Buddhist Monks: Collected Papers on the Archaeology, Epigraphy, and Texts of Monastic Buddhism in India* (Honolulu: The University of Hawai'i Press), 238–257.

———. 2004. "Dead Monks and Bad Debts: Some Provisions of a Buddhistic Monastic Inheritance Law." In *Buddhist Monks and Business Matters: Still More Papers on Monastic Buddhism in India* (Honolulu: The University of Hawai'i Press), 122–169.

Schroeder, Leopold von, ed. 1970–1972. *Mäitrâyanî Samhitä.* Wiesbaden: Franz Steiner Verlag GMBH.

Selby, Martha Ann. 2005. "Narratives of Conception, Gestation, and Labour in Sanskrit Āyurvedic Texts." *Asian Medicine* 1(2): 254–275.

Sharma, Narendra Nath, trans. 1976. *Āśvalāyana Gṛhyasūtram with Sanskrit Commentary of Nārāyaṇa.* Delhi: Eastern Book Linkers.

Shastri, A. Mahadeva, ed. 1979. *Paraśurāmakalpasūtra with the Commentaries 'Vṛtti' by Śrī Rāmeśvara 'Nīrakṣīraviveka' by Param Hans Mishra 'Hans'.* Baroda: Oriental Institute. First published in 1950.

Shastri, Dakshina Ranjan. 1963. *Origin and Development of the Rituals of Ancestor Worship in India.* Calcutta: Bookland Private Limited.

Shastri, Vishvanath. 1971. *Shraddakalpa of Chaturvarga Chintamani.* Part I. Translated by Sri Hemadri Pandit. Varanasi: Banaras Hindu University.

Siegel, Lee. 1987. *Laughing Matters: Comic Tradition in India.* Chicago: University of Chicago Press.

Singh, Purushottam. 1970. *Burial Practices in Ancient India (A Study in the Eschatological Beliefs of Early Man as Revealed by Archaeological Sources).* Varanasi: Prithivi Prakashan.

Singh, Thakur Udaya Narain, trans. 1992. *Gobhila Gṛhyasūtram with Sanskrit Commentary.* Delhi: Choukhamba Sanskrit Pratishthan.

Smith, Brian K. 1986. "The Unity of Ritual: The Place of the Domestic Sacrifice in Vedic Ritualism." *IIJ* 29: 79–96.

———. 1989. *Reflections on Resemblance, Ritual, and Religion.* New York: Oxford.

———. 1994. *Classifying the Universe: The Ancient Indian Varṇa System and the Origins of Caste.* New York: Oxford University Press.

———. 1996. "Ritual Perfection and Ritual Sabotage in the Veda." *History of Religions* 35(4): 285–306.

Sprockhoff, J. F. 1980. "Die feindlichen Toten und der befriedete Tote" In *Leben und Tod in den Religionen. Symbol und Wirklichkeit.* Edited by Gunther Stephenson, 263–284. Darmstadt: Wissenschaftl. Buchgesell.

Staal, Frits. 2008. *Discovering the Vedas: Origins, Mantras, Rituals, Insights.* New Delhi: Penguin Books.

Staal, Frits, C. V. Somayajipad, M. Itti Ravi Nambudiri, and Adelaide De Menil. 1983. *Agni: The Vedic Ritual of the Fire Altar*. Berkeley: Asian Humanities Press.

Stietencron, Heinrich von. 1976. "Vom Tod im Leben und vom Leben in Tod." In *Der Mensch und sein Tod*. Edited by Johannes Schwartländer, 146–161. Göttingen: Kreuz-Verlag.

Strong, D. M. 1902. *The Udāna or the Solemn Utterances of the Buddha*. London: Luzac.

Suktankar, Vishnu Sitaram. 1927–1966. *The Mahabharata*. 19 Vols. Poona: Bhandarkar Oriental Research Institute.

Tachikawa, Musashi. 2006. *Vedic Domestic Fire-ritual: Sthālīpāka (Its Performance and Exposition)*. Delhi: New Bharatiya Book Corporation.

Thapar, Romila. 1982. "Householders and Renounces in the Brahmanical and Buddhist Traditions." In *Way of Life: King, Householder, Renouncer Essays in Honour of Louis Dumont*. Edited by T. N. Madan, 273–298. New Delhi: Vikas Publishing House.

Thite, Ganesh Umakant. 1975. *Sacrifice in the Brāhmaṇa-texts*. Poona: Poona University Press.

———, trans. 2004. *Āpastamba-Śrauta-Sūtra*. 2 Vols. Delhi: New Bharatiya Book Corporation.

———, trans. 2006. *Kātyāyana-Śrautasūtra*. 2 Vols. Delhi: New Bharatiya Book Corporation.

Tull, Herman W. 1989. *The Vedic Origins of Karma: Cosmos as Man in Ancient Indian Myth and Ritual*. Albany: State University of New York Press.

Upadhyaya, Kashi Nath. 1971. *Early Buddhism and the Bhagavadgita*. Delhi: Motilal Banarsidass.

Varma, V. P. 1960. "The Vedic Religion and the Origins of Buddhism." *The Journal of the Bihar Research Society* 46: 276–308.

Vidyālaṇkār, Kailāśacandra. 1976. *Pitṛ-Pūjā: ārya pūjā-paddhati meṃ udbhava aur vikās*. Delhi: Bhāratīya Granth Nikelan.

Vidyāratna, Rāmanārāyana, ed. 1874. *The Grihyasūtra of Āśvalāyana, with the Commentary of Gārgya Nārāyana*. Calcutta: C. B. Lewis Baptist Mission Press.

Wasson, R. Gordon. 1968. *Soma: Divine Mushroom of Immortality*. New York: Harcourt Brace Javanovich.

Weber, Albrecht, ed. 1852. *The Vâjasaneyi-Sanhitâ in the Mâdhyandina- and the Kâṇva-çâkhâ with the Commentary of Mahîdhara*. Berlin: Ferd. Dümmler's Verlagsbuchhandlung.

———, ed. 1964. *The Çatapatha-Brāhmaṇa in the Mādhyandina-Çākhā with Extracts from the Commentaries of Sāyaṇa, Harisvāmin and Dvivedaganga*. Varanasi: Chowkhamba Sanskrit Series Office.

———, ed. 1973. *Die Taittirîya Saṃhitâ. Indische Studien: Beiträge für die Kunde des indischen Alterhums*. Vol. XI–XII. Hildesheim: Georg Olms Verlag. First published in 1871.

White, David Gordon. 1986. "'Dakkhiṇa' and 'Agnicayana': An Extended Application of Paul Mus's Typology." *History of Religions* 26(2): 188–213.

Winternitz, M., ed. 1887. *Āpastambīya Gṛhyasūtra with Extracts from the Commentaries of Haradatta and Sudarśanārya.* Vienna: Alfred Hölder.

Witzel, Michael. 1987. "On the Localization of Vedic Texts and Schools." In *India and the Ancient World.* Edited by Gilbert Pollet, 173–213. Leuven: Departement Orientalistiek.

———. 1989. "Tracing the Vedic Dialects." In *Dialectes dans les littéritures indo-aryennes.* Edited by C. Caillat, 97–265. Paris: Collège de France.

———. 1997. "The Development of the Vedic Canon and its Schools: The Social and Political Milieu." In *Inside the Texts and Beyond the Texts: New Approaches to the Study of the Vedas.* Edited by Michael Witzel, 257–348. Columbia, MO: South Asia Books.

Woodward, F. L. 1914. "The Buddhist Doctrine of Reversible Merit." *The Buddhist Review* 6: 38–50.

———, trans. 1996a. *The Book of the Gradual Sayings (Aṅguttara-Nikāya) or More-numbered Suttas.* Vol. V. London: Pali Text Society. First published in 1936.

———, trans. 1996b. *The Book of Kindred Sayings (Saṃyutta-Nikāya) or Grouped Suttas.* Vol. IV. London: Pali Text Society. First published in 1927.

———, trans. 2000–2001. *The Book of the Gradual Sayings (Anguttara-Nikāya) or More-numbered Suttas.* 2 Vols. London: Pali Text Society. First published in 1932–1933.

Index